Bert Van Roosebeke

State Liability for Breaches of European Law

GABLER EDITION WISSENSCHAFT

Ökonomische Analyse des Rechts

Herausgegeben von
Professor Dr. Peter Behrens
Professor Dr. Manfred Holler
Professor Dr. Claus Ott
Professor Dr. Hans-Bernd Schäfer (schriftführend)
Universität Hamburg, Fachbereich Rechtswissenschaft II

Die ökonomische Analyse des Rechts untersucht Rechtsnormen auf ihre gesellschaftlichen Folgewirkungen und bedient sich dabei des methodischen Instrumentariums der Wirtschaftswissenschaften, insbesondere der Mikroökonomie, der Neuen Institutionen- und Konstitutionenökonomie. Sie ist ein interdisziplinäres Forschungsgebiet, in dem sowohl Rechtswissenschaftler als auch Wirtschaftswissenschaftler tätig sind und das zu wesentlichen neuen Erkenntnissen über Funktion und Wirkungen von Rechtsnormen geführt hat.

Die Schriftenreihe enthält Monographien zu verschiedenen Rechtsgebieten und Rechtsentwicklungen. Sie behandelt Fragestellungen aus den Bereichen Wirtschaftsrecht, Vertragsrecht, Haftungsrecht, Sachenrecht und verwaltungsrechtliche Regulierung.

Bert Van Roosebeke

State Liability for Breaches of European Law

An economic analysis

With a foreword by Prof. Dr. Hans-Bernd Schäfer

Deutscher Universitäts-Verlag

Bibliografische Information Der Deutschen Nationalbibliothek
Die Deutsche Nationalbibliothek verzeichnet diese Publikation in der Deutschen Nationalbibliografie; detaillierte bibliografische Daten sind im Internet über <http://dnb.d-nb.de> abrufbar.

Dissertation Universität Hamburg, 2006

1. Auflage März 2007

Lektorat: Brigitte Siegel / Sabine Schöller

Der Deutsche Universitäts-Verlag ist ein Unternehmen von Springer Science+Business Media.
www.duv.de

Umschlaggestaltung: Regine Zimmer, Dipl.-Designerin, Frankfurt/Main
Gedruckt auf säurefreiem und chlorfrei gebleichtem Papier
Printed in Germany

ISBN 978-3-8350-0653-9

Voor Opa
"Dat is 't een en 't ander"
"Opgepast is niet gelachen"

Foreword

With this work, which was written under my academic supervision at the Graduate College for Law and Economics, Bert Van Roosebeke has covered a topic which is rather unusual to the literature of law and economics in a number of ways.

This work does not – as does the huge majority of law and economics scholarship – deal with individual behaviour, as addressed by private law. Rather does the author analyse state behaviour as governed by European made state liability jurisdiction and law. He does so with the law and economics instruments traditionally used in the analysis of contract law, tort law and criminal law. The methods of analysis are truly interdisciplinary as well: legal, empirical as well as model-theoretical methods are applied to the questions under discussion.

The starting point for the academic discussion on state liability was the European Court of Justice's landmark Francovich judgement in 1991. In that judgement, the ECJ – against the declared political opinion of EU member states – controversially paved the way for a liability of EU member states for damages caused by the non-transposition of European directives into national law. The judgement was followed by a rich and lengthy discussion among legal scholars, in which the competency of the ECJ to introduce such non-contractual state liability was controversially debated. Following this first judgement, the ECJ widened the scope of application of non-contractual state liability in subsequent judgements. In its Brasserie du Pêcheur judgement of 1996 the ECJ decided that not only procedural wrongdoings – such as the lack of transposition of a directive – but also substantive errors by a member state might give rise to non-contractual state liability. In principle, the ECJ decided that breaches, which are sufficiently serious give rise to non-contractual state liability.

In recent years, the ECJ has continued widening the application of this "Francovich doctrine". In its Köbler case of 2003, it decided that in principle, even judicial errors in a decision of a national court adjudicating at last instance might justify state liability claims.

As a reaction to the Francovich judgement of 1991, member states altered article 228 of the EC-Treaty in Maastricht. As before, it remained one of the European Commission's main tasks to guard the application of European Treaties and secondary legislation by the member states. However, the treaty now foresaw in the use of public fines, which were to sanction member states which continuously ignored an ECJ-judgement, categorising a member state's behaviour as a breach of European law.
However, the Heads of State decided against explicitly mentioning a state liability clause in the Treaties. Hence, primary European law does still not foresee for more than public fines, which can only be applied after a lengthy procedure of acting by the Commission.

This constellation is the starting-point of Bert Van Roosebeke's economic analysis. The co-existence of two mechanisms – one private, the other one public – both governing breaches of European law by state acting, puts forward a number of interesting questions: What is really the aim of both mechanisms? Is this aim economically justifiable? Do the instruments applied really lead to the goal aimed at? Which method of both (the public or the private one) has a comparative advantage over the other one?

Bert Van Roosebeke poses and answers these questions, which are basic to the traditional analysis of law and economics and transposes them to the sphere of state acting. His work can only be the starting point of such an analysis. The public choice literature has offered us a fair understanding of public acting. Bert Van Roosebeke's attempt to apply this knowledge to the teleological law and economics literature – though challenging – remains promising and deserve scholars' effort and attention.

Prof. Dr. H.B. Schäfer

Preface

This dissertation was written in the Graduate Programme in Law and Economics at the University of Hamburg under the supervision of Prof. Dr. Hans-Bernd Schäfer and at the George Mason University School of Law in Arlington, Virginia.

First and foremost I would like to thank Prof. Dr. Schäfer for the freedom, support and trust he granted me. I hope he's not all too disappointed by the result. I am also grateful to the Deutsche Forschungsgemeinschaft for the financial support and to Prof. Dr. Adams for assuming the role of second referee during the doctoral procedure.

The excellent atmosphere at the Graduate College has done its part in promoting this work. Not only the inspiring academic setting-up of the Graduate Programme, but especially my colleagues – both lawyers and economists – have proven to be of great help. I especially would like to thank Heike Schweitzer, Hans-Wilhelm Krüger and Ohad Soudry for the many discussions whose end was mostly not related to their beginning, but without which this thesis would probably still be in the making.

I also would like to thank my former colleagues at the Deutsche Bundesbank, whose annoying questions on the exact status of this work made sure I didn't forget to give it the finishing touch. The questions by Mario Jung, Thomas Kaufmann, Silvia Marenow and Stefan Duckheim were so annoying that they deserve special reference.

Most of all however, I would like to thank Bettina Scheuer, without whom this work would have been finished much earlier. At the same time, the annoyance of her questions exceeded everything mentioned before. She was indispensable to me during the writing of this work, and will most definitely remain so afterwards.

Bert Van Roosebeke

TABLE OF CONTENTS

PART I: INTRODUCTION 1

1. INTRODUCTION 1
2. BASICS OF THE EUROPEAN UNION 4
   2.1 The Acquis Communautaire 4
   2.2 Institutions of the European Union 5
      2.2.1 The European Commission 5
      2.2.2 The Council of the European Union 6
      2.2.3 The European Parliament 7
   2.3 Decision-Making in the European Union 8

PART II: A FIRST LOOK AT BREACHES. ON THEIR EXISTENCE, EXPLANATIONS AND THE COURT'S ANSWER 15

3. (WHAT AND WHY) DO MEMBER STATES BREACH? 15
   3.1 Breaching what? 15
      3.1.1 Treaties, Regulations and Decisions 15
      3.1.2 Directives. 16
      3.1.3 ECJ-Judgements 18
   3.2 Who breaches? 19
   3.3 Statistics: how many breaches? 21
   3.4 Why do Member States breach? Theory and Empirics. 25
      3.4.1 Intentional Breaches 27
         3.4.1.1 Direct political disagreement: a preliminary test of explanation.. 27
            A.) Data collection and bias problems. 28
            B.) The tests-results and interpretations 31
         3.4.1.2 Indirect political disagreement: log rolling/package dealing and free riding 35
         3.4.1.3 Change of political leadership 39
         3.4.1.4 Preference building and change 40
         3.4.1.5 Ignorance 40

3.4.2 Non-intentional Breaches 41
3.4.2.1 Non-intentional "structural" factors 41
A.) Degree of Federalism 41
B.) Administrative well-functioning 43
3.4.2.2 Non-intentional inherent factors 43
A.) Vague law 43
B.) Conflicting principles of law 44
3.4.3 Empirical Testing 46
3.4.3.1 Operationalisation of the dependent variable: breaches. 46
3.4.3.2 Operationalisation of the independent variables 46
A.) Direct political disagreement 46
B.) Indirect political disagreement: Logrolling 47
C.) Change in political leadership 49
D.) Preference building and voting ignorance 50
E.) Non-intentional structural factors 51
3.4.3.3 Method 52
3.4.3.4 Test Results 55
3.4.3.5 Conclusion 65

4. TREATING BREACHES: THE LAW'S AND THE COURT'S ANSWER. 67
4.1 Rules of Primary European Law regarding Breaches of European law by the European Community and its Member States. Damage Compensation and Fines before EC-Courts. 67
4.1.1 Recourse for Member States or the Commission against Member States: fines for non-compliance with ECJ-Judgements. 68
4.1.1.1 Sources of Law 68
4.1.1.2 Responding to breaches: Article 226 Nice Treaty (old 169) 69
4.1.1.3 Growing teeth. The Renewal of Article 228: Penalty Payments for Breaches. (old article 171) 71
4.1.1.4 Member state v. Member state. 79
4.1.2 Recourse for Individuals against the EC: Damage Compensation in Primary Community law. 81
4.1.2.1 Right of Action: Art. 230 Consolidated Treaty (173) 81
4.1.2.2 Right of Compensation: Art. 288 Nice Treaty (215) 82

4.2 ECJ-Jurisdiction: Damages before National Courts: a Recourse for Individuals against Member States. The Introduction of liability of Member States under European Law *84*
4.2.1 Direct effect and supremacy doctrine, Van Gend&Loos 84
4.2.2 Procedural: Francovich and non-implementation of Directives 85
4.2.3 Substantive: Brasserie du Pêcheur, Factortame and liability for legislative action 88
4.3 The Political History of State Liability in the European Union *96*

PART III: THE AIM OF STATE LIABILITY REGULATION. WHAT ARE WE REALLY LOOKING FOR? **103**

5. INTRODUCING NORMATIVE LAW AND ECONOMICS: SEARCHING FOR AN AIM OF STATE LIABILITY LAW 103
5.1 Introduction *103*
5.2 A First Analogy: Efficient Breaches in Contracts and Breaches of European law. *104*
5.2.1 Terminology 104
5.2.2 Dealing with Breached Contracts 105
5.2.3 Breaches of European law and lessons of contract law? 108
5.3 A Second Analogy: The Economics of Tort Law *112*
5.3.1 Traditional Economic Analysis of Tort Law: Reasoning and Goals ... 113
5.3.2 Introducing the State 116
5.3.3 Combining contract law with tort law to understand state liability as a law enforcement instrument. 121
5.3.4 Moving from Ex-post to Ex-ante, or from Enforcement to Compliance 123
5.4 A Third Analogy: The Economics of Crime and Punishment *127*
5.5 Summarising: Is there an economic reasoning in the Private Francovich and Public Art. 226-228 Enforcement? *131*
5.6 Concluding: Aim and Economic Sense of Member State Liability in Enacting Community Law. *132*

6. Are Breaches really that Bad? A Rationale not to allow Breaches......... 138
6.1 An Elementary question and aspects of contract law: why do we need enforceability?......... 138
6.1.1 Kaldor-Hicks efficient agreements 138
6.1.2 Second best solutions......... 140
6.1.3 Inefficient Legislation 140

PART IV: INTRODUCING POSITIVE LAW AND ECONOMICS. REACHING THE AIM......... 145

7. Evaluation of the Current Situation: Two Distinct Enforcement Mechanisms. 145

8. Procedural Aspects. Private and Public Enforcement: Complements or Substitutes? 146
8.1 Evaluation of public enforcement......... 146
8.1.1 What is public enforcement of law and how can it work against a State? The specificity of the European Union......... 147
8.1.2 Borrowing from Criminal Law. Eight Arguments in Favour of Public Enforcement. 150
8.1.2.1 Of Costly Information, Free-riders, Fishermen and Force......... 151
8.1.2.2 Rational Private Ignorance and Public Goods......... 158
8.1.2.3 Indifference and rights vs. interests......... 162
8.1.3 Problems of the Commission's Public Enforcement......... 164
8.2 Evaluation of private enforcement......... 166
8.2.1 The European Court of Justice and private enforcement......... 166
8.2.2 Information as a comparative advantage of private enforcement...... 168
8.2.3 The Credibility Problem of the Private Threat: on procedural hurdles, participation restrictions, group action and punitive damages...... 169
8.2.3.1 Procedural critique......... 169
8.2.3.2 Procedural difficulties and the role of group action in the European Union......... 171
8.2.3.3 Punitive Damages as a Demand Stimulator......... 180
8.2.4 Few cases: does it work or not at all??......... 184

9. SUBSTANTIVE ASPECTS OF PUBLIC ENFORCEMENT: DETERRENCE BY FINES? 187
9.1 Details on the specificities of art. 226-228 .... *187*
9.2 The lack of first and second order deterrence by article 228 and proof thereof. *190*
9.3 Law and Economics of crime *194*
9.4. Existing public state sanctioning: international economic sanctions *195*

PART V: STATE LIABILITY IN TORTS AS A LAW ENFORCEMENT INSTRUMENT. DOES IT WORK? **203**

10. SUBSTANTIVE ASPECTS OF PRIVATE ENFORCEMENT: DETERRENCE BY DAMAGE COMPENSATION? 203
10.1 Introduction *203*
10.2 Distinct features *204*
10.2.1 Different budget restraints 204
10.2.2 The Efficacy of Tort Systems in deterrence 207
10.3 A formal Public Choice Approach *208*
10.3.1 Treaty provisions and regulations: Nontariff Barriers and Free Trade Regulation 210
10.3.2 Transposing Directives: Francovich and the effect on producers' costs 212
10.3.3. The Formal Framework for non-tariff barriers 215
A. Decisions under the absence of liability 215
B. Introducing member state liability 222
10.3.4 Policy Conclusions 234
A. The Status Quo *234*
B. Recommendations *236*

SUMMARY **241**

LIST OF CASES **246**

BIBLIOGRAPHY **249**

FIGURES

Figure 1: Vote Allocation in the Council 9
Figure 2: Categories of Breaching 18
Figure 3: Voting Outcomes and Political Opinions 26
Figure 4: Council Voting Record and Breaches per Member State 32
Figure 5: Scatter Diagrams: Breaches vs. No-Votes 33
Figure 6: Voting Outcomes with Logrolling 36
Figure 7: References for Preliminary Rulings to the Court 45
Figure 8: Descriptive Summary Statistics of Dependent Variables 54
Figure 9: Initial Test Results of a Binomial Regression Model 56
Figure 10: Corrected Test Results of a Binomial Regression Model 58
Figure 11: A Summary of Situations causing Liability and the respective Cases 96
Figure 12: Costs of Voting 118
Figure 13: The Degree of Intent in Tort and Crime: A Scale of Culpability 129
Figure 14: Log-Rolling between two Countries as a Reason not to allow for Breaches 142
Figure 15: Logrolling with three Countries causing Inefficiencies 143
Figure 16: Market Effects of Regulation 211
Figure 17: Directives increasing domestic Producers' Costs on the Market 213

Note: This dissertation takes account of legal acts and jurisprudence up to July 1st 2005.

PART I: INTRODUCTION

1. Introduction

Law is useless without enforcement. The process of making national law equally enforceable not just against individuals or friends of the mighty but also against the mighty themselves, has been a long lasting journey. Nowadays, this is a corner stone of the constitutional democratic state. Making supranational or even international law enforceable against States is a story still unfolding. The latter can be observed daily in the context of the United Nations work. Successes with for example the International Criminal Tribunal for the former Yugoslavia are followed by less successful initiatives like the International Criminal Court. The former, being supranational law - and more specific *European Community legislation* is the subject of this dissertation.

A number of important European institutions have stated that implementing European legislation is of highest importance[1]. To fulfil this desire, two mechanisms have been created.

The first one is a so called *"public enforcement procedure".* As « guardian of the Treaty », the European Commission was given the power to bring to the European Court of Justice any Member State which infringes Community law (articles 226 and 228 of the EC Treaty). Before going to the European Court of Justice, the Commission has to enter into formal consultations with the Member State, first with a « letter of formal notice », which is a request for information, then with a « reasoned opinion », which sets the Commission's definitive position on the alleged infringement. More than 90% of the cases are solved before reaching the European

---

[1] The European Council annexed a *Declaration on the Implementation of Community Law* to the Maastricht Treaty. The European Court of Justice stated in its Opinions on the Treaty on a European Economic Area that *the role and effectiveness of Community law are fundamental to the future legal and institutional architecture of western Europe.* The European Commission stated in 1978 that *the application of EC law was to be considered as important as its creation.* The European Parliament has constantly insisted on the importance of compliance with European Community Legislation and has passed a Resolution on 9th February 1983 on the responsibility of the Member States for the application of and compliance with Community Law. As a consequence

Court of Justice, illustrating that both the Commission and the member states appreciate a "diplomatic" solution of infringement problems.[2]
In 2001, the European Commission opened 2180 new cases of examination against Member States of the European Union under suspicion of having breached European legislation[3]. It received 1027 complaints from individuals against Member States[4]. In the same year, the Commission referred 157 cases to the European Court of Justice. The teeth of these proceedings against Member States are the possibility of fines.

The trigger point of this dissertation is the analysis of one of the most famous and contended products of jurisdiction of the European Court of Justice**: the liability of Member States of the European Community for breaches of European legislation.** This so called *"Francovich doctrine"* has been developed by the European Court of Justice as an alternative -since private- law enforcement mechanism to the European Commission's public enforcement activities.

Before dealing with these different enforcement mechanisms in greater detail in Part IV, I will first discuss some of the most basic institutions and instruments of decision-making in the European Union in **Part I**.

Part II will clarify factual questions on breaches. I will explain what exactly constitutes a breach of European law and will deal with some statistical data on the occurrence of breaches. Following that, an attempt will be made to explain theoretically why Member States breach decisions they (in)directly supported. In an empirical chapter, the explanatory power of these theories will be examined. A detailed legal analysis will conclude this second part. This analysis will cover both primary European law and jurisdiction by the European Court of Justice dealing with breaches of Community law. With the use of the work produced by political science and legal scholars, I will also explain the philosophy of the court, which, in conferring rights upon individuals in order to deter Member States from breaching European legislation, used liability as a law enforcing instrument and will briefly sketch the political history of the State liability doctrine.

---

of this resolution, the Commission publishes annual reports documenting the application of Community Law by the Member States.

[2] Tallberg (2003)

[3] Source: the European Commission's 2001 annual report on the application of Community Law.

[4] id.

The focus of this dissertation will however not lay on the justice aspects of European State liability law, but on the **incentive effects** it is thought to provide. In **Part IV**, This dissertation takes a closer, comparative look at the workings of the different enforcement mechanisms and attempts to embed this analysis in the law and economics literature in **Part III**. It is not easy to fit state liability into the classical framework of the law and economics literature. The decision-making phase in the European Union shows analogies with contract-like negotiations, obliging me to address contract law. The more interesting post-decision-making phase shows characteristics of both the economic analysis of torts and crime. Therefore, I will draw analogies *with* and use the findings *of* the economic analysis of tort law and criminal law, of law enforcement, of international sanctions and use public choice arguments since the actor dealt with here is the State, and not the individual typical to classical Law and Economics literature.

Finally, in **Part IV** respectively **Part V**, I will turn to the methods of economics and the economic analysis of law to analyse more closely the effectiveness of both the Commission's acting and the private liability instrument in deterring unwanted state behaviour.

2. Basics of the European Union

2.1 The Acquis Communautaire

The law of the European Community, or the *acquis communautaire*, consists of three types of legislation. Firstly, there is **primary legislation**, written down in Treaties. (Treaty of Rome (1957) amended by the Single European Act (1987), the Treaty on European Union - 'Maastricht Treaty' (1992), the Treaty of Amsterdam (1997) and the Treaty of Nice (2002). These are to be ratified by the Member States' national parliaments. They have direct effect[5] *(unmittelbare Wirkung)*, meaning that this supra-national law becomes legislation that is to be applied before national courts by national judges.

Secondly, there is **secondary legislation** in the form of regulations (*Verordnungen)*, directives *(Richtlinien)* and decisions. Regulations and decisions do not require any action by national parliaments[6]. Directives mention an aim to be reached within a certain time limit[7]. It is up to the Member State to decide with national legislation on the form and means of achieving this aim[8]. This secondary legislation is adopted by the Council of the EU; or by the Council and the European Parliament in a co-decision procedure[9]. The European Commission has the monopoly right to initiate proposals for regulations and directives[10].

Thirdly, **case law** by the European Court of Justice or the European Court of First Instance forms a final form of EC-legislation. Supremacy of Community law has lead this case law to be of utmost importance, also to domestic legal systems.

Further, a distinction should be made between the **vertical and horizontal direct effect** of European legislation. Legislation with vertical direct effect can be invoked by an individual against a Member State in national court. Legislation having horizontal

---

[5] The direct effect doctrine is developed by standing jurisdiction of the European Court of Justice. Chapter 4 gives more details on this doctrine. (see section 4.2.1, page 84)

[6] Article 249 Nice Treaty

[7] id.

[8] id.

[9] id.

[10] Article 251 Nice Treaty

direct effect can also be invoked directly by an individual against another individual in a national court. Treaties, Regulations and decisions all have both these effects[11]. Directives are a special case. They do not have a horizontal direct effect since, upon timely and correct transposition by Member States, they become national legislation which is in any case applicable in national courts. As will be seen below, upon incorrect or late transposition, they have vertical direct effect[12], meaning that individuals[13] can invoke the directive against the Member State in question[14] in national courts.

2.2 Institutions of the European Union

2.2.1 The European Commission

The European Commission is without doubt one of the most important driving forces in the European Union. The Treaties have delegated competencies to the Commission in four different areas:

- **Legislative:** The Commission has the so-called "right of initiative", which is in effect a monopoly right to propose legislation to the Council and the European Parliament.[15] In this function, every Commissioner is to bear in mind the general interest of the Union and its citizens, not those of specific member states, industries or other pressure groups.[16] Before making legislative proposals, the Commission has to apply the "subsidiarity principle", i.e.: it has to ascertain that the problem can be solved more efficiently on the European level than by national, regional of local action.

- **Executive:** As the European Union's executive body, the Commission is responsible for managing and implementing the EU budget and the policies and

---

[11] The doctrine of direct effect was laid down by the European Court of Justice in Case C-26/62, Van Gend & Loos *v.* Administratie Der Belastingen. European Court of Justice (1963b)

[12] See section 4.2.1 at page 23

[13] In its jurisdiction, the European Court of Justice has set out conditions for individuals to hand in a liability claim against a Member State. These conditions are mentioned on page 86.

[14] Note that individuals do not have to be nationals of a Member State of the European Union, neither that the Member State in question should be the one where the individual is a national of.

[15] Articles 192 and 208 of the consolidated Treaty authorise the European Parliament resp. the Council to "request the Commission to submit any appropriate proposal on matters on which it considers that a Community act is required for the purpose of implementing this Treaty." This request however, does not bind the Commission.

[16] Articles 211, 213 Consolidated Treaty

programmes adopted by Parliament and the Council. In these fields, the Commission enjoys considerable discretion; discretion it has typically used to strengthen its influence. European competition law may serve as an example for this.

- **Enforcement:** Together with the European Court of Justice, the European Commission is responsible for ensuring the proper application of Community law by the member states.[17] Through this task, the Commission has earned the title *"Guardian of the Treaties".* The exact details of this enforcement process are discussed below in section 4.2.1 on page 67.

- **Representation:** The Commission is the outwards face of the European Union and represents the European Union on the international stage, for example by negotiating agreements between the EU and other countries.

2.2.2 The Council of the European Union

The **Council of the European Union** is the EU's main decision-making body and like the European Commission and Parliament, it was set up by the founding treaties in the 1950s. The Council represents the member states and in theory, its nine different assemblies are attended by the competent ministers from each of the EU's national governments.

The nine different Council constellations are :

- Economic and Financial Affairs ("ECOFIN")
- Employment, Social Policy, Health and Consumer Affairs
- Competitiveness (Internal Market, Industry and Research)
- Transport, Telecommunications and Energy
- Agriculture and Fisheries
- Environment
- Education, Youth and Culture
- General Affairs and External Relations
- Justice and Home Affairs

In the first seven configurations, the ministers negotiate and vote upon legislative action in the form of directives and regulations (often in a co-decision procedure with the European Parliament). These matters largely represent the first pillar of the European Union, i.e.: those matters of which the member states have decided to pool their sovereignty and delegate decision-making powers to the EU institutions.

Both remaining meetings represent the second and third pillar: the Common Foreign and Security Policy (CFSP) and the judicial co-operation in criminal matters. Here, member states have decided to exercise "intergovernmental co-operation" rather than delegate power to Brussels. Hence, meetings in these groups have the character of co-operation and co-ordination, rather than law-making. The same can be said of the ECOFIN Council, where the economics and finance ministers carry out the co-ordination of the economic policies of member states.[18]

In day-to-day practice, more than 90% of this work is performed by national diplomats and bureaucrats of the *Permanent Representations*, which negotiate on a daily basis in the Council in Brussels. More difficult matters on which no consensus could be reached, are referred to the *COREPER I and II* (Committée des Représentants Permanents) where, eventually, the member states' ambassadors to the European Union will enter the negotiation process. Only when a solution can still not be reached, the ministers themselves will discuss the matter on their regular Council meetings.

The Council (of the European Union) is not to be confused with the "European Council", which is an international organisation non connected to the European Union. The Russian Federation for example, is a member of the European Council.

2.2.3 The European Parliament

Based in France (Strasbourg), Belgium (Brussels) and Luxembourg, the European Parliament as well dates back to the founding treaties of the 1950s. Since 1979, the members of Parliament (MEPs) are directly elected by the citizens they represent. Just as in *traditional* national parliaments, MEPs sit not in national blocks but in Europe-wide political groups that bring together all the main political parties operating in the EU member states. In the legislative period 2004-2007, the Parliament counts 732 members.

---

[17] Article 211 consolidated Treaty.

[18] Such co-ordination has gained special importance in the light of the adoption of the Euro and the single monetary policy.

The parliament's legislative task has been considerably smaller than the one national parliaments typically enjoy, but has grown in importance over time. Nowadays, one of the most common procedures for adopting secondary legislation is the *co-decision procedure* (see both sections below). At least on paper, this places the European Parliament and the Council on an equal footing. Recent years have seen the Parliament becoming more self-confident and it has increased its influence in decision-making, both vis-à-vis the Council and the Commission.

Besides its role in decision-making, the European Parliament also functions as a body of democratic supervision (over the Council, but especially over the Commission) and decides -jointly with the Council- over the European Union's annual budget.

2.3 Decision-Making in the European Union

Decision-making processes for primary and secondary European legislation are distinctly different. Primary legislation is decided upon by all heads of states in high-profile summits, which typically take place about every four to five years.[19] The passing of treaties requires unanimity amongst all member states, but it remains a matter of every single member state to decide upon the practical legal proceedings of its ratification. Whereas for some member states, only the national parliament has to ratify the treaty text, in others, referenda have to be held for the member state in question to ratify the consensus text.[20]

The passing of secondary legislation is the typical day-to-day work taking place in the European institutions in Brussels. As regulated in article 251 of the Nice Treaty, the Commission has the monopoly right on the initiation of proposals on directives and regulations. It makes use of this right by delivering proposals to the member states in

---

[19] Catching strong media attention for about two weeks, these Treaty changes are in effect prepared for intensively over a long period of time on a lower political level in so called Intergovernmental Conferences.

[20] Consider for example the famous case of Ireland, where the failure of a national referendum on the Treaty of Nice obliged member states to re-negotiate the Treaty text. Whereas referenda might strengthen the treaty's democratic legitimation as well as member states' negotiation power vis-à-vis other member states, they also make it more difficult for political representatives to reach compromises.

the Council, where negotiation amongst member states as well as with the Commission will take place. In the course of this process, the Commission might alter its legislative proposal, might decide to withdraw it if a majority for it seems unlikely, or might manage to make the Council adopt the proposal. In the majority of issues, this is done not by simple, but by *qualified majority vote* (QMV).[21]

The east-extension of the European Union and the (foreseen) enactment of a European Constitution have caused the allocation of votes between member states and the definition of a "qualified majority" to have changed rather frequently in recent times. It is sufficient here to mention the system in power at the moment of writing.[22]

Starting from November 1st 2004, and until the entry into force of the European constitution, the number of votes each country can cast (including the new member states) is regulated as follows in the Treaty of Nice:**Fehler!**

Germany, France, Italy, United Kingdom	29
Spain and Poland	27
The Netherlands	13
Belgium Czech Republic, Greece, Hungary and Portugal	12
Austria and Sweden	10
Denmark, Ireland, Lithuania, Slovakia and Finland	7
Cyprus, Estonia, Latvia, Luxembourg and Slovenia	4
Malta	3
TOTAL	**324**

Figure 1: Vote Allocation in the Council

[21] For some details of this voting rule, see page 47. Preparing for a larger European Union, the Nice Treaty has extended the number of issues where qualified majority voting is applicable. However, qualified majority voting is still <u>not</u> applied in some sensitive areas such as the common foreign and security policy, taxation, asylum and immigration policy.

[22] Previous voting systems are explained for on page 47.

Under this system, a qualified majority will be reached:
-if a majority of the number of member states approve AND
-at least 72,3% of votes is cast in favour.

In addition, a member state may ask for confirmation that the votes in favour represent at least 62% of the total population of the Union. If this is found not to be the case, the decision will not be adopted.

Although the Constitution is to enter into force on November 1st 2006, the current consensus is that these decision-making rules will remain valid until 1 November 2009, the date of commencement of the new Commission which will be set up after the European elections of 2009.

Parallel to the Council's voting, the European parliament has a legislative say in an increasing number of areas as well.[23] The complicated, so-called **co-decision procedure** describes two ways in which the Parliament participates in passing secondary legislation. The most relevant way is described in article 251.

Following this article, the European Parliament can deliver its opinion on a legislative proposal of the Commission. The Council can then either accept the Parliament's amendments (and adopt the act with a qualified majority) or reject them, in which case it will communicate a common Council position to the Parliament.

In the second round, it is up to the Parliament to approve the Council's common position[24] (meaning the act will be considered as adopted) or -acting by simple majority- reject the common position. In the latter cases, the legislative proposal will simply disappear and not be adopted. Alternatively, the Parliament can again propose amendments to the Council's common position, on which the Commission will deliver it's opinion.

If, in the next round, the Council agrees with *all* Parliamentary amendments, the act will be considered adopted. Note that the Council can approve the amendments by qualified majority. However, the Council has to act **unanimously** on the amendments on which the Commission has delivered a negative opinion.

---

[23] Articles 251 and 252 Consolidated Treaties
[24] Non-action by the Parliament will be interpreted as approving of the Council's common position.

If these conditions are not fulfilled (meaning: a qualified majority did not agree with *all* amendments, or at least one member state does not agree with the critical amendments), a final provision foresee for the instalment of a **Conciliation Committee.** This committee is to reach agreement on a joint compromise, which - passing the normal voting rules in both organs- can become secondary Community legislation.

This voting mechanism, which seems forever unstable as a result of continuous (r)evolutions in the political framework of the European Union will (again) soon reach its end. This time, the change seems to be of a more enduring and qualitative nature, as it is embedded in nothing less than a European Constitution.

2.4 The European Constitution

On October 29th 2004, the Heads of State of the 25 member states and the 3 candidate countries signed the Treaty establishing a Constitution for Europe which was unanimously adopted by them on 18 June of the same year.

This Treaty can enter into force only once it has been adopted by each of the signatory countries in accordance with its own constitutional procedures. This ratification can comprise either or both of the following two types of mechanism:

- the "parliamentary" method: adoption by a Parliamentary vote;
- the "referendum" method: a referendum is held, submitting the text of the Treaty directly to citizens, who vote for or against it.

First of all, the Constitution, in articles I-33 to I-35, changes the denomination of secondary Community legislation. Whereas at present, article 249 of the EC Treaty lists five basic acts (directive, regulation, decision, recommendation and opinion), article I-33 distinguishes between **legislative acts** and **non-legislative acts.** As a sub-group of legislative acts, two sources of law exist: **laws** and **framework laws**.

European laws correspond to what is currently known as a regulation. Such law is thus directly applicable in all member state and does not need to be transposed into domestic law. The definition of a European framework law corresponds to that of directive. It lays down the results to be achieved but leaves it to the Member States to choose the measures to be taken to achieve these results within a given time limit. Article I-34 lays down the procedures for adopting laws and framework laws, in most cases on the basis of the ordinary legislative procedure described immediately below.

Non-legislative acts are acts of general application for the implementation of legislative acts. They largely correspond to decisions, recommendations and opinions and generally fall in the decision-power of the Commission. (Article I-35)

One of the Constitution's main novelties are the changes in the legislative procedure. Repealing the existing system (with the allocation of votes to member states and the definition of a qualified majority), it intends to replace it by a **double majority system**: majority of the Member States and of the population of the Union.

Such majority will be reached in the Council with

- at least 55% of the members of the Council, comprising at least fifteen of them and representing Member States comprising at least 65% of the population of the Union. A blocking minority must include at least four Council members.[25]

Besides, the constitutional treaty proposes to extend the qualified majority vote to approximately 20 additional provisions.[26] Although many of those are rather uncontroversial and include issues in areas such as culture, the internal market or freedom, security and justice, they also include controversial points, such as changes by qualified majority to the statute of the European System of Central Banks in articles III-187.

As a potential opening for even more qualified majority votings, a new switchover clause in article IV-444 (the *"Bridge Clause"* or *"Simplified Revision Procedure"*) will make it possible to make the transition to the qualified majority vote in certain areas, after a final unanimous vote at the European Council .

The role of the European Parliament largely remains unchanged and is regulated in Article III-396. This article is close to identical to the co-decision procedure under the old rules.

---

[25] Article I-25 of the constitutional Treaty

[26] As described in article I-23, §3: "The Council shall act by a qualified majority except where the Constitution provides otherwise." Important fields where decision are still unanimous are: taxation, the enhanced co-operation between member states , social policy, agreements with international organisations or third countries and institutional changes in the monetary area.

As on the moment of writing, it remained uncertain whether the Constitutional Treaty would ever pass the ratification process in all member states and enter into force. Both the French and Dutch population declined to accept the constitution in national referenda on May 29th 2005 and June 1st 2005. For the moment, the constitution project has been put on hold.

PART II: A FIRST LOOK AT BREACHES. ON THEIR EXISTENCE, EXPLANATIONS AND THE COURT'S ANSWER.

3. (What and Why) Do Member States breach?

Under the current regime of European legislation and its interpretation, Member State liability for breaches of EC-legislation can occur in different cases, depending on the type of legislation breached. European *directives* form a distinct group of legislation breached, compared to a second group containing European *regulations*, *decisions* and *the Treaties*. A third group are judgements by the European Court of Justice. This chapter offers an overview of the possible infringements of European law qualified as "breach" as well as a short overview of some of the typical breaching actors. The chapter will finish with a theoretical discussion and empirical analysis of the dimension of the importance of breaches of European legislation and possible **explanations** for those breaches.

3.1 Breaching what?

Given the decision-making process as described above, six types of acts by Member States can be distinguished between, all of which constitute a breach of European legislation. These five types of *infringements* concern three sources of law against which is breached:

3.1.1 Treaties, Regulations and Decisions

The European Council (in a possible co-decision procedure with the European Parliament) decides on regulations[27], the European Commission on decisions[28] and

---

[27] Cf. footnote 6

[28] Article 211 Nice Treaty. Decisions are no legislative acts. They are of a purely administrative nature, but bind the individuals, companies or governments they address.

the Member States might decide on Treaties[29]. Expect for ratification of Treaties, these sources of law do not require acts by Member State's Parliaments: they become directly applicable in national courts[30]. Member States can thus not break European law in the legal implementation of these sources of law. In the practical implementation however, they might break these sources of law by their (non) acting, be it on the legislative or the executive level.

Treating the legislative acts, it is indeed so that national laws might be passed that violate Treaty provisions, decisions or regulations. We then speak of infringing national measures that are taken or not reversed.

On the executive level, an act or non-act of the administration or executive organs of the Member State might be a breach of European legislation. Thus, one can speak of absent or insufficient application or enforcement of these sources of law.[31]

In both cases, the terminology for this act is to speak of ***"violations".***

3.1.2 Directives.

Contrary to treaty provisions, regulations and decisions, Member States *can* breach European law in legal implementation issues by failing to transpose a European directive timely and/or correctly into national law[32]. Indeed, these directives, agreed and voted upon in the European council (in an increasing number of cases by a qualified majority voting procedure and not unanimously)[33] are not directly applicable, but require Member States to realise the aims set forward in them by means of national law within a given period of time, specified in the directive[34]. Member States are thus left a considerable amount of sovereignty concerning the form and manner of transposing the directives into national law[35]. Once a Member State has correctly

---

[29] This is governed by the Vienna Convention on the Law of Treaties which entered into force on 27th January 1980.

[30] Cf. Footnote 5

[31] As an illustration of such case, consider European Court of Justice (1991a), Case C-64/88, *European Commission v. France*, where France was found to be acting in breach of Community law, since it found that France had failed to enforce controls in French ports related to minimum mesh sizes of nets, the minimum size of fish permitted to be sold and other provisions regulated in Council Regulations No. 2057/82 and No. 2241/87.

[32] The combination of article 249 Nice Treaty with article 10 of the same treaty allows us to draw this conclusion. Article 249 obliges Member States to transpose European directives. Article 10 demands Member States to take "appropriate action to fulfil the obligations arising out of this treaty".

[33] Article 205 Nice Treaty

[34] Cf. footnote 6

[35] The "effect utile" doctrine developed by the European Court of Justice stipulates that such transposition must happen with means which are the most effective. See European Court of Justice (1963b), Case C-26/62, *Van Gend & Loos v. Administratie Der Belastingen.*

transposed a directive, a new piece of national legislation has been created that is enforceable against fellow individuals, by or against the Member State[36] in national courts.

In the legal implementation process of directives, Member States can fail to correctly transpose a European directive in different ways:

1. The Member State did not take any action at all. No efforts were taken to transpose the European directive into national law. This infringement is known under ***"no notification of transposing measures".***

2. The Member State took action: it created a national law in order to transpose the European directive, but did so too late. This case will be referred to as a ***"late transposition"*** of a directive.

3. The Member State took action: it created a national law in order to transpose the European directive. However, the national law might be found not to reflect the content of the directive to a sufficient extent. This might be so because the national law is found incorrect or incomplete. In this case of an *incorrect transposition* of a directive, the infringement is referred to as ***"not properly incorporated"*** directives.

Remains, of course, the case of a combination of an incorrect and late transposition: the Member State did not transpose the directive correctly neither timely.

However, just as it is the case with treaty provisions, regulations and decisions, Member States can also breach European directives in the practical implementation process. These cases, referred to as ***"not properly applied"*** directives, involve two categories of acting.
Firstly and most obviously, by taking national measures that are opposed to directives, Member States actively violate European law. As these transposed directives have become domestic law, this inconsistency of the national measure with

---

[36] Whether a piece of legislation is enforceable against fellow citizens, by or against the Member State of course depends on the nature of the piece of legislation. A directive mentioning the aim of safer car-traffic for example, might urge a Member State to oblige the wearing of seatbelts. In this case, the Member State can enforce this law against its citizens. In directives aiming at increasing the level of consumer protection, the national legislator might create the right for consumers to return

other domestic legislation will be treated with in national (and not in Community) law. Secondly, also passiveness by the Member State might constitute a breach of European law. Especially in the field of implementing directives, Member State have an obligation to proceed against violators and to guarantee the individual rights of victims of such violators. Again, as directives have been implemented into domestic law, the non-application will be treated with in domestic, not Community law.

3.1.3 ECJ-Judgements

Under primary European law, which will be dealt with below, the European Court of Justice has the authority to find a Member State guilty of breaching provisions of European Community law[37]. The Member State will be obliged to adopt its acting in accordance with the judgement by the Court. If this is not done within due time, the Member State act composes an infringement of European legislation referred to as ***"judgements not yet complied with".***

		Primary European Law	**Secondary European Law**			**Tertiary European Law**
		Treaties	Regulati on	Decisions	Directives	Judgements ECJ
ACTIVE	legislative	*Violation*	*Violation*	*Violation*	*Late transposition or not properly incorporated*	*judgements not yet complied with*
	executive				*Not properly applied*	
PASSIVE	legislative	*Violation*	*Violation*	*Violation*	*no notification of transposing measures*	
	executive				*not properly applied*	

Figure 2: Categories of Breaching

purchased items to the shop within a week of the purchase. Legal conflicts on this topic will be contested between individuals.

[37] Articles 226-228 Nice Treaty.

3.2 Who breaches?

One might argue that the distinction made above between directives, judgements and regulations/treaties/decisions is not very useful. If this analysis of liability rules were really concerned with how to set incentives for actors to act in way conceived as preferable, it might be more useful to distinct between those actors breaching European law.

Different actors might be found breaching European legislation. A first and obvious distinction is to be made between the European Communities on the one hand and its Member States on the other. Just as the member states of the European Union, the European Communities can be found liable against individuals in non-contractual affairs as is regulated in articles 230 and 288 of the Treaty. This Community liability is not the topic of this work and will not be treated in full detail. However, in chapter 4.1.2 Recourse for Individuals against the EC: Damage Compensation in Primary Community law, on page 81, this community liability will be briefly dealt with as it has proven important for the development of non-contractual liability of member states.

Coming back to breaches committed within member states, it should be recognised that "the member state" is indeed a black box with its own dynamics which are not always easy to predict. Think for example of the role of the bureaucracy as an executive agent within the executive branch[38].

However, a horizontal and vertical dimension of "the State" can be identified. First, one should distinguish between breaches committed by the national *legislator* (the case of wrong/late/no transposition of directives; of regulation contradictory to European regulations, treaties or decisions), by the *executive* (the case of acts contradictory to European regulations, treaties or decisions or of improperly applied directives) or by the *judicial* (case of judgements contradictory to European legislation)[39]. On all three horizontal levels, "the State" can be held responsible for breaches of Community law, the European Court of Justice decided[40].

---

[38] Niskanen (1971) and Niskanen (1975)
[39] See European Court of Justice (2003b), Case C-224/01, *Gerhard Köbler V. Republik Österreich*
[40] European Court of Justice (1996a), *Brasserie du Pêcheur*, at para. 34

On the vertical dimension, some member states might be organised in a federal way, which in practice leads to multiple executive or legislative agents[41,42]. Also in non-federal states however, decentralised entities and public emanations will exist, and might breach European law. Hence, also on the vertical level, there might be a number of different actors within a member state which might breach Community law. As described lucidly by Anagnostaras (2001a), the European Court of Justice has decided not to intervene in too much detail in the question exactly which breaching actor might be hold liable in damages. All the Court decided was that this remains to be regulated by national state liability rules, given that the principles of effectiveness and equivalence are respected[43].

This work will deal mainly with decisions made by member states' elected politicians in a central government. Decisions and thus also the incentive effects of the bureaucracy and of the jurisprudence will not be considered in this analysis. Moreover, this work considers incentives for politicians in executive (government) and in legislative (coalition partners in parliament, opposition) to be identical. This assumption is made solely for the purpose of simplicity and does not seem to be too far-fetched. Most Member States of the European Union are governed by majority governments, meaning that the executive political parties bearing a loss or enjoying a benefit from breaching European law are also the ones having the majority -and are thus politically responsible- for passing the law in the legislative body[44]. In order for that reasoning to function, a certain amount of governmental discipline is silently assumed. Governmental coalition are thought of as one (1) unit with identical interests. If this were not the case, minorities in the parliament would be able to pass legislation with the help of at least one governmental party and against another governmental party. Then, parliament has different interests than the executive,

---

[41] As an example, consider Germany where the states (*Länder*) enjoy legislative and executive compentencies also in matters regulated by European law. By their (non) acting, these Länder can breach European law. The same goes for other (more or less) federal European Union member states such as for example Belgium, Spain and Austria.

[42] Note that in federally organised states, the sub-national executive and legislative powers cannot be subject to the European Commission's public enforcement mechanisms under article 226-228 Consolidated Treaty since only the (federal) member state is a signing party of those treaties. In cases of alleged breaches by sub-national agents, the Commission can proceed against the federal member state which in turn can hold the regional actor accountable under national legislation.

[43] These principles will be examined more closely on page 94.

making the case more complicated. Clearly, this too is not too realistic: different parties in coalition governments do have different agendas and despite governing agreements, cabinet crises do occur. Thus, one party of the coalition might benefit or suffer more from some certain act and decide to breach a government leave the coalition.

3.3 Statistics: how many breaches?

Now, after having outlined *who* might breach Community law *how*, let's turn our attention to the seriousness of the breaching problem.

The only data source on breaches of Community law available to scholars of compliance with European law are the *Annual Reports on Monitoring the Application of Community Law*, published by the European Commission[45]. According to the annual reports, more than 15.700 infringements proceedings have been initialised by the Commission[46] since 1978. An annual average of about 1000 complaints by individuals are received and the European Court of Justice rules on about 80 infringement cases per year since the 1990s[47].
Based on these reports, there seems to be a prevalent agreement among scholars that the European Union does have a problem with Member States not complying with European law. Whereas a first group of scholars (Snyder (1993), Weiler (1992), Mendrinou (1996), Tallberg (2000), Tallberg (2002) and Tallberg (2003)) judge the problematic as serious and systematic, a second group of scholars argues that the level of state non-compliance with European law is of the same extent as of state non-compliance with domestic laws. (See Keohane and Hoffmann (1990) and Neyer, Wolf et al. (1999))

---

[44] At least in some member states, institutional and/or political tensions between government and parliament are seen by some members of parliament to explain part of the problem on non-compliance with Community legislation. See European Parliament-Commissie juridische zaken en interne markt (2002)

[45] See http://www.europa.eu.int/comm/secretariat_general/sgb/droit_com

[46] As will be seen below, the European Commission plays an important role in the enforcement of European law. (see 4.1 Rules of Primary European Law regarding Breaches of European law by the European Community and its Member States. Damage Compensation and Fines before EC-Courts. on page 67)

[47] Börzel (2001)

The impressive figures from the Commission's reports are played down in a recent study by Börzel (2001), which offers a justified critique on the trustworthiness of the data in the annual reports. She claims that the data in the annual reports cannot be used as an indicator, neither for the absolute actual level of non-compliance nor for relative changes in compliance over time in the European Union. Börzel identifies problems of "unrevealed non-compliance" and of "incomplete data" as the main reasons to be cautious in using the data as indicators of non-compliance with European law.

Firstly, *unrevealed non-compliance* means that not all cases where Member States breach European legislation show up in the annual reports because not all of them are proceeded against by the European Commission. This thesis is confirmed by the fact that under its Article 234 authority, the European Court of Justice has preliminary ruled many acts by Member States to be breaches of law without those acts having caught the attention of the European Commission before[48]. Börzel suggests this lack of detection by the Commission might be partially the result of limited resources of the Commission in tracing breaches. Tallberg and Jönsson (2001) however mention a political motive, as both Member States and Commission are interested in future cooperation[49]. The Commission might thus show mercy with some breaches of law in order to ensure a Member State complying with another provision deemed more crucial by the Commission. Those breaches might thus very well be "revealed" by the Commission, but no action is taken to repeal them. Börzel also recognises this by stating that "the Commission prefers quiet negotiations and bargaining to formal sanctions in order to induce compliance. It considers an official opening of Art. 226 proceedings only *when all other means have failed.*"[50]

Irrespective of which explanation is more accurate, it is clear that some breaches will not enter the annual reports and hence those reports can only provide an image too

[48] When a case is brought before a national Court in one the Member States, this Court might (in lower instances) or even has to (when no appeal is possible) refer a question to the European Court of Justice under article 234 for a preliminary ruling when it believes unclarity on the interpretation or relevance of European Community legislation exists.
[49] Tallberg and Jönsson (2001) at pp. 14-15
[50] Börzel (2001), pp. 812

positive of the present level of non-compliance by Member States[51]. Also, as indicated by the article 234 proceedings, and as will be discussed in detail below, there is an alternative law enforcement instrument of a more private nature to the European Commission's efforts which have a public nature.
Börzel's second critique is on the incompleteness and inconsistencies of the data provided in the annual reports. The fact that the Commission has repeatedly changed the way in which data is reported, combined with some inconsistencies in reporting makes cross-time analyses difficult, but not impossible.

Börzel argues that when the reports are analysed correctly, the conclusion is that the European Union does *not* have a systematic implementation problem and that only four Member States are found to consistently not comply with European law[52]. She argues that the number of breaches mentioned in the reports did indeed increase dramatically over the years, but that this was due in part to the increasing amount of European legislation ("increased breaching opportunities") and to the more active enforcement efforts of the Commission in light of the implementation of the internal market programmes.

Claiming that one should measure non-compliance as a percentage of all legislation, and trying to prove that there truly is no big compliance problem, Börzel mentions the high percentages of "implemented directives". These well-known tables show the percentage of directives which were implemented timely by Member States.[53] The figures are indeed rather impressive, in a positive way. In 1992, the "worst scholar" was Greece, which implemented "only" 92% of directives within due time. Figures have remained high since.

Deducting from this fact, as Börzel does, that there isn't really a problem with non-complying states and that mainstream scholarship has been too critical on states, seem however a somewhat hastened conclusion.

---

[51] Note that these data could still be useful when analysing relative changes of compliance over time, also when some breaches remained "unrevealed". In order to be so however, there should be no adverse selection in the data offered: the efforts made by the Commission in detecting breaches should remain equal over time. This however, is not the case.
[52] Börzel identifies Italy, France, Belgium and Greece
[53] European Commission (2003)

As has been said repeatedly: figures "only cover a fraction of the violations of Community Law in the Member States"[54] and only show infringements *detected and made public*. There is no doubt that many infringements remain unaccounted for. Exactly how many those might be, remains totally unknown and makes conclusions on the "seriousness" of the problem subject to a large deal of speculation. Therefore, the conclusion made by Börzel that the "level of non-compliance is rather modest and has remained stable over time"[55] seems somewhat rushed, especially what concerns the first part of it.

Interesting as Börzel's paper might be, nothing is said on the deterrence effect of the Commission's enforcement efforts. Larger number of infringements are corrected for more intense enforcement efforts by the Commission, but what could be the dynamics of this problem? Could one expect Member States to anticipate the Commission's efforts in tracing breaches, causing such higher efforts to lead to lower numbers of breaches? If so, Börzel's argument that "infringements are frequent *because* of the Commission's efforts", has to be to corrected to: "infringements are high *despite of* the Commission's enforcement efforts".

If the later is the case, the deterrence effect of such enforcement efforts can be said to be modest, making the problem more relevant than Börzel judges it to be.
One can illustrate this, using the above mentioned example of transposed directives. As will be seen below, the European Court of Justice has made Member States liable in damages to private individuals for breaches of European law, given that those breaches are *sufficiently serious*. In its jurisdiction, the Court has established that the mere failure of a Member State to transpose a directive in due time into national is a sufficient condition for such *sufficiently serious breach* and hence for liability. The *incorrect* transposition of a directive however only leads to liability when it is so grave that Member States are found to have "manifestly and gravely disregarded the limits of exercise of power". As this is a condition rather difficult to prove, and given that the European Court of Justice has been rather cautious in the application of liability to incorrect transposition in order not to interfere too much in the legislative authority of national parliaments, Member States have found themselves on the safe side by just transposing *something* in due time.

---

[54] Börzel (2001), pp. 808
[55] id. pp. 804

The figures mentioned above do not control for incorrect transpositions, they count for all what Member States call "transpositions of directives". Hence, in my opinion the high number of transpositions does not reflect a high implementation of European law; and secondly: increased enforcement efforts do not necessarily have a deterrence effect.

Be that as it be, Börzel's interesting analysis makes the discussion on private and public enforcement of European law even more interesting. If non-compliance figures were really as low as Börzel claims, what could be the role of enforcement strategies to this (claimed) fact? What is the role of private enforcement about which Börzel doesn't speak at all? Is it useful at all? If non-compliance figures were not as positive as Börzel claims -which is what most scholars believe- is this because of the absence of any deterrence effect in the Commission's enforcement efforts? Could private enforcement possess such deterrence effect?

Given that the empirical data on breaches is somewhat unclear, let us now turn to some theoretical explanations in the next chapter: why would Member States breach European law? Some theoretical arguments as well as empirical proof will be presented.

3.4 Why do Member States breach? Theory and Empirics.

Economists have spent much effort understanding decision-making in the Council and on the primary legislative level[56], but have so far largely neglected the analysis of reality following this legislation-drafting. Economists often assumed states to act according to the legislative acts they decided upon. This assumption however, is questionable. Indeed, decisions "voluntarily" agreed upon are not always respected.

To start with, member states can be said to agree either **directly** or **indirectly** with decisions taken in the Council. When member States truly support a legislative proposal and thus vote in favour of it, they are said to support it directly. When member states do not support the content of a proposal, they might still vote in favour

[56] A large branch of literature to be mentioned here concerns the theory of power indices. See for example Garrett and Tsebelis (1999), Steunenberg, Schmidtchen et al. (1999), Holler (1984) and Shapley and Shubik (1954).

of it, and will hence support it indirectly. States will do so in the process of logrolling. They will help States favouring the proposal passing it, in the hope to receive their help (i.e.: votes) upon passing another proposal they favour themselves. Finally, member states might neither support a proposal nor vote in favour of it. If the proposal passes with a (qualified) majority, it is also legally binding member states that voted against. Those member states can however also be said to have indirectly supported the proposal since they agreed that decisions will be passed with a (qualified) majority vote. This voting rule, as well as all primary legislation has been passed with the explicit consent of all. The following figure summarises the possible voting outcomes and their meanings.

Vote **True Opinion**	**YES**	**NO**
YES	*Direct support*	-
NO	*Indirect support* Logrolling Indirect political disagreement	*Indirect support* Direct political disagreement

Figure 3: Voting Outcomes and Political Opinions

Member states thus do not directly support all proposals passed in the council. This **direct political disagreement** can be seen as a first and most obvious explanation for breaches of (in this case) secondary European legislation.

Following, this hypothesis will be tested by means of a simple correlation-test between breaches and no-votes. After that however, other reasons for member states breaching (not only secondary) European law will be discussed, which are not necessarily linked to voting behaviour in the Council. Those will be : Change in political leadership, log-rolling, preference building, voting ignorance, reasons of a structural kind such as the degree of federalism and administrative well-functioning and reason linked to the inherent character of the law such as vagueness and conflicting principles of law. These will first be theoretically explained and operationalised, after which their explanatory power will be tested.

A distinction will be made between intentional and non-intentional breaches, where "intentional" is thought to indicate the presence of a willingness to breach in a political decision-process which might be subject to the influence of a tort system. Non-intentional factors are not directly linked to an active political decision concerning European law. They might be structural characteristics of the political arena which differ amongst member states (in which case they enter a regression analysis as variables), or might be the very basics of "law", which incentive mechanisms wouldn't be able to change (those would enter a regression analysis as constants).

3.4.1 Intentional Breaches

3.4.1.1 Direct political disagreement: a preliminary test of explanation

At first sight, a rather obvious reason for Member States to choose not to comply with European law, is their lack of support *for* and their vote *against* a provision of European legislation. This however is only relevant to those parts of secondary legislation that can pass the decision-making process after a (qualified) majority vote. All remaining secondary law and all primary law are subject to Member States' veto-right: if one member state had voted against such legislative proposal, it would have failed.

Indeed, not all secondary legislation is agreed upon by all. Countries might thus act very "logical" and "consequent" in that they choose not to comply with parts of European law they did not support.

The first question to be asked is thus whether more breaches are observed by Member States having voted against a legislative proposal. If this were the case, lack of political will to comply with European law could be said to be an important reason for breaches to occur.

In order to test this hypothesis, two tests can be thought of.
A **first test** should check the voting behaviour of member states on precisely those directives and regulations they were later found to have breached. Alternatively, a **second test** calculates the correlation coefficient between the number of "no"-votes by a member state (irrespective of the issues they concern) and the number of breaches committed by that very member state.

A.) Data collection and bias problems.

Interesting as these tests might be, data-related problems occur with both of them, making it difficult to perform the test or to draw any conclusions from their results.

Firstly, there are considerable data collection problems. It is quite a cumbersome task to find out how member states have voted on a legislative proposal in the Council. Minutes of the Council's meeting are readily available since 1999 only and on request for the years preceding 1999. However, there is no truly systematic record of vote-casting by member states[57]. As reported by Mattila[58], voting in the European Council is rather rare. The Chair of the Council can accept a legislative proposal in speaking, if he "knows" there is a sufficient majority under member states. As all other member states, member states opposing or abstaining on the subject could then still request for the publication of their vote in the minutes of the meeting. Entries of member states' voting behaviour can thus only be found in the minutes when their publication has been explicitly requested by a member of the Council or the Commission. In reality, such is pretty rare, leaving one on many occasions with nothing but a guess as to how exactly member states might have voted.

Mattila and Lane (2001), discussing the time period from 1994 to 1998, claim that only in 16 to 25 per cent of the decisions, there was one or more Council members that voted against the majority or abstained from voting. This relatively small share of contested decisions might be interpreted such, that Council members do not necessarily want to make their dissent public, and indicates that the numbers of no-votes counted here are most probably subject to a downward bias of true disagreement.

For the second test, data collecting on the number on "no-votes" was done by manually looking through the Council's meeting minutes and by counting, for every member state, the number of "no" votes. Abstentions where also counted as "No's" since to my estimate, they should be interpreted as a strongly critical voice, as the council has mostly done an effort to reach decisions by consensus. Moreover, the

---

[57] The Council Minutes are available online at: http://register.consilium.eu.int
[58] Mattila (2004)

numerous statements[59] delivered and made public by national delegations were also carefully read through and then judged on their "sceptical" nature. This was done since in many occasions where a qualified majority was reached, member states have decided not to make public detailed voting details, but did publish some statements. Those often make conclusions on (especially negative) voting behaviour possible[60].

Matching these data on the number of no-votes with data on the number of breaches also proved to be rather difficult. The only source of information on these numbers of breaches is the annual reports published by the Commission. When considering the latest available annual report (2002), an obvious problem is the time delay in the enforcement of secondary legislation. Indeed, most of the potentially breached against secondary legislation mentioned in the 2002 annual report passed the Council before 1999, the earliest data for which voting records are available[61]. Only three (3) different directives and four (4) different regulations that originate from 1999 or later are mentioned in the 2002 annual report. It is thus impossible at this point of time to satisfactorily match voting records with breaches of exactly those parts of legislation that was voted upon, reducing the relevance of the first test to one of anecdotal nature. Only around 2006, sufficient data from both the decision-making and the enforcement side might be available to do so, given constant enforcement efforts by the Commission.

As a proxy for breaches committed during the 1999-2003 period, we will use the number of "*Infringements for which proceedings were commenced*" as mentioned in Table 2.1. of Annex II of the 2002 Annual Report. This data covers the *enforcement-period* 1998-2002, meaning that most of the secondary legislation covered by these enforcement efforts passed the Council at the latest in the first half of 90ies.

---

[59] *Statements* are to be distinguished from voting-records. Also member states voting in favour of a proposal can provide a statement, explaining their behaviour.

[60] Note that the reasons for member states to vote against or to abstain are not confined to political disagreement. Member states sometimes mention problems of a legal kind, or sometimes even think the proposed legislation is not going far enough. This makes moral judgement on "breaches" of European law by member states rather difficult. A member state might hence be found to breach European law, only because it did not want to join an act which it found of poor legal quality.

[61] For data on breaches, see Annex IV, part 3 (*"Infringements for non-conformity"*) and part 4 (*"Infringements for incorrect application of national measures implementing the directives"*) of the "XXth report on monitoring the application of Community Law" (2002) to be found at: http://www.europa.eu.int/comm/secretariat_general/sgb/droit_com/pdf/rapport_annuel/20_rapport_annuel_en.htm. For voting-records, see http://register.consilium.eu.int

Moreover, another weak point of this approximation is that the data not only includes breaches of directives and regulations, but also of treaty provisions no single member state voted against.

Secondly, besides these data collection problems, it cannot be excluded that the data is subject to a data selection bias. Data from breaches has to be taken from the Commission's annual reports. For example, one could imagine the Commission's enforcement agents to be especially vigilant against member states' actions after those have voted against a legislative proposal in the Council. If this were true, the cases of breaches reported would over-proportionally reflect exactly those cases where member states voted against.

Also, enforcement efforts by the Commission are not likely to remain constant over time, as Börzel (2001) already indicated[62]. These changing efforts will most probably affect different member states to different degrees, polluting the relation between the number of no-votes and breaches. This is also the main reason why observations in the test are limited to the period starting 1999. With some extra effort in data-collection on voting-records[63], one could run this test for the period from 1994 to 2002. However, those years would include the first years of Sweden's, Austria's and Finland's membership, during which these countries might well have been subject to more intense scrutiny by the Commission than others. Hence, breaching data would have had a bias against those countries in these years, overstating the number of breaches.

Finally, the annual reports by no means reflect all breaches committed. They just show a (probably non-random) sample of breaches detected by the Commission.

This test is not to say that there are no other variables influencing breaching except for voting behaviour. It is rather a simple forerunner to a more complete regression analysis, attempting to explain member states' breaching behaviour. Such similar test has been performed by Mbaye (2001) and will be repeated with more recent data below. What we are especially interested in here is the strength and direction of

---

[62] See page 23

[63] There is data available on the number of suspected breaches from 1994 on. The first annual report available online which reports data in a way comparable to later reports dates back to 1994. See data sources in footnote 61. Council voting records prior to 1999 are not available online, but can be requested with the Council's services.

influence of the number of "no-votes" on breaches reported. Mbaye has chosen "power in the Council" as one of the explanatory variables. This variable is however broader than the one used in this section, also including possibilities of logrolling which are not accounted for here.

B.) The tests-results and interpretations

Starting with this first test, seven different sources of secondary law (three directives and four regulations) sum up to fourteen (14) cases of reported breaches by the different member states. Of these 14 cases, no single voting record can be traced back where one of the allegedly breaching member states has been reported abstaining or voting against the proposed directive or regulation it later breached.

In one case in 2001, France was reported abstaining on the vote on a Council Regulation amending Council Regulation 404/93 on the common organisation of the market in bananas. In the Commission's 2002 annual report, France was then said to be allegedly breaching Commission Regulation (EC) No 896/2001 of 7 May 2001 laying down detailed rules for applying exactly that amended Council Regulation 404/93.

To say this proofs anything is quite far-fetched, even more so when considering that from the remaining thirteen (13) cases, in nine (9) cases no indications whatsoever were found that those member states who were later found suspected of breaching had abstained or voted against the legislative proposal. In four (4) cases, no voting records could be found, as the sources of law were Commission regulations for which no explicit vote by member states in the Council took place. All of those took reference to the application of Council regulations prior to 1999, for which also no voting records are available.

Both the lack of a sufficient number of observations and of data availability, which makes drawing conclusions from this first test impossible, force us to take recourse to the second test, allowing the introduction of proxies to substitute for this lack of data. Instead of "matching" the voting record on every source of law with breaches reported against this very source, the *total* number of no-votes is simply related to the *total* number of breaches by every member state.

The conclusions of the second test are at first sight somewhat surprising. The following table shows the collected data. The data on the number of breaches has also been adjusted for the letters of formal notice sent to member state, in order to capture not only delays of implementation, but enduring breaches. The separation of the data into two categories might also correct for an over-activeness by the Commission, which might be issuing "too many" letters of formal notice.

Member State	no - votes and abstentions	fn+ro+ref Number of Breaches	ro+ref Number of Breaches
IRE	11	625	253
LUX	12	541	240
FI	13	367	82
GR	14	791	334
P	15	711	276
FR	18	913	439
B	19	693	287
ESP	19	597	205
I	19	913	406
NL	20	385	118
A	26	626	237
D	32	678	250
S	32	369	78
DK	34	265	47
UK	35	542	214

fn = letters of formal notice
ro = reasoned opinions
ref = references to the European Court of Justice

Source: 2002 *Annual Report on Monitoring the Application of Community Law, Minutes of the Council Meetings: 1999 - 2003*

Figure 4: Council Voting Record and Breaches per Member State

Correlation tests between the number of abstentions and no-votes on the one side and the number of breaches on the other side yielded following results:
Correlation (no-votes and abstentions; breaches including formal notice) : - 0,354
Correlation (no-votes and abstentions; breaches excluding formal notice): - 0, 379
R square values are 0,13 and 0,14 respectively.

First of all, it is of course, over-simplifying to assess the breaching behaviour of any state as the result of only one variable: its voting record. Without doubt, other factors will influence breaching as well, as illustrated by the low R square of the correlation, making it of little statistical significance. Indeed, the voting behaviour can only explain for 12,5 resp. 14,3 percent of breaches. Many more factors do influence member states' breaching behaviour and this causes the low explanatory power of a simple correlation coefficient between "no-votes" and detected breaches unless those other variables correlate perfectly with the number of no-votes. Given the low R-square value, this is obviously not the case. These other variables will be discussed below.

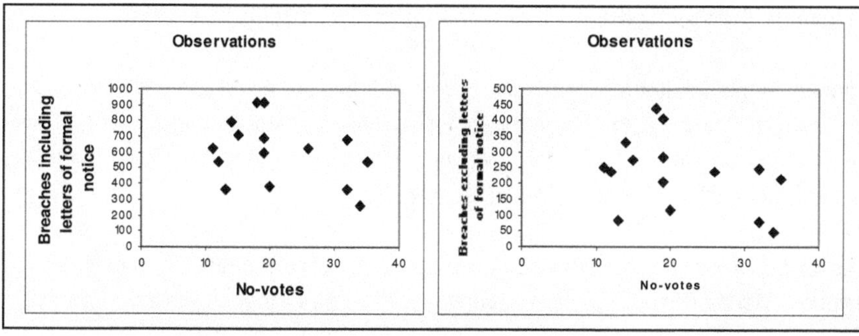

Figure 5: Scatter Diagrams: Breaches vs. No-Votes

Secondly, and most surprisingly, the correlation between no-votes and breaches committed is of a (very weak) negative kind. Hence, the more a member state is observed to vote against legislative proposals, the less one can expect this member state to breach European

law. To illustrate the weakness of the correlation, consider following scatter diagrams.

Anticipating data-related critique, the same test was also conducted with voting-data taken from Matilla (2004). He as well counted no-votes (correcting for abstentions), but did so for the period 1995-2000. Unfortunately, there is no comparable data available on the breaches by member states for the full length of this period. Realising the inaccuracy, a correlation of voting data from 1995-2000 with breaching data from the 1998-2002 annual reports, delivered following –very similar- results. The R-square values are given between brackets.

Correlation(no-votes including abstentions; breaches including formal notice) : -0,051 (R-square: 0,003)

Correlation(no-votes including abstentions; breaches excluding formal notice): -0,096

(R-square: 0,01)
Correlation(no-votes excluding abstentions; breaches including formal notice) : -0,212
(R-square: 0,04)
Correlation(no-votes excluding abstentions; breaches excluding formal notice): -0,258
(R-square: 0,07)

Keeping in mind that the explanatory powers of these correlations are extremely low, some explanations could still be thought of in order to explain this counter-intuitive result. They do remain rather speculative, and can serve only to gain insight in the dynamics of more complex regression analysis.

It is to be noted that the tree countries reported to vote negative most often are Sweden, Denmark and the United Kingdom. All three of them are known to have a Euro-sceptical[64] population, and to scrutinise European legislation on "what's in for them" in a quite sober way. Whereas delegates of some other member states might at times be carried away by a convinced ideology in favour of the "European Idea", it might be the case that delegates of countries more sceptical to the European idea only vote in favour of a proposal when they really support it, hence explaining their higher number of no-votes. The backbone of this explanation is thus kind of turning around the starting explanatory variable: member states might vote "in favour" too fast, without really estimating correctly during voting what are the consequences for their country. When they later find that the piece of legislation (they voted in favour of) actually harms national interest, they might decide to breach it. Simplifying, this reasoning leads to the hypothesis that "the more a member state votes in favour, the more it can expected to breach European law". Logrolling practices are non-ideological situations were this can be thought of, as will be discussed below.

Finally, as has been highlighted in detail, the quality of the data is questionable. Only proxies could be used, which are subject to an adverse selection bias and to a large share of incompleteness. Only since 2002, negative votes seem to be reported in the Council's meeting minutes on a quite regular basis, although for an non-attendant of

---

[64] In fact, these three countries were the only of the fifteen member states not to adopt the Euro as national currency. The levels of public support in these member states, as measured by the Eurobarometer mentioned in footnote 80, are amongst the lowest in the European Union.

those meetings, it remains impossible to assess whether *all* negative votes reported are truly *all* those cast. Before that date however, they were only very exceptionally reported. Also, member states might hold different traditions in voting, which might again diminish the comparability of the number of negative votes across member states. Some member states might avoid voting against a proposal in order not to offend advocating member states when they know there is a qualified majority in favour.

3.4.1.2 Indirect political disagreement: log rolling/package dealing and free riding

It is clear from the preceding that the available data cannot support the hypothesis that "direct political disagreement" is a sufficient explanation for breaches of secondary European law. If at all, the (bad) data available rather seems to point to the contrary, that is to say: that countries that vote in favour of legislative proposals more often, breach them more often as well. Hence, one should introduce more explanatory variables. We start by looking at situations where member states have supported a proposal indirectly.

An additional reason to look into this is primary European law: all Member States of the European Union have signed and ratified these treaties. That is: they have all voted in favour. Voting against can hence not explain any breaching of primary European law. There is however a similarity between the way in which both primary and secondary legislation are negotiated: in both cases, Member States might agree with something which is not in their interest, offering a rationale for breaches.

Primary European legislation is negotiated in a setting where every Member State has to give its explicit consent, and thus at least de jure, has a veto-right. In the reality of the European Union however, this veto-right does not guarantee that all Member States agree with *all* provisions of such primary legislation. Indeed, as it is fair to assume that a country only becomes member of the European Union -and thus signatory of the treaties- if the *overall* benefits of such membership exceed *overall* costs to this country, this does not imply that this country profits from *all* pieces of legislation decided upon in the European Union. However, other Member States will benefit from exactly these contested pieces of legislation, which is the reason why they passed the Council or Treaty making process in the first place.

More correctly, the need to reach (qualified) majorities and -to a lesser extent- the existence of the veto-right will lead to package dealing, meaning that by not using a veto, Member States agree with proposals unfavourable to them on the condition that they will gain in another situation at the cost of another member state. This *logrolling process* might partially explain the phenomenon of Member States not respecting their obligations stemming from European law. It might very well be the case that the directive, regulation or treaty provision is simply not it the (perceived) interest of a Member State, but passed with the support of that very member state, only for it to get another proposal passed which does work in its advantage. Note that this procedure is often said to be a major explanation for the high pace with which the body of European legislation has grown[65].

Thus, also if Member States formally agreed with a proposal (i.e.: voted in favour), they do not necessarily do so in content. Packages are made, where a member state M votes *for* something, actually being against; only to make another Member State S vote in favour of another proposal which this member state S dislikes, but benefits M. This praxis is called *logrolling.* Consider an illustrating example with two member states M and S voting on two legislative proposals: A and B.

State / Proposal	M	S	Vote result	Total Welfare Effect
A	-10	+20	No	+10
B	+30	-10	No	+20
A&B	+20	+10	Yes	+30

Figure 6: Voting Outcomes with Logrolling

Each single proposal is a welfare improvement, but will not pass when it is voted upon separately unless side payments exist[66]. For both proposals, one of the member states will vote against as it affects its country negatively. Bundling proposal A and B to one package however, guarantees it passing the voting and creates a welfare gain

[65] As stated by Salmon (2002): *"Many policies exist that are not wanted per se by a majority of member states but are accepted as parts of logrolling compromises."*

[66] For decision-making in the Council, it seems to be realistic to assume that no direct side-payments exist. Rather than by money payments, Member States are "compensated" by other, favourable regulation.

of 30. Not all logrolling will result in efficient deals however, as a more detailed welfare analysis provided for in part on page 141 will show.

This phenomenon makes empirical research more complicated. Its existence has been proven for the USA by Stratmann (1992). The extra difficulty it brings is that also if a country has voted in favour of a proposal, it might actually be against and the *direct political disagreement* test mentioned above on page 26 cannot truly explain breaches.

What is of specific importance to the occurrence of logrolling in the context discussed here is the explanation for breaches it may offer. Whereas economic studies of the European Union have mainly focussed on proving the relevance of logrolling in decision-making and the explanations it might offer for some observations such as the lack of transparency and the growing size of (European) government[67], very few have considered its influence on *post*-decision incentives.

It is however clear that this co-operation amongst member states in the form of logrolling creates an incentive to free-ride. If both parties were to profit from a legislative proposal, they wouldn't have had to take recourse to logrolling to reach a decision on the issues. Clearly, every country has an incentive to breach that part of the package-deal which is of disadvantage to it. In this specific example, after package A&B passed, country M can be expected to breach obligations from proposal A; and country S from proposal B.

Clearly, the same intuition holds when changing the setting from a two-country group to a more realistic N-country group. Moreover, one could even argue that, the larger the deciding group, the more free-riding will occur. Indeed, the more participating countries, the higher the monitoring costs for the country or institution having an interest in enforcing the deal. Member states do have quite some possibilities *not* to enforce a given piece of legislation. Even after transposing it officially into national legislation, administrative acts or non-acts can effectively undercut the becoming effective of that legislation.

---

[67] Reference is made to Tullock (1959), Schwartz (1975), Coleman (1966), Stratmann (1992) and Stratmann (1997)

The enormous implications of this free-riding reflex on the European Union should be clear to the reader. A large deal of decision-making on both the primary and secondary levels are subject to the logrolling phenomenon. As the European Union enlarged from fifteen to twenty-five countries in May 2004, and given the outcome of the constitutional debate, (qualified) majority voting *-and hence logrolling-* will only gain importance in the process of passing secondary legislation. In practice, the inevitably opposed interests of member states on changing issues will lead to nothing less than a market in votes. This will in turn provide member states with the free-riding effects discussed, causing a tremendous potential problem of enforcement. If no efficient relief is provided for, an ever growing body of legislation (because of logrolling) might be subject to a high degree of free-riding, in effect putting the rule of law out of place.

In the absence of any legal remedy to this free-riding, the only costs of breaching to member states might be a loss of reputation. Indeed, the member state trying to pass its legislative proposal in the council will be most interested in the log-rolling member states not only supporting the proposal in the Council but also doing so afterwards, in reality[68]. For free-riding to occur, detection should be difficult to detect, since it has a negative effect on future co-operation between member states, diminishing the "value" of a country's vote on the market for support. To some, it might seem questionable however, if political decision makers can be thought of as considering such long-term effects. Depending on the efficiency of law-enforcement mechanisms in place, detection might take quite some time, affecting reputation and negotiation power only on the long term.

Incentives to free ride not only exist in the case of logrolling by means of package-dealing, but also in more "classical" forms of co-operation. Consider (contrary to the example offered above) a co-operation on one issue only. There is thus no packaging or logrolling: all parties to the co-operation on the one issue voluntary agree to co-operate since they all expect a long-term benefit of doing so. Still, these agreements might not be self-enforcing because most countries will expect a short-term benefit of free-riding, i.e.: they will try to reap the benefits of other states respecting these agreements, but not to do so itself. This benefit is not necessarily from a monetary, but might also be from a political nature. It would be naive to believe that political decision makers are interested solely in the welfare of their country. Politicians are not equally interested in all interests, and will thus pay more attention to some groups' interests than to others.

Consider as an example the free movement of goods. Every member state's economy profits from the other Member States of the European Union respecting this free movement, but politicians have a short-term incentive to close of domestic markets for foreign producers. Domestics producers profit from this nationalistic reflex, since the absence of foreign competitors grants them more market power on the domestic market. Employees of these domestic producers might also profit from this, but domestic consumers will face prices higher than those under a tougher, international competition. Some benefits to limiting international free trade might however also exists, consider for example the uncertainty on the quality of imported nutrition. The political justification given for limiting international free trade is often exactly this negative externality, but in fact mostly has its origin in the furthering of domestic producers' interests, on the costs of foreign producers and domestic consumers, public support the latter having diverse interests and not being as centrally organised as producers are.

3.4.1.3 Change of political leadership

Different political leadership might be a **third explanation** for breaches of obligations which member states voluntarily entered into. A Member State's government might simply have a different opinion on a certain matter than its predecessor in power and therefore decide not to respect an obligation entered into by that predecessor. This might especially be the case for issues with a high political profile where the opinion of the incumbent government is distinctly different from the one of its predecessor. Although there is rarely a public statement of new-in-power representatives denouncing one of his/her predecessor's decisions in the international arena, it seems well possible, if not likely, that politicians are highly irritated by some

[68] Of course, a issue of purely national nature would leave the member state in question indifferent whether other member states comply or not. Most issues regulated in the Council and in the Treaties however, do have some kind of international interest, mostly through the European common market.

obligations entered into in the past[69]. If respecting them disables them to execute (parts of) their political programme, it seem rather "logical" for politicians to at least *consider* de-facto ignoring the obligation. Hence, the more often a member state has seen a new government coming to power, the higher one might estimate the chances for such deliberate ignoring of past commitments to occur.

3.4.1.4 Preference building and change

Fourthly, the application of the general wording of the law to a specific case might cause problems for politicians to respect European law. There might be something like *preference building* by voters on an issue about which they didn't have an opinion before this specific case arose. Also, a *preference change* might take place among voters, due the sensitivity of the actual case concerned. For examples of this *preference building*, think about sudden upsurges of nationalistic reflexes, often leading to a public outcry for protectionist or discriminatory measures.

The question raised here is whether politicians will care enough about this preference of (parts of) the public to act accordingly. For sure, they care about re-election and thus care to some extent about the opinion of their voters. However, parliamentary elections in reality are votes on something like a package of ideas, and not only on one issue. Every candidate or party stands for a specific combination of a number of issues, and it is not always so that a difference in opinion on one specific issue would significantly alter voting results. However, the more parties governments exists of, the higher the likelihood that the change in public opinion might be important enough to at least one party in government to change its behaviour and act against the support of a piece of European law.

3.4.1.5 Ignorance

Finally, Member States might have made a "mistake/misjudgement" in voting. A bad study of the situation or problem treated in the legislative proposal or of the wording

---

[69] A rare and well-observed exception is President Bush' "withdrawal" of predecessor Clinton's signature under the treaty establishing the International Court of Justice. Although such signature is to be followed by an official ratification for the treaty to become binding, it clearly was a refusal to be bound by the treaty and a reversal of a precedent decision.

of a proposal might have made them vote "ignorantly". Later, when the law is to be applied, they could then be confronted with the true implications of it and might decide to breach the obligation. This is basically a story of *untrue consent* and might have been pretty explanatory at the start-up of the European Union, where Member States maybe didn't truly realise the impact of the obligations they were entering into. Nowadays however, one might say that the lax attitude with which positions *for* or *against* a legislative proposal are taken has made place for a thorough analysis of facts and implications.

3.4.2 Non-intentional Breaches

Besides these five reasons why a Member State might knowingly decide to breach its obligations stemming from European law, another category of explanations for breaches should be considered. This category can be named **non-intentional breaches** and can stem from interpretational uncertainties and difficulties in the law or conflicting principles of European law as well as from structural factors.

3.4.2.1 Non-intentional "structural" factors

A.) Degree of Federalism

A considerable number of European Union member states are federal states, and also in those organised rather centrally, local or regional agents exist which have a considerable influence on the compliance with European legislation. A number of decision-making models recognise this and among others, Hooghe and Marks (2000) present a multi-level-governance (MLG) model distinguishing between three levels of action. They see a supranational, a national and a sub-national level. The latest level can be organised locally, regionally, or both.

It is clear that the actors on the sub-national level do influence compliance by member states with European law, as they themselves enjoy a certain level of discretion power. As noted by Paraskevopoulos (1998), a higher number of actors involved in implementation increases the probability of infringement problems.

This seems true for a number of different reasons. First of all: the national member state might have only limited power to convince one of its regions to act according to European law. Most regions do enjoy an extent of freedom in certain areas of political decision-making and the national state's complaints on a certain regional act might very well remain without avail. This lack of influence isn't necessarily a problem since the delegation of powers to sub-national actors in some areas of decision-making has mostly been agreed upon and is typically subject to constitutional arrangements. The problem however, is that a region can not be held accountable by the European Commission under its public law enforcement proceedings. Only national, member states have signed the relevant treaties and are the official parties to both primary and secondary legislation. Only they can be held accountable on the basis of European law, and eventually, obliged to pay fines resulting from breaches. When such case would occur, the national state would most surely try to get any fine refunded by the sub-national actor truly responsible, but the "directness" of the action is somewhat missing. As will be discussed below however, given the direct effect of European Community legislation, private enforcement through the Francovich doctrine remains in principle available against regional actors though. How exactly such sub-national actor might be held accountable will depend on member states' specific state liability provisions in the respective domestic legislation.

In my opinion, a greater problem lays not in the ex-post enforcement of European law on the sub-national level, but in the ex-ante process of compromising. Indeed, when deciding on a matter in the Council, member states first have to negotiate a national position with all relevant sub-national partners. At the end of those national deliberations, one national position will result, which might not be in the interest of a large share of sub-national actors. In essence, this is nothing else than a domestic version of the logrolling process described above. When this national position would eventually find its way through the Council, for the same reasons of (in)direct political disagreement described above, even those very regional actors who drafted the successful national position might decide to breach the law.

It should thus be considered why all member states are allowed to represent only one (1) national position, and not divide their votes over the sub-national actors responsible. This would most definitely offer centralist member states a larger decision making power in the Council, and might trigger even more log-rolling with its questionable efficiency effects. However, in as far as this empirical analysis would prove federalism to be an important factor in explaining infringements, this measure might ease tensions among sub-national actors dissatisfied with European regulation, at the risk of increasing political tensions on the national level amongst sub-national partners.

B.) Administrative well-functioning

The compliance of states with European law is not only dependent on politicians' behaviour. A great deal of the law enforcement dossiers opened by the European Commission are initiated for reasons which are not necessarily political, but might in essence be the result of administrative problems.

Some literature, headed by the prominent Chayes and Chayes (1991) and Chayes and Chayes (1993) even goes as far as to question whether breaches of legal standards are really so often caused by intentional political choice. They claim these breaches more often result from of a malfunctioning, inefficient or corrupt bureaucracy. It should be noted however, that these authors in such fields as international relations or compliance theory most often focus on international public law outside the European Union and that their arguments might not be easily applied to the European Union.

3.4.2.2 Non-intentional inherent factors

A.) Vague law

Law is inherently vague. It is thus often not totally clear what exactly is meant by legal provisions. This vagueness is important in the case of the transposition of directives, where it might often be unclear what exactly is necessary to guarantee a correct transposition. In case of doubt on the correctness of a transposition, the European Court of Justice might have to decide whether an act by a Member State suffices as transposition. The discussion of this issue brings further questions with it. Does it make sense to hold Member States liable for bad transposition if it was unclear to them what exactly is required? Why do we have directives at all? Also, there seems to be a dynamic effect which looks a bit like a moral hazard problem. Once could indeed argue that Member States have an interest in keeping directives unclear, so they would not be held liable upon breaching those "unclear" provisions later. The inherent vagueness of (Community) law will play a considerable role in analysing its consequences for liability legislation later on.

B.) Conflicting principles of law

The second non-intentional, inherent cause for breaches are conflicting principles of law. Indeed, in realistic cases, different principles of European law might find application, and it might be very difficult to correctly assess which principle should get priority over the other one. To facilitate understanding just consider these two real cases:

The Treaty guarantees free movement of goods in articles 28 and 29. Limits to this freedom are confined to the situations described in article 30, which foresees that "The provisions of Articles 28 and 29 shall not preclude prohibitions or restrictions on imports, exports or goods in transit justified on grounds of public morality, public policy or public security; the protection of health and life of humans, animals or plants; the protection of national treasures possessing artistic, historic or archaeological value; or the protection of industrial and commercial property. Such prohibitions or restrictions shall not, however, constitute a means of arbitrary discrimination or a disguised restriction on trade between Member States."

The European Court of Justice did not rule liable a member state for an alleged breach of the free movement of goods consisting of the impossibility, during a 30-hour period, for a transport-company to use a motorway as a result of a demonstration. The Court ruled that in balancing the free movement of goods against fundamental rights, there had been no breach of EC law[70].

Another, more famous example is the Brasserie du Pêcheur case[71]. In this case, Germany proceeded with the argument of public health against free movement of goods. Balancing both principles, the European Court of Justice didn't accept Germany's public health arguments and found that free movement should have been given way. Germany's act was found to be in breach of Community law.

---

[70] See European Court of Justice (2003d), Case 112/00, *Schmidberger v. Republic Österreich*

Interpretational uncertainty on law will thus always exist. European law is pretty young however, and one might argue that this level of uncertainty concerning the interpretation of it was very high in the initial phase of the European Union but has steadily decreased over time as more an more jurisdiction of the European Court of Justice became available.

The following statistics taken from the European Court of Justice's annual reports provide us with the following view on the development of preliminary questions to the Court.

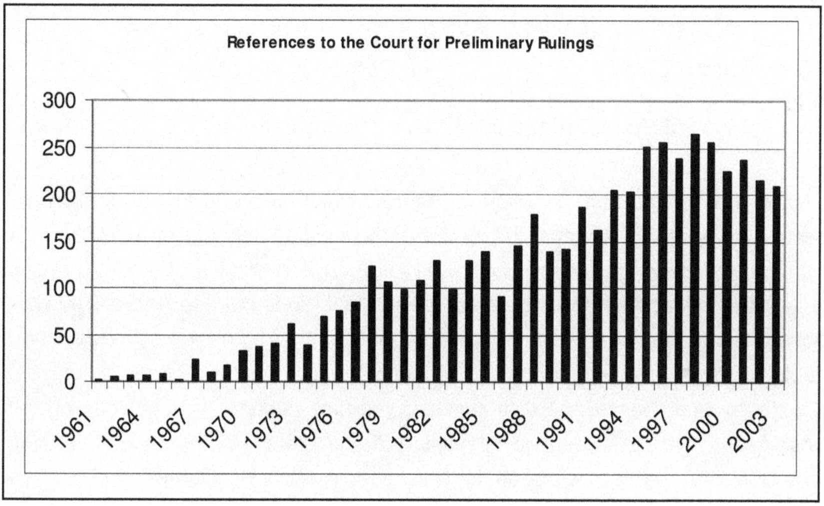

Figure 7: References for Preliminary Rulings to the Court

The data shows that, after a sharp increase of references for preliminary rulings to the European Court of Justice in the 1980's and especially in the 1990's, the last couple of years seem to witness a steady decrease of references again. Indeed, in 2003, the number of references has decreased to approximately the level of 1993. Cautiously, this evolution can be interpreted as illustrating the relative decrease of uncertainty concerning European law. This might have consequences for

[71] See European Court of Justice European Court of Justice (1996a), joined cases 46/93 and 48/93, *Brasserie du Pêcheur v. Bundesrepublik Deutschland and The Queen v. Secretary of State for Transport, ex parte Factortame and others.*

enforcement procedures, which might move from *public enforcement* (which deals with this uncertainty by a slow and lengthy procedure offering the possibility to first start negotiations between commission and Member States - compliance bargaining[72] - and later get a judgement from the European Court of Justice, to only apply fines after a breach of this judgement) to *private enforcement* with immediate damage compensation in case of a sufficiently serious breach. This could be a practical justification for the existence of the art. 228 compensation system.

3.4.3 Empirical Testing

Now, after having theoretically described all variables, let's turn to an empirical test of their explanatory power.

3.4.3.1 Operationalisation of the dependent variable: breaches.

Breaches are defined and identified in the same manner as in the correlation test described on page 27. However, breaches were collected not only for the 1999-2003 period, but for the longer period from 1994-2002. This is done so, since the reason why this was *not* done in the simple correlation test, does not apply here. The bias-effect mentioned on page 29 is anticipated against in the regression by introducing a variable measuring the length of membership in the European Union. As before, two categories of breaches will be distinguished: the first category will comprise of both letters of formal notice, reasoned opinions and court referrals, the second category will exclude formal notices to correct for a potentially overactive Commission.

3.4.3.2 Operationalisation of the independent variables

A.) Direct political disagreement

I include this variable in the regression analysis with the same reservations as those made in section "B.) The tests-results and interpretations" on page 30. It should as well be noted that the same data-sets will be used, i.e.: once the data covering 1995-2000, collected by Matilla (2004) and once the data I assembled running from 1999-

---

[72] As described by Tallberg and Jönsson (1989), this compliance bargaining is an established process of negotiating the legislation's interpretation.

2003. As the years do not match the sample dates for the independent variable (1994-2002), for both Matilla's data-set and mine, an average was calculated which was inserted as variable for every year. The direct political disagreement variable is thus constant over time but varies over member state. The analysis of results will report which measurement (if at all) had more explanatory power.

B.) Indirect political disagreement: Logrolling

Contrary to direct political disagreement, this variable is not directly observable. It is indeed impossible to judge whether a "yes-vote" by a member state is truly a vote *in favour* or whether the member state is only voting so as part of a logrolling deal. Hence, proxies have to be taken resort to. Three measurements are included as to indicate the degree of indirect political disagreement: a power-index, economic strength and a measure of corporatism.

The ability of a member state to engage in logrolling is thought to increase with its relative possibility to influence decision-making in the council. The more likely the support of a certain member state makes it for a legislative proposal to reach a sufficient majority, the more often it will be requested to do so; in exchange of course, for other, favourable legislation.

Measuring this ability is the subject of a growing and rather complex body of literature calculating "degrees of bargaining power" or "power indices"[73]. Obviously, this **power index** will depend on institutional settings such as voting rules, requested majorities regarding votes and member states as well as on the number of states involved in the voting process.

For the purpose of clarity, it should be pointed out that for the data-period covered in this test (1994-2002), two different voting rule-systems were in place.
First, 1994 was the last year of a decision-system adopted in the Single European Act. This amendment of the Treaties, agreed upon in 1986, is marked by the increasing adoption of qualified majority voting as a way of passing decisions in a ever growing European Union, facing the entry of new member states such as Spain and Portugal. Every member state received a number of votes it could cast in the

council and if 23 or more votes were cast against a proposal, it was supposed to have failed.

From 1995 on, which was the year of the accession of Sweden, Austria and Finland, a voting rule was adopted stating the necessity of 62 of 87 votes to pass secondary legislation[74]. The division of votes over member states is as follows: ten votes were allocated to France, Germany, Italy and the United Kingdom; Spain received eight votes; Belgium, Greece, the Netherlands and Portugal five; Austria and Sweden four; Denmark, Ireland and Finland three votes and Luxembourg two votes.[75]

Without going in too many unnecessary details here, it is clear that two different measures for member states' power indices are necessary: one for 1994 and one for the years following. Most importantly, the measurement should be consistent over these two periods, in order to enable a sensible regression analysis. Choosing from the array of available power index measurements, the Shapley-Shubik index was selected; since this one easily allowed the consistent calculation of both 1994 and post 1994 power indices for all member states at that time[76]. Unfortunately, the Shapley-Shubik index varies per member state but is constant over time for the period 1995-2000.

As a second measurement for a member state's ability to participate in log-rolling, its **GDP** as a percentage of the EU's GDP was inserted as variable for every year.

---

[73] Reference is made to the literature already mentioned in the footnote on page 25.

[74] For the sake of simplicity, the (ever increasing) role of the European Parliament in passing legislation is ignored here. Let it suffice to state that in an increasing number of cases, the council has to co-operate with the Parliament in order to pass legislation.

[75] The east-enlargement of the European Union has again led to a change of decision making procedures in the Council. As arranged in the Treaty of Nice and the 2000 Intergovernmental Conference, twenty-seven further issues will be decided upon with a qualified majority system. Social and tax policy, as well as foreign policy remain subject to a veto rule however. Following these new rules, which entered into effect starting November 1st 2004, a proposal will need a certain number of votes (which will change as new countries join) as well as the support of a majority of member states which should represent at least 62% of the European Union's population. Another important change concerns the co-decision procedure, which awards more power to the European Parliament. All twenty-seven issues now subject to qualified majority voting, became subject to this co-decision procedure. Those issues already decided through qualified majority voting in the past remain to be decided by the European Commission and the Council alone.

[76] This is by no means to say that no other measurements of power are available, enabling the calculation of power indices in both 1994 and the post-1994 era. Rather, the commonly accepted Shapley-Shubik index was readily available to the author. Readers might feel invited to run this test with other power indices and to inform the author of any results.

Gross domestic product was inserted in 1990 US Dollar, which where converted at Geary Khamis Purchasing Power Parity.[77]

Finally, as a degree of the likelihood of a member state free-riding, a measurement of corporatism is included. The higher this level of corporatism, the more a member state's government is subject to political pressure by interest groups, which will attempt to convince those in power to take action in their interest. As these groups are typically regionally or nationally organised, and as European legislation promotes the internal market, this taking action in their interest might often be in conflict with European law. Hence, a large degree of corporatism might lead to more breaches of European law.

Measures of **corporatism** are taken from Siaroff (1999) and are again subject to the same problem as the power index mentioned above. No consistent way of measuring corporatism could be found, for all member states, covering all years from 1994 to 2002. Hence, avail was taken to Siaroff, who provides one measurement per country, per decade. For breaches reported in 1994-1997, the corporatism index for the late 80s was introduced, for those reported in 1998-2002, the index for the mid 90s was thought to be relevant. This seems defendable as the Commission's enforcement actions are subject to some delay. Breaches mentioned in the 1994 report are unlikely to have passed the Council after 1990.[78]

C.) Change in political leadership

For a change, this is a variable that is directly observable. The number of parliamentary **elections** on national level was counted in the time period starting 20 years before every observation. This number of years seems high enough in order not to allow coincidence to gain too much of an importance[79], and low enough to remain relevant to the breach.

---

[77] Source for the GDP data was the Groningen Growth & Development Centre at http://www.ggdc.net/dseries/GDP.shtml

[78] This decisions was found to have no consequences for the significance of the regression results.

[79] Most member states re-elect parliaments every 4 to 5 years. To avoid the variable jumping too often, a longer time span was chosen, running from 1980 to 2002. Source of the information was the non-governmental organisation IDEA (International Institute for Democracy and Electoral Assistance) at www.idea.int

Federal member states would have a far higher amount of elections, as their regional parliaments will be on the ballot every couple of years as well; therefore it was thought to be inappropriate to count regional elections as well. The same goes for presidential elections, which were ignored in order to avoid auto-correlation problems with variables such as the one taking account of the "federal" character of a member state. Note that a parliamentary election not necessarily leads to a change of parties in power. The number of elections, however, can serve as a proxy for the stability of a member state's political landscape.

D.) Preference building and voting ignorance

What has been described as preference building and ignorance are two variables rather difficult to measure objectively. Preference building seems rather similar to something like "scandal-sensitivity" and repeating what has said before, it seems like this is more likely to occur under coalition governments. In a coalition government, even very small parties are a "veto-actor", meaning they can prevent or push for decisions by the government they could never implement by themselves. The more parties a coalition government exists of, the higher the likelihood that an issue which became a "scandal" is deemed to be of crucial importance to one of the coalition-parties and that it will push for the government to give way to the "public outcry", also if this goes at the expense of breaching European law.

This seems even more likely considering the "specialisation" of some, especially smaller parties on some issues, where they are unwilling to compromise. If these issues come in the cross-fire of debate, that party will see few alternatives than to try to convince coalition partners to act, also if this is in breach with European law. Also, approaching elections seem like an ideal point of "scoring some points" with a standard public through measures of which the compatibility with European legal standards is not the main concern.

Hence, the phenomenon of "serving the public", even if contrary to European law is not unique at all to coalition governments, but the willingness to do so might well be thought to be larger the more parties a government is made up of.

A measurement of the **number of parties in government** is taken from the *European Journal of Political Research's* annual special editions on "political data".

Note that it expresses the number of parties in national governments only: regional data is already confined in the degree of federalism which is also entered as a variable (see below). The number of parties in government during the observed year were entered as variable.

As an additional indicator, the current **public approval** for membership in the European Union was inserted as a percentage, taken from the autumn version of the bi-annual Eurobarometer published by the European Commission[80] as well as the **number of years of membership** in the European Union, as an admittedly rude proxy for the ignorance upon voting. Member states having a longer membership record might be better apt at correctly assessing the true consequences of decisions taken in the Council.

E.) Non-intentional structural factors

Non-intentional structural variables enter the regression analysis: they are thought to have some explanatory power in explaining the number of breaches committed. However, the breaches they explain are not dependant on member states' politicians' behaviour but rather have the character of "given factors" than of variables liability legislation attempts to influence. Although by no means offering them as an excuse, even if member states were willing to act totally according to European law, they would still be found in breach of it every now and then, partly because of these factors.

finding an index for the degree of **federalism** proves to be rather difficult. Hooghe and Marks (2000) provide such index, which is the composite index of four variables measuring the degree of regional governance. These four variable are: Constitutional federalism (from 0 to 4 points), special territorial autonomy (0 to 2 points), the role of regions in central government (0 to 4 point) and the holding of regional elections (0 to 2 points). The composite index hence sums up to a value from 0 (centralized authority) to 12 (dispersed authority). Unfortunately, the data reflects the situation for every member state only for the year 1990, and is hence constant over time. Changes in the federal character of member states over the observed period of time can thus not be accounted for.

Administrative well-functioning is entered by two variables: one is a corruption index, the other an index of bureaucratic inefficiency. The **corruption index** is collected from the Internet Center for Corruption Research, which is a co-operation between Transparency International and the University of Passau[81]. It varies over time and over member states. The index reflecting **bureaucratic efficiency** is by Daniel Kaufmann, Aart Kraay and Massimo Mastruzzi and was collected from the World Bank Institute[82]. It provides estimates for the years 1996, 1998, 2000 and 2002. All observations will be used for both the year of the observations and the preceding one, with the exception of the 1996 observation, which will be used from 1994 to 1996.

3.4.3.3 Method

After gathering all the data, it was ranked per country and per year, running from 1994 to 2002. Given 15 member state and 9 years of observation, 135 observation were made. Each observation consisted of the number of breaches (both corrected and fully reported) as dependant variable and the eleven explanatory variables which were just mentioned.

Although at first sight the data seems to show characteristics of panel-data models, we decided not concentrate on these methods. Undeniably, methods such as the fixed or random effects models might -in principle- be very apt at analysing data covering different countries. What they basically aim at is to take account of *unobserved effects*. In our case, these models might incorporate the unobserved difference between -say- France and Greece. In which way exactly France is then different from Greece is not explained by the model.[83]

Two reasons made us decide against applying this approach.
First of all, data quality is rather poor in the sense that its availability is sub-optimal. For the reasons described above, only 3 out of 11 explaining variables show varying observations for all points of time (the 9 years from 1994 to 2002). These variables

---

[80] Accessible at: http://europa.eu.int/comm/public_opinion/
[81] Data is to be found on the website of The Internet Center for Corruption Research (1994-2002).
[82] See The World Bank Institute (2003)
[83] For a detailed analysis of panel-data see Baltagi (2001) and Wooldridge (2002)

are member states' GDP, its duration of membership in the EU and the support amongst its population for EU membership. The variables measuring direct political disagreement and corporatism were only observed once respectively twice over the whole sampling period. Quality of bureaucracy was measured 4 times. A number of other variables was by nature invariable: measures for federalism, the number of parties in government and the number of elections over the past 20 years are constant over time.

Secondly, and more importantly, through its specific nature, the phenomenon captured by the data is not best analysed by panel-data models. Of interest to us here are cross-section differences. Differences over time, for example differences between breaches in 1995 as compared to 2002 are not of major interest to us here. Available data is not suited to analyse these time-dependent evolutions. The -described- institutional background of breaching proceedings does not allow for such analysis aiming at the dynamics of adjustments, as panel-models aim at. It would be a misconception to attach too much importance to explaining changes in the number of breaches in a specific year by means of cross-sectional *and* cross-time changes in explanatory variables. Every observation of the number of breaching procedures has a long history, which might, for *every* year, go back to year one (1) of membership in the European Union. It would therefore be inappropriate to attach too much importance to intertemporal dynamic changes.

Making allowance for all specificities of the data at hand, we decided to treat data as a cross-national, event count time-series. The event count aspect is important, as it means that observations cannot turn negative. The number of breaches observed are zero or positive.

In our dataset, both aim variables (full and corrected number of breaching procedures) were inserted together with the 11 explanatory variables for each member state and for each year the member state was member of the European Union. Event count data are most often analysed by means of a Poisson regression. Mean and variance of our aim-variables are not identical in our case (see Figure 8). We account for this overdispersion problem by using a negative binomial regression in Eviews. Most of the few available studies on compliance apply simple OLS on a pooled dataset, which does not lead to significantly different results.[84] Mbaye (2001) applies a negative binomial method.

Series: BREACH		Series: BREACHCOR	
Sample 2 127		Sample 2 127	
Observations 126		Observations 126	
Mean	119.5476	Mean	42.39683
Median	122.0000	Median	43.00000
Maximum	238.0000	Maximum	117.0000
Minimum	22.00000	Minimum	0.000000
Std. Dev.	42.14975	Std. Dev.	24.74254

Figure 8: Descriptive Summary Statistics of Dependent Variables

We hence estimate
BREACH = F(CORPORATISM, CORRUPTION, DPD, ELECT, FEDERAL, NPC, SSINDEX, SUPPORT, YOM, YEAR)

Where:
Corporatism measures the degree of corporatism in every member state,
Corruption measures the degree of corruption in every member state,
DPD measures the degree of Direct Political Disagreement in every member state (the averaged number of no votes in the Council),
ELECT measures the number of parliamentary elections between 1980 and 2002 in every member state,
FEDERAL measures the degree of federalism in every member state,
NPC measures the number of parties in the governing coalition in every member state,
SSINDEX is the Shapley-Shubik power index for every member state,
SUPPORT measures the level of support of membership to the European Union in every member state,
YOM measures the number of years of membership in the European Union of every member state and

---

[84] Lampinen and Uusikylä (1998) and Giuliani (2003)

YEAR represent the year in which the observation was made.

The same function was estimated for BREACHCOR as dependent variable.

Before running the analysis, tests on collinearity in the independent variables were performed. As might have been expected, running a cross-correlation revealed strong collinearity between the degree of corruption and the quality of bureaucracy as well as between GDP and the voting power index in the Council. As there is reason to believe that both pairs of variables do measure the same two phenomenon twice each, we argue it is defendable to leave out the one variable that correlates the weakest with the aim variable. Hence we leave out the variables bureaucratic quality as well as GDP. Cross correlation coefficients between all other variables showed no proof of collinearity. As a final control for multicollinearity, variance inflation factors were calculated[85].

This VIF-factor is equal to $\frac{1}{1-R_i^2}$, where R_i^2 is the R-square value from the regression of the i-th explanatory variable on all other explanatory variables. The rule of thumb is that any VIF-value exceeding 10 is a clear evidence of multicollinearity. In our calculations, no variable showed a value exceeding 6.

3.4.3.4 Test Results

The tables below show the results of a binomial regression model on each of the dependent variables (breach and breachcor). The variable "Breachcor" excludes the letters of formal notice issued by the Commission. The variable "breach" might be disproportionally high, if the Commission were overactive or were to make too many mistakes in tracing breaches.

---

[85] See Gujarati (2003) at page 351

Dependent Variable: BREACH
Method: ML - Negative Binomial Count
QML (Huber/White) standard errors & covariance

	Coefficient	Std. Error	z-Statistic	Prob.
C	-19.72116	16.47907	-1.196740	0.2314
CORPORATISM	0.093716	0.057494	1.630003	0.1031
CORRUPT	-0.147714	0.017623	-8.381643	0.0000
DPD	-0.154591	0.044949	-3.439258	0.0006
ELECT	0.033154	0.023501	1.410713	0.1583
FEDERAL	-9.20E-05	0.011838	-0.007774	0.9938
NPC	-0.014003	0.016687	-0.839179	0.4014
SSINDEX	4.710197	1.305485	3.608005	0.0003
SUPPORT	-0.002306	0.002167	-1.064167	0.2873
YEAR	0.012528	0.008211	1.525616	0.1271
YOM	0.005994	0.003615	1.657953	0.0973

R-squared	0.597136	Mean dependent var	119.5366
Adjusted R-squared	0.557213	S.D. dependent var	42.55494
S.E. of regression	28.31702	Akaike info criterion	9.532305
Sum squared resid	89005.76	Schwarz criterion	9.806664
LR statistic (11 df)	1579.898	LR index (Pseudo-R2)	0.579063
Probability(LR stat)	0.000000		

Dependent Variable: BREACHCOR
Method: ML - Negative Binomial Count
Included observations: 123
QML (Huber/White) standard errors & covariance

	Coefficient	Std. Error	z-Statistic	Prob.
C	-78.40044	34.36695	-2.281275	0.0225
CORPORATISM	0.071423	0.137382	0.519887	0.6031
CORRUPT	-0.246799	0.039170	-6.300733	0.0000
DPD	-0.255487	0.097885	-2.610060	0.0091
ELECT	0.026356	0.046057	0.572236	0.5672
FEDERAL	0.024184	0.027640	0.874991	0.3816
NPC	-0.037661	0.035250	-1.068391	0.2853
SSINDEX	5.459797	3.197967	1.707271	0.0878
SUPPORT	-0.002419	0.004717	-0.512823	0.6081
YEAR	0.041696	0.017178	2.427302	0.0152
YOM	0.015910	0.007822	2.034111	0.0419

R-squared	0.491218	Mean dependent var	42.53659
Adjusted R-squared	0.440798	S.D. dependent var	24.92918
S.E. of regression	18.64199	Akaike info criterion	8.620974
Sum squared resid	38575.14	Schwarz criterion	8.895333
LR statistic (11 df)	1567.057	LR index (Pseudo-R2)	0.601919
Probability(LR stat)	0.000000		

Figure 9: Initial Test Results of a Binomial Regression Model

First of all, it is notable that a number of variables prove insignificant. While corruption, direct political disagreement and power in the Council are significant in explaining commenced breaching procedures, others are not. Corruption, direct political disagreement, the length of EU Membership as well as the year of observation explain significantly for the reduced number of breaching procedures. A large number of variables are insignificant in explaining both total and reduced number of breaching procedures. These are: the degree of corporatism and federalism, the number of elections and parties in government as well as popular support for EU membership.

In the following, we decide to leave out these insignificant variables and run both regressions again with the variables which proved significant. Again, the table below shows the results.

Dependent Variable: BREACH
Method: ML - Negative Binomial Count
QML (Huber/White) standard errors & covariance

	Coefficient	Std. Error	z-Statistic	Prob.
C	-22.72732	15.43177	-1.472762	0.1408
YEAR	0.014163	0.007728	1.832614	0.0669
CORRUPT	-0.133513	0.013154	-10.14993	0.0000
DPD	-0.083922	0.023082	-3.635791	0.0003
SSINDEX	3.454088	0.814639	4.240023	0.0000
YOM	0.002882	0.002029	1.419969	0.1556

R-squared	0.575129	Mean dependent var	119.7520
Adjusted R-squared	0.553525	S.D. dependent var	42.25664
S.E. of regression	28.23537	Akaike info criterion	9.506788
Sum squared resid	94073.89	Schwarz criterion	9.665174
LR statistic (6 df)	1571.318	LR index (Pseudo-R2)	0.572290
Probability(LR stat)	0.000000		

Dependent Variable: BREACHCOR
Method: ML - Negative Binomial Count
QML (Huber/White) standard errors & covariance

	Coefficient	Std. Error	z-Statistic	Prob.
C	-76.27391	33.99314	-2.243803	0.0248
YEAR	0.040658	0.017025	2.388175	0.0169
CORRUPT	-0.222228	0.026866	-8.271558	0.0000
DPD	-0.207677	0.044876	-4.627762	0.0000
SSINDEX	5.530185	1.690449	3.271430	0.0011
YOM	0.012715	0.003781	3.363204	0.0008

R-squared	0.498713	Mean dependent var	42.60000
Adjusted R-squared	0.473224	S.D. dependent var	24.73635
S.E. of regression	17.95348	Akaike info criterion	8.601723
Sum squared resid	38034.62	Schwarz criterion	8.760109
LR statistic (6 df)	1554.810	LR index (Pseudo-R2)	0.594340
Probability(LR stat)	0.000000		

Figure 10: Corrected Test Results of a Binomial Regression Model

The results for both dependent variables are not identical, but do show significant similarities.

Three variables significantly explain for (corrected) breaches in the same manner: corruption, direct political disagreement and the power index for Council-voting. R-square values for both regressions are around the 0,5 mark. The regression analysis explains for half of all breaches.

The estimated coefficients seem reasonably explainable.

Starting with **corruption**, a rise in a member state's corruption is shown to lead to an expected rise in the number of breaches of European law it will commit[86]. Bearing in mind that this variable is highly correlated with the variable measuring bureaucratic efficiency, this empirical finding seem all the more understandable.

Corruption (and bureaucracy) are one of the most influential factors in explaining both total and corrected infringement proceedings. The variable is significant to a high extent, both statistically and economically. Its practical significance changes only slightly when distinguishing between both phases of enforcement. This finding stresses the role of the administration in daily compliance of member states with European Community law. On the "lower level" of administration, a great deal of decisions are made which might be contradictory to both primary and secondary European law. A better organisation of the administration partly seems to prevent such breaches. The analysis reveals that the influence of corruption is three times higher in explaining the number of well-funded breaches (measured by the standardised coefficient in explaining corrected number of breaches). This might be due to both the Commission's endurance in these cases or to a higher seriousness of breaches in these countries.

The importance of the corruption variable, proven already in studies concentrating on non-European international public law[87] can thus be confirmed for the European Union as well.

Direct political disagreement is also a statistically significant variable. Interestingly, this variable's impact is negative. This negative impact means that, the *more* often a member state was observed voting against proposals in the Council, the *less* often the Commission could be expected to initiate infringement proceedings against such member state. This relation goes also for the corrected dataset.
This negative relation is clearly rather counterintuitive: one would expect a member state's *no-vote* to be a clear signal of political disagreement, which might eventually be followed by consequent acting in the form of breaches of Community law. Moreover, this member state's signal is easily detectable by the Commission, which could be expected to keep an eye on those member states voting against more often.

---

[86] The index measuring corruption *increases* with lower levels of corruption. Hence, the negative beta for this variable means that more corrupt countries (a lower index observation) can be expected to breach more often.

For the member states in question, this again would lead to more breaches being reported.

All of this seems incorrect: keeping everything else constant, the more a member state votes against, the less enforcement proceedings are opened against that member state.

As a first possible explanation for this negative impact of the voting record on breaches, data problems cross one's mind. These however, can be excluded. Measuring errors by Matilla are unlikely: when using the alternative variable measuring direct political disagreements, assembled independently of Matilla by myself, the same conclusion is reached. Moreover, both variables (Matilla's measurement and mine) correlate highly: the correlation is significant, even at the one percent level.

At the other hand, this variable of direct political disagreement does not correlate at a significant level with any other variable in the regression. No other variable, which might offer a more straightforward explanation for this strange relation, can serve as a "substitute" for the measure of direct political disagreement. Hence, some explanation should exist to account for the negative relation between the number of no-votes and the number of initiated enforcement proceedings by the Commission. To approach such explanation, let's develop some thoughts on the aim of voting no publicly in the Council.

Voting in the Council cannot be compared with voting in a parliamentary setting. In the Council, the president "detects" or "fails to detect" a sufficient majority in favour of a certain legal proposal and a traditional voting is more an exception than it is a rule. Voting no publicly hence serves the purpose of clearly signalling discontent. Given the regression results however, this signalling does not seem to lead to the Commission concluding that the member state in question might very well breach Community law and should be scrutinised.

This conclusion might be misleading. The Commission might very well be "alarmed" by a member state publicly voting no, and might observe this member state more closely than it does other member states. When the Commission detects an alleged

---

[87] See Chayes and Chayes (1991) and Chayes and Chayes (1993)

breach, it will contact the member state over diplomatic contacts to communicate its findings. If that member state signals a willingness to comply, the Commission will not see a necessity to send a letter of formal notice. In this way, a negative relation between public no-votes and infringement proceedings might be established.
The political logic behind this seemingly absurd behaviour is the signalling purpose towards the home audience that public no-votes might serve. The member state's representative wants to "score points" with voters at home by showing his disagreement with the matters decided and consequently breaching those decided matters. Possibly, the member state is mainly concerned with the political effects at home of his no-vote, but is not willing to stubbornly continue breaching after the Commission has detected the infringement and communicated its findings in diplomatic meetings. The member states steps back in line quickly once the Commission notes the infringement, as an enduring conflict is seen as useless. At the same time, the political aim of the "exercise": signalling political toughness at home, was reached. This phenomenon can be called "cheap signalling".

A second, more plausible explanation for the negative impact of no-voting on the number of infringement proceedings is given by the theory of log-rolling.

Log-rolling occurs by member states which help a proposal pass the council, and in return expect other member states' votes for proposals they particularly favour. The occurrence of log-rolling is typically associated with the increasing size of government or of legislative work. Although theoretically possible, log-rolling is more likely to help proposals pass instead of preventing them from passing.[88] This implies that all those member states voting *no* on a particular legislative proposal did not participate in log-rolling. The opposite is not necessarily true: those member states voting in favour might have voted yes for intrinsic reasons, and not because of log-rolling participation.

As described above, log-rolling participation provides incentives for ex-post opportunistic behaviour. Member states taking part in log-rolling can be expected to

---

[88] Indeed, instead of gathering votes to make proposals pass, member states might attempt to gather votes of other member states in order to prevent proposals from passing. In exchange, these former member states might -later- help other member states in preventing proposals from passing. In this way, "negative" log-rolling would serve as a mechanism preventing the growth of government. Mainstream literature on log-rolling however agrees that "positive" log-rolling is by far more common than this form of log-rolling.

breach more often. Exactly this might explain for the negative relation between direct *no-votes* and the number of initiated infringement proceedings. If public no-votes serve as an inverse proxy for the (unobservable) participation in log-rolling, the negative relationship which at first looks counterintuitive, becomes explainable. Voting *no* more often means less participation in log-rolling which implies less incentives for ex-post breaching.

Clearly, this reasoning points at an interesting conclusion: for member states, the incentive to breach Community law after participating in log-rolling exceeds the incentive to do so after having voting against the same proposal.

The Shapley-Shubik power index for voting in the Council is the final significant variable explaining for both dependent variables.

Of special interest to us is the direction of its influence, which is positive. This means that the higher the SSINDEX (or the highly correlated GDP) of a member state, the more breaches we can expect the Commission to report on this member state. Also when explaining for the corrected number of breaches, the SSINDEX plays a positive role.

This positive sign of the GDP-variable requires some analysis. Two possible explanations seem to exist for this positive relation.

Firstly, relatively powerful member states might breach Community law more often than their smaller counterparts do. This again, might be the case because of two reasons.

A.) Larger member states are confronted with more situations where breaches can occur, also if they do not intend to breach. There are simply more situations similar to those of Mr. Francovich or the Zollamt Kiel in countries the size of Italy than in those with the size of Luxemburg. Since Italy has to transpose the same number of directives as Luxemburg however, this reasoning can only partly explain for GDP or SSINDEX as a positive explanatory variable for the number of breaches. The GDP argument seems applicable especially to breaches of primary European law which happen unwillingly.

B.) Larger member states might however *willingly* breach more. Often, uncertainty exists on the proper interpretation of provisions of Community legislation. A certain member state might hold its interpretation for correct whereas the Commission thinks the same about its own one. When such difference on interpretation arises, the public enforcement mechanism managed by the Commission functions as a "re-negotiation mechanism"[89]. To a certain extent, both the member state and the Commission have an interest in not letting the conflict escalate, and there might very well be willingness on both sides to accommodate. Clearly, when considering its chances in such re-negotiation process, a large member state might feel more confident than a smaller one in its ability to convince the Commission of its interpretation. Hence, where smaller member states might "comply" with Community law "spontaneously", larger member states might decide to "go for it" and attempt to impose their interpretation on the Commission.

Secondly, the Commission might concentrate some of its scarce enforcement resources on larger member states. It might expect an exemplary effect on smaller member states by doing so, or might target the more influential member states to avoid interpretations of Community law to gain ground which it (the Commission) judges inappropriate.

It would be most interesting of course, to find out which of these different reasonings accounts for which share of breaches: whether it is the Commission's *over*-activeness, the higher likelihood of breaches in large member states or the (large) member state's renegotiation attempts which cause this positive relationship between GDP and number of breaches. Although this seems quite challenging, the results of the second regression (explaining the corrected number of breaches) might offer us some insight.

The size of a member state thus positively correlates with the number of infringement proceedings beyond the formal notice phase, but considering standardised coefficients, the explanatory power of a member state's size has more than doubled. What could explain for this difference?

In this context, it is important to realise that the dataset on corrected breaches really reflects a sort of "stubbornness" by the member state vis-à-vis the Commission. Most

---

[89] Tallberg (2003)

cases passing the phase of a letter of formal notice will not be solved within a short period of time, because both parties do see a certain likelihood of winning the conflict.

Comparing the results of the analysis on total breaching procedures and on the corrected breaches thus offers a possibility to at least partly separate some effects of GDP on (reported) breaches. If the Commission were really more active against bigger member states, we could expect GDP to play a bigger role in explaining all reported breaches than in explaining breaches corrected for letters of formal notice. The two assumptions behind this reasoning are that

- The Commission would start more infringement procedures against big states and would hence simply make more "mistakes" than in its proceedings against smaller member states. Those "mistakes" would be clarified soon (often by a member state's informal answer) and the case would disappear from the statistics in the data-set "corrected breaches".
- In a reasonable number of cases, the infringement is pretty obvious and further persistence of the member states (also when it is large and influential) would make little sense.

Since such decrease in importance of GDP does not occur in the second regression model, we can conclude that the increase in explanatory power of SSINDEX/GDP between both phases can be explained by

- An absence of increased Commission's attention for larger member states

in combination with

- The apparent willingness of larger member states to take cases to the European Court of Justice and not to give in to the Commission's interpretation of a case.

This willingness to take on the Commission has repercussions for the suitability of the public enforcement mechanism. Obviously, the potential conflict with the Commission does not fully deter larger member states to breach. As will be seen in the legal chapter following immediately, financial sanctions are not readily available in this phase of the public enforcement mechanism yet. In a private enforcement mechanism, breaching might have direct financial consequences, and this might deter larger member states as well.

Finally, some attention should be given to two variables helping to explain corrected breaching procedures. The significance of the year only for this variable points to the fact that the year cannot explain for the number of initiated proceedings by the commission. There hence seems no support for the hypothesis that the Commission has become more active in starting breaching procedures.

Also the length of membership in the EU is significant for the corrected number of breaches only. Length of membership thus cannot explain for all initiated proceedings. We find no support for the theory that "younger" member states are observed more intensively than younger ones. The longer a country is member of the EU, the more corrected breaching procedures can be expected to exist against this state. This seems no surprise, as the likelihood of being found in breach is simply increasing with the length of exposure to EU legislation. However, another explanation might be that older member states might be less willing to comply directly with the Commission's remarks uttered in letters of formal notice

The regressions seem to fulfil most classical assumptions. A test of the residuals of the first regression which was run confirms they have a mean very close to zero. Heteroskedasticity, the problem were residuals have varying variances can also be eliminated. With the use of Eviews, a graphic control of the residuals shows a histogram with residuals being normally distributed.

3.4.3.5 Conclusion

To summarise this chapter one can say that, however interesting the process of decision making on primary or secondary European legislation is, the story is not finished after the passing of such pieces of legislation. Member states do not always comply with the legislation passed and might do this either knowingly or in good faith, arguing on the correct interpretation of a legal provision.

In this chapter, an attempt was made to explain for the number of breaches by member states by means of different explanatory variables. A number of variables of which was thought that they might contribute to an increased breaching behaviour proved to be of no significance. The degree of federalism and corporatism of member states, the frequency of governmental elections or the number of parties in government as well as the level of EU-membership support proved insignificant. A

number of other variables correlated with each other and were replaced by only one variable.
The size of a member state's economy and hence also its (correlating) voting power in the Council positively relate to the number of infringement proceedings initiated against a member state. Only part of this relation is due to the Commission's over-activeness in the form of concentrated enforcement efforts. A considerable part of the relation can be explained only be a willingness by member states to enter into conflict with the Commission on interpretational questions. This confirms critique by some that the Commission's action is really rather a political negotiation process than a law enforcement one.

The effectiveness of member states' bureaucracy is one of the most important factors explaining infringements of Community law and highlights the importance of "lower executive powers" in this area. This variable also highly correlates with the corruption index.
The number of no-votes in the Council negatively explains the number of breaches detected, and can be interpreted as a measure for the participation in log-rolling processes. Logrolling hence does occur in the European Union and there seem to be problems with the ex-post commitment to deals made. Interestingly, the incentives to breach Community law after participating in log-rolling seems to be *bigger* than after having voting against the same proposal.

Historical reasons explain why older member states have more serious conflicts on infringements with the Commission than younger member states. It can not be excluded however, that older member states fear the conflict with the Commission less than younger ones do. There are no indications found for an higher observations of younger member states by the Commission.

All in all, although non-intentional or structural factors such as the effectiveness of bureaucracy do play a large role in explaining for breaches, intentional decisions play a considerable role in explaining breaches. In the law and economics philosophy of tort law, exactly these intentional decisions will be aimed at with legal provisions, which we will turn to in the next chapter.

4. Treating Breaches: The Law's and the Court's Answer

European legal scholarship has written extensively on the doctrine of state liability for breaches of European law.[90] *Especially after the European Court of Justice's Francovich decision*[91] *in 1991, scholarly interest in the field of state liability exploded, making authors start articles "requiring apology for any more"*[92] *or title them "Once more unto the Breach"*[93]*. This chapter aims at providing an in-depth analysis of the primary legislation as well as of the European Court of Justice's jurisprudence on the matter of non-contractual liability of Member States.*

4.1 Rules of Primary European Law regarding Breaches of European law by the European Community and its Member States. Damage Compensation and Fines before EC-Courts.

The Treaty foresees in different types of actions against a number of different breaching parties. Firstly, member states are identified as potential breachers. Both the Commission or other member states can take action against those and initiate a public enforcement act at the European Court of Justice. This procedure will be treated immediately below.

A second possibility in primary law is for individuals to proceed against a breaching Commission. These cases as well are to be heard at the European Court of Justice and proved to be of high importance for the development of further relevant doctrines. This individual proceeding against the Commission will be treated in the second section of this chapter.

---

[90] See for example: Betlem (1996), Dougan (2000), Harlow (1996), Craig (1997), Steiner (1993), Lewis (1996)

[91] European Court of Justice (1991b), joined cases 6/90 and 9/90, *Francovich and Bonifaci v. Italy*

[92] Harlow (1996)

[93] Craig (1997). The title of the article, *Once more unto to Breach* refers to a famous Star Trek episode with the same title.

4.1.1 Recourse for Member States or the Commission against Member States: fines for non-compliance with ECJ-Judgements.

4.1.1.1 Sources of Law

The guidance given by European primary legislation on how to treat Member States breaching European legislation and on the consequences of those breaches is to be found in articles 10, 211 and 226-228 of the Consolidated Treaty.

Article 10 of the Treaty sets the duty of a Member State to respect European legislation. It reads:
"Member States shall take all appropriate measures, whether general or particular, to ensure fulfilment of the obligations arising out of this Treaty or resulting from action taken by the institutions of the Community. (...) They shall abstain from any measure which could jeopardise the attainment of the objectives of this Treaty."

Article 211 regulates the competencies of the European Commission, one of which is to *"ensure that the provisions of this Treaty and the measures taken by the institutions pursuant thereto are applied".* The Commission thus has the right and the duty to monitor member states' compliance with European Community legislation. How to respond to non-compliance is detailed in articles 226 and 228, which are treated below.

Besides for the European Commission, another enforcing agent is foreseen for in article 227. Member states which are of the opinion that other member states have breached Community legislation can, under certain circumstances dealt with under title 4.1.1.4 on page 79, bring the case before the European Court of Justice.

Note from the outset, that there is no provision whatsoever in the treaties explicitly providing individuals with a right of compensation of damages caused by a member state breaching European Community law.

4.1.1.2 Responding to breaches: Article 226 Nice Treaty (old 169)

Articles 226 of the Consolidated Treaty sets the procedural rules for the European Commission to initiate proceedings in the European Court of Justice against a Member State which it considers to be acting in breach of Community law.

Article 226 provides:
"If the Commission considers that a Member State has failed to fulfil an obligation under this Treaty, it shall deliver a reasoned opinion on the matter after giving the State concerned the opportunity to submit its observations.
If the State concerned does not comply with the opinion within the period laid down by the Commission, the latter may bring the matter before the Court of Justice."

In practice, article 226 is applied in the following four stages:

- Firstly, in an unofficial pre-controversial stage, the Commission will contact a member state allegedly breaching community law through diplomatic contacts and give the member state the possibility to explain its position. An attempt will be made to solve the matter silently, by reaching an accommodation with the member state.

- If this attempt proved unsuccessful, in a second stage, the Commission will send the member state allegedly breaching community law a *letter of formal notice* on the specific alleged infringement. The member state is typically given a period of two months to reply to this letter, a reply in which it can accommodate to the Commission's arguments or argue why it thinks its behaviour does *not* constitute a breach of Community law.

- When unsatisfied with the member state's reply, the Commission can proceed to a third stage in which it will issue a *reasoned opinion* which sets the final legal opinion of the Commission, arguing formally why it believes the behaviour concerned is a breach of Community law.

- When the member states chooses not to comply with this reasoned opinion, the Commission can turn to a fourth and final stage, which is to *refer to case* to the European Court of Justice.

The Commission has taken pride in the fact that it has managed to solve most cases before taking resort to the fourth stage, the referral to the European Court of Justice.

Or, as noted by Snyder (1993): *"the main form of dispute settlement used by the Commission is negotiation, and litigation is simply a part, sometimes inevitable but nevertheless generally a minor part, or this process"*.[94]

Under article 226, the European Commission's actions very much resemble those of a public enforcement agent. The Commission can start proceedings against member states on own initiative or does so in response to individual complaints. Given the Commission's limited resources in tracing breaches of Community law, increasingly, attention has been given to these individual complaints. The Commission has placed a standard form for complaints on the internet, to facilitate individuals in passing information on alleged breaches to the Commission[95] and repeatedly mentioned in its "Annual Reports on Monitoring the Application of Community Law" that individual complaints account for an important share of breaches detected.[96] On the other hand, the Commission's enthusiasm for individual complaints remains somewhat ambiguous. Repeatedly, it has stated that this involvement of individuals by no means should be interpreted as a granting of rights to individual complainants.

As the Commission mentions in its 13th annual report, the *"primary purpose* [of the article 226 procedure] *is not to protect an individual who wishes to rely on Community law. Individuals have other redress procedures before national authorities and the national courts, operating as the ordinary courts of Community law, with the possibility of going so far as to have the State ordered to pay damages for the breach of Community law. But the complaint to the Commission is still an indispensable instrument, not only for the Commission but also for the individual citizen."*[97].

In its 18th annual report of 2001, the tone is even clearer:
"But the primary objective of the infringement procedure is still, as before, to cause the offending member state to come into line with Community law. Nor does it have any effect on the discretionary power that the Commission is acknowledged to have by the Court of Justice as regards commencing infringement proceedings.

---

[94] Snyder (1993) at page 30
[95] See http://www.europa.eu.int/comm/secretariat_general/sgb/lexcomm/index_en.htm
[96] As an example, in its 20th Annual Report (2002), the Commission stated that individual complaints account for 60% of all detected infringements in 2002 and 60% in 2001. See European Commission (2003)
[97] European Commission (1996)

This is all the more important as the nature of the procedure may sometimes leave complainants feeling frustrated: they, of course, are aiming for a different result – the satisfaction of their individual interests which they see as threatened by the member state's alleged unlawful conduct.'[98]

After some individual complainants felt their rights were not properly respected by the Commission, the Court of First Instance ruled that:
"So far as concerns the applicant's argument on proceedings under article 226 EC [...], it must be noted that individuals are not party to proceedings concerning failure to fulfil obligations and for that reason cannot invoke rights to a fair hearing involving application of the audi alteram partem principle."[99]

It is thus clear that the enforcing process stays a public one: the individual complainant delivers information to the Commission but is not granted any rights in the procedure that might or might not follow.

The path foreseen for in article 226 is of a mixed nature. It clearly shows diplomatic characteristics, attempting to solve conflicts silently without calling upon a Court to publicly judge on them. This "exit" however still persists, leaving the whole procedure with an air of an non-political, objective, law enforcement mechanism of which article 228 provides the teeth in the form of penalty payments.

Before treating article 228, it should thus be clear that this public organisation of enforcement activities by the Commission is but one way for guaranteeing enforcement of Community legislation and that there is no reason to ex-ante assume this way is the ideal one. For more concrete arguments on the suitability of central or public law enforcement activities see section 8.1.2 on page 150.

4.1.1.3 Growing teeth. The Renewal of Article 228: Penalty Payments for Breaches. (old article 171)

Since 1967 in the Treaty establishing the European Economic Community and until 1992 under the Single European Act, primary European law did not foresee in

---

[98] European Commission (2001) at page 7.
[99] European Court of Justice (2001a), T-191/99, *Petrie and Others v. Commission*

damage compensation, fines or any other system of punishment and/or deterrence for breaches of Community law by member states. Article 171 of the Single European Act only vaguely regulated that

"if the Court of Justice finds that a Member State has failed to fulfil an obligation under this Treaty, the State shall be required to take the necessary measures to comply with the judgement of the Court of Justice."

In other words, there was no basis in primary European law to convict a member state to the payment of a fine for breaches of European Community legislation or for non-compliance with a judgement of the Court of Justice .

One year after the landmark *Francovich* decision, in 1992, this article 171 was changed (and renumbered to 228) in the Maastricht treaty in order to enable the European Court of Justice to order *lump-sum payments or penalties* to be paid following non-compliance by member states with one of its judgements. The article now reads:

1. If the Court of Justice finds that a Member State has failed to fulfil an obligation under this Treaty, the State shall be required to take the necessary measures to comply with the judgement of the Court of Justice.

2. If the Commission considers that the Member State concerned has not taken such measures it shall, after giving that State the opportunity to submit its observations, issue a reasoned opinion specifying the points on which the Member State concerned has not complied with the judgement of the Court of Justice.

If the Member State concerned fails to take the necessary measures to comply with the Court's judgement within the time-limit laid down by the Commission, <u>the latter</u> may bring the case before the Court of Justice. In so <u>doing it shall specify the amount of the lump sum or penalty payment</u> to be paid by the Member State concerned which it considers appropriate in the circumstances.

If the Court of Justice finds that the Member State concerned has not complied with its judgement <u>it may impose a lump sum or penalty payment on it</u>.

(underscore added)

It should be noted that this change can be well thought to be a reaction by Europe's heads of state on the Francovich doctrine –which will be treated shortly- developed by the European Court of Justice. By developing a renewed and more credible *public* alternative to the new *private* enforcement mechanism, member states hoped to ease the European Court of Justice in possible future developments of the Francovich doctrine.[100] In other words, after the change of article 171 to 228, it was made more difficult for the Court to extent the non-contractual liability doctrine based on the argument that no credible alternative for enforcing Community legislation existed. Moreover, member states gave a significant political signal by not picking up the Francovich doctrine with any provisions in primary law. Individuals were not granted the written right in Community law to proceed against member states for breaches of Community law and no mention is made of damage compensation to be paid to individuals for state acts not compatible with European law.[101]

However interesting the inclusion of lump sum payments or penalty payments in article 228(2), it is safe to say that these growing teeth of the public law enforcement mechanism remain rather unsharp. A mere breaching of European Community law by a member state cannot lead to the imposition of penalty payments upon that member state. In case of a breach, the Commission has to go through the due process of formally notifying the member state, then has to await its answer before it can draft a reasoned opinion. Only after haven given the member state some more time to comply with the Commission's reasoned opinion, the Commission can proceed by taking the unsolved case to the European Court of Justice for the first time.

Then, when the Court decides to follow the Commission's opinion and judges the member state's behaviour to be contrary to European Community legislation, the old article 171 -or new article 228(1)- applies and the member state is to take measures within due time to comply with the Court's judgement.

Once again, only after this has not happened within due time, the new article 228(2) applies and the Commission shall notify the member state, which again, is to submit its observations. Finally, the Commission can issue a reasoned opinion, mentioning the points where it feels the member state has failed to comply with the Court's judgement and a deadline by which the member state is to comply.

If compliance has still not occurred by that time, the Commission can finally bring the case before the European Court of Justice, specifying a lump-sum or penalty

---

[100] Tallberg (2002)

[101] Clearly, this has not hindered the Court in pursuing its interpretation, as will be shown below.

payment if feels is appropriate for the member state to be convicted to pay.[102] There are no legal guidelines prescribing the height of the fine, the Commission recommends a fine to the Court which can change it at will. Upon proposing a fine, the Commission has typically taken account of the seriousness and the duration of the breach as indicators for the height of the punishment.[103]

A mechanism for the collection of these penalty payments is not foreseen for in the treaties. If a member state were to refuse to pay the fines it was convicted to, there seems little more than political pressure from the Commission and other member states to take resort to. Also, in the article 228 proceedings, the Court does not have the power to order injunctive measures or to order a member state to take action.[104]

Given the length of the procedure, it might not be surprising that very few cases have occurred where member states were convicted under article 228(2). A short overview of cases is given.

The first article 228(2) case to occur involved Greece and is known under the name *Kouroupitos*, a river in the prefecture of Chania in Crete (Greece) [105]. In a first stage, Greece failed to comply with directives 75/442/EEC and 78/319/EEC which oblige member states to ensure the disposal of waste and to take appropriate measures in respect of toxic and dangerous waste. Amongst others, member states are required to draw up plans for the attainment of certain objectives. Greece failed to do so and after the Commission started public enforcement proceedings under articles 226-228, the case was brought to the European Court of Justice a first time, where Greece lost.[106] After not substantially altering its behaviour following this judgement, in 2000, Greece was taken to the European Court of Justice by the Commission for a second time, applying article 228(2) to fine Greece.

The Court

1. Declared that [...] the Hellenic Republic has not implemented all the necessary measures to comply with the judgment of the Court of 7 April 1992 in Case C-45/91

---

[102] For some more information on the Commission's praxis of setting the height of penalty payments see page 187.

[103] See [1997] OJ C63/2, *Information from the Commission – Method of calculating the penalty payments provided for pursuant to article 171 of the EC Treaty* in conjunction with [1996] OJ C242/6, *the Memorandum on applying article 171 of the EC Treaty.*

[104] Interestingly, the Court does possess these powers in interim proceedings under article 243.

[105] European Court of Justice (2000b), Case C-387/97, *Commission v. Greece*

[106] European Court of Justice (1992), Case C-45/91, *Commission v. Greece*

Commission v Greece and has failed to fulfil its obligations under Article 171 of the EC Treaty;
2. Orders the Hellenic Republic to pay to the Commission of the European Communities, into the account EC own resources, a penalty payment of EUR 20.000 for each day of delay in implementing the measures necessary to comply with the judgment in Case C-45/91, from delivery of the present judgment until the judgment in Case C-45/91 has been complied with.[107]

Three observations concerning this case are worth mentioning.
Firstly, the Court lowered the Commission's proposed daily penalty payment from 24.600 € to 20.000 €. No explanation is given by the Court on the exact calculation of this sum.
Secondly, although Greece's non-compliance with the judgement started almost 8 years earlier in 1992, it was to pay 20.000€/day starting only from the delivery of the 2000 judgement. This is not in accordance with the Commission's guidelines on the calculation of fines as explained on page 187. Greece hence did not have to pay any penalty payments for the period of 8 years in which it ignored the Court's judgement and knew it was breaching European Community law. Even more, in as far as it was clear since 1981 (the year Greece joined the European Union) that Greece's act was not in accordance with the 1978 directive, the country was not punished for breaching the law during 19 years!
Thirdly, Greece eventually paid the Commission about 5.000.000 €, meaning it took Greece another 250 days to comply with the 8 year old judgement.[108]

Also in another case, in 2001, a financial penalty has been imposed on a Member State for not complying with an earlier judgement by the European Court of Justice. Spain was found not having taken the necessary measures to ensure that the quality of inshore bathing water in Spanish territory conforms to the limit values set in accordance with Article 3 of Council Directive 76/160/EEC of 8 December 1975 concerning the quality of bathing water.[109] In a second case, Spain was found to not have complied with this judgment in Case C-92/96 and was ordered to pay:
"a penalty payment of EUR 624.150 per year and per 1% of bathing areas in Spanish inshore waters which have been found not to conform to the limit values laid down

---

[107] Judgement in Case C-387/97
[108] For implications of this, see pages 111 and 187.
[109] European Court of Justice (1998), Case C-92/96, *Commission v. Spain*

under Directive 76/160 for the year in question, as from the time when the quality of bathing water achieved in the first bathing season following delivery of this judgment is ascertained until the year in which the judgment in Commission v Spain is fully complied with".[110]

Again, the Court altered the Commission's calculated penalty payment (the Commission had proposed a daily fine of 45.600 €) and even provided for a yearly, not a daily fine. Experts claim this fine might end up to amount to over 9.000.000 €.

The Spanish government seemed taken by surprise by the whole action and even contended (unsuccessfully) that the Court should:

- dismiss the action in its entirety;
- in the alternative, dismiss the application for imposition of daily penalty payments
- in the further alternative, order that the daily penalty payment should not exceed € 11.400.[111]

A third case, still pending before the Court, is one where the Commission has demanded the record daily penalty payment of 309.750 € to be summoned against Italy. The case relates to the discriminatory treatment of former foreign language lecturers in several Italian universities. In its judgement on Case C-212/99 of 26 June 2001, the Court declared that since Italy had not recognised the acquired rights of foreign language assistants who had become associates and mother-tongue linguistic experts, by granting such recognition to all national workers, Italy had failed to fulfil treaty requirements relating to non-discrimination on the grounds of nationality. In January 2004, Italy did adopt a law to comply with that judgement, but the Commission finds that law insufficient and has again proceeded against Italy. On February 4th 2004, the Commission decided to bring the case to the Court under article 228(2).[112]

A final word should be spent on the form of the financial penalty payment set by the European Court of Justice. Article 228(2) foresees that the Commission specifies the amount of the *lump sum* or *penalty payment* to be paid by the Member State which it

---

[110] European Court of Justice (2003a), Case C-278/01, *Commission v. Spain*
[111] id. at para. 19
[112] See the European Commission's press release IP/04/164 from February 4th 2004

considers appropriate given the circumstances. Until recently, in cases where the Court has imposed penalties upon member states, those always took the form of daily fines. In other words: member states were demanded to start paying fines, starting from the date of the second judgement of the Court, and hence had no incentives to comply with Community law until that judgement. This lack of deterrence effect might be about to be repaired.

In his opinion to the European Court of Justice on Case 304/02,[113] Advocate General Leendert Geelhoed proposed to dramatically change the regime of financial sanctions against breaching member states. Case 304/02 is a public enforcement procedure, led by the Commission against France, and is a follow-up of a previous case where the Court in 1991 found France to be acting in breach of Community law between 1984 and 1987 since it did not sufficiently carry out controls in order to ensure compliance with Community fishery conservation measures.[114]
Following this finding of a breach, in a second period of time from 1991-2000, France was involved in a dialogue with the Commission concerning the measures it was taking in order to enforce Community rules. The Commission found these measures to be insufficient and hence, brought France to Court again for a second time in order to sanction it with financial penalties.

Under "standard" jurisdiction by the Court, France could expect daily penalties for every further day it would not comply with the regulation in question, starting from the day of the judgement in Case 304/02. As has been discussed before, in effect, this would allow France breaching Community law from 1984 to the day of judgement in 2004 without any financial consequences.

Advocate General Geelhoed finds exactly this to be not in line with the philosophy behind article 228, and proposes the following:[115]

- In relation to the conduct of France between 1991 and 2000, and (...) given the persistent, serious, and structural nature of the infringement, the Advocate General proposes that, for the first time, the Court impose a lump sum fine of **€ 115.522.500.** To arrive at this figure the Advocate General has taken the

113 European Court of Justice (2002), Case 304/02, *European Commission v. France*
114 European Court of Justice (1991a), Case C-64/88, *European Commission v. France*
115 European Court of Justice Press and Information Division (2004)

daily fine proposed by the Commission and multiplied it by 365 to give the amount payable over a year.

- As regards possible continued infringements after a judgement in case 304/02, the Advocate General recognises that the Commission needs further information in order to determine this fact. As monitoring and enforcement practices cannot be changed instantaneously, he considers a daily penalty to be inappropriate and proposes a penalty to be imposed every six months. On the basis of the daily fined proposed by the Commission, he arrives at a six monthly fine of **€ 57.761.250**.

The size of these proposed penalties is impressive, and it remains to be seen whether the European Court of Justice will follow this non-binding advice by its advocate-general.

From an economic point of view, Geelhoed's proposals are to be welcomed as they effectively close a hole in the application of article 226-228 proceedings. By installing financial sanctions also for the period of non-compliance between the initial judgement by the Court (informing the member state that its act is a breach of Community law) and its second one (setting the financial penalty), it attempts to create a deterrence effect which is absent now.

It is to be remarked, that Geelhoed's calculation of the lump-sum payment is still rather conservative. Instead of calculating one year's penalty using the Commission's daily penalty proposal, he could as well have argued that the lump-sum penalty is to cover to breach in the period 1991-2000. Hence it should cover nine years at not one, at should amount to the even more astronomic sum of **€ 1.039.702.500.**

All in all, it should be obvious to the reader that although article 228(2) is a serious improvement in the possibilities of the Commission to make member states comply with Community law, it remains a painstakingly slow and long procedure. As to April 2005, there is no possibility to convict member states to the payment of fines for a breach of European law. Only the non-compliance with a judgement by the European Court of Justice can give rise to such demands. The Court's judgement in case 304/02 will show us whether this will remain the case.

4.1.1.4 Member state v. Member state.

A final possibility for a public actor to proceed against member states breaching European law is given by article 227 of the Treaty. This article allows for member states to proceed against each other.

Article 227 reads as follows:
A Member State which considers that another Member State has failed to fulfil an obligation under this Treaty may bring the matter before the Court of Justice.
Before a Member State brings an action against another Member State for an alleged infringement of an obligation under this Treaty, it shall bring the matter before the Commission. The Commission shall deliver a reasoned opinion after each of the States concerned has been given the opportunity to submit its own case and its observations on the other party's case both orally and in writing.
If the Commission has not delivered an opinion within three months of the date on which the matter was brought before it, the absence of such opinion shall not prevent the matter from being brought before the Court of Justice.

Clearly, this possibility is not suited to improve relations between member states and has not been used to a large extent. Very few cases have occurred where member states have chosen to take this path all the way to the Court. Following Craig and de Burca (2003), in more recent years, Belgium (without the support of the Commission, but with the support of four other member states) brought an unsuccessful action against Spain in relation to its requirements concerning rules of origin for Rioja wine.[116]

The best-known article 277 case however, dates back to the 1970s. On October 1st 1977, a French fishing vessel was boarded by British Fishery protection officers while fishing in the UK's territorial waters. The captain of the vessel was summoned and convicted in the UK for using fishing-nets with mesh which were smaller than prescribed for in the British Fishing Nets Order of 1977.

Following that incident, the French government started an article 227 procedure and –as foreseen in that article- brought the case to the European Commission. In March

[116] European Court of Justice (2000a), Case C-388/95, *Belgium v. Spain*

1978, the Commission delivered a reasoned opinion in which it found the British Fishing Nets Order to be a breach of Community law. The United Kingdom refused to comply with this reasoned opinion, and hence, France took the case to the Court in June 1978.

France, with the support of the Commission, successfully claimed that by adopting the Fishing Nets Order, the UK acted unilaterally, although it was only to do so after having consulted and having received approval of the Commission[117]. As a result, the Court judged that

"by bringing into force on 1 April 1977 the Fishing Nets (North-East Atlantic) Order 1977, the United Kingdom of Great Britain and Northern Ireland has failed to fulfil its obligations under the EEC Treaty."[118]

Note that article 227 does not foresee in any sanctions or injunctive measures. The Court can hence only judge whether it understands the behaviour of a member state to be in breach with Community legislation. Member states not complying with such judgement are subject to Commissionary acting under article 228.

Primary legislation dealing with member states' breaching of European law thus only allows for public enforcement procedures. Both the Commission and member states are granted the right to proceed against breaching member states and a penalty payment system is arranged for to be used by the Commission only. Penalties are given for non-compliance with judgements only, not for breaches of Community law.

In the following, we will have a short look into the primary law dealing with cases where the European Community itself failed to respect European Community law. This area of law has proven to be the link between the article 226-228 proceedings and the Francovich doctrine.

---

[117] The basis for this was given in Council Regulation no. 101/76

[118] European Court of Justice (1979), Case 141/78, *French Republic v United Kingdom of Great Britain and Northern Ireland*

4.1.2 Recourse for Individuals against the EC: Damage Compensation in Primary Community law.

Although the treaty does **not** grant individuals a right of action or compensation against Member States, there is such individual right against the Community. Even though this is not the topic of this work, this right will be elaborated upon, since it has proved to be the basis for granting individuals a right of action and compensation against Member States.

4.1.2.1 Right of Action: Art. 230 Consolidated Treaty (173)

Article 230 grants Community institutions as well as its individuals the right to request, within two months of publication, the European Court of Justice to review the legality of acts of Community institutions. The Court can decide to annul the measure, if it finds its illegal.

"*Any natural or legal person may (...) institute proceedings against a decision addressed to that person or against a decision which, although in the form of a regulation or a decision addressed to another person, is of direct and individual concern to the former. The proceedings provided for in this Article shall be instituted within two months of the publication of the measure, or of its notification to the plaintiff, or, in the absence thereof, of the day on which it came to the knowledge of the latter, as the case may be.* "

In early days, this article 230 had a greater meaning than it has now. In a judgement of 1963, the European Court of Justice held that for article 288 to be applicable, the norm in question had to be annulled first.[119] This necessity disappeared in subsequent cases at the Court and article 228 actions became independent of article 230 proceedings. This came clear without doubt by the Court's Schöppenstedt judgement.[120]

[119] See European Court of Justice (1963a), Case C-25/62, *Plaumann v. Commission*

[120] See European Court of Justice (1971), Case C-5/71, *Aktien-Zuckerfabrik Schöppenstedt v. Council*

4.1.2.2 Right of Compensation: Art. 288 Nice Treaty (215)

Whereas article 230 grants individuals the right of *action* against the Community (and alone the Community)[121], article 288 regulates their right of compensation.

Contractual liability is governed by the law applicable to the contract in question.[122] In the case of non-contractual liability, " *the Community shall, in accordance with the general principles common to the laws of the Member States, make good any damage caused by its institutions or by its servants in the performance of their duties.(...)"*
That these cases are to be heard in the European Court of Justice is mentioned in article 235.

In the mentioned Schöppenstedt case, the European Court of Justice has established the general principal for non-contractual liability of the Community. This principle became known as the **Schöppenstedt Test**. Liability, thus the Court, does not simply result from the Court declaring a measure null and void. Non-contractual liability arises only on the condition of a
"sufficiently flagrant violation of a superior rule of law for the protection of the individual".[123]
Whereas a discussion on what exactly constitutes a "superior rule of law" is not considered of elementary importance here[124], attention should be devoted to the meaning of a *"sufficiently flagrant violation".*

From the start on, one of the crucial factors for the Court was the degree of discretion left to the decision-maker. As was shown in the Bayerische NHL case, in practice, this meant that to be tested was whether the institution had "manifestly and gravely disregarded the limits on the exercise of its powers"[125].

---

[121] The organs of the European Community mentioned in article 230 are the European Parliament, the Commission, the Council and the European Central Bank.

[122] Clearly, contractual liability is not what we are interested in. The topic of relevance here is the liability of the Community and the member states for acts which did not take place between contracting partners. In other words: of interest here is the non-contractual liability.

[123] European Court of Justice (1971), Case 5/71, *Zuckerfabrik Schöppenstedt v. Council* at para. 11

[124] Interested readers are referred to Craig and de Burca (2003) at pages 549-552

[125] European Court of Justice (1978), Case 83/76, *Bayerische NHL et al. v. Council and Commission*

In the case at hand, a Council regulation imposed an obligation upon certain actors in the agricultural business to buy milk powder at a certain (high) price. This was done so as an effort to reduce the excessive stock of milk-powder. It its judgement, the Court repeated that, although it had declared the regulation null and void in the past, this alone is not sufficient a condition for the Community to incur liability. The Court once again stated that: *"the Community does not incur liability on account of a legislative measure which involves choices of economic policy unless a sufficiently serious breach of a superior rule of law for the protection of the individual has occurred."*[126] The Court did not see this condition to be fulfilled in this case.

In paragraph 4 of its ruling, the Court explains why it feels such serious breach condition is a meaningful argument: *"This restrictive view is explained by the consideration that the legislative authority (...) cannot always be hindered in making its decisions by the prospect of applications for damages whenever it has occasion to adopt legislative measures in the public interest which may adversely affects the interest of individuals."*

The Court thus took account of the specific, public nature of political decision-making. A more detailed economic assessment of this "legitimate harm of decision-making" will be given on page 119.

The lack of subsequent non-contractual liability cases against the Commission have prevented the Court from clarifying more precisely under article 228 what it understands to be a "sufficiently serious breach" and how important exactly the role of "discretion power" is. The Court however has applied these conditions concerning *Community* non-contractual liability on *member states* non-contractual liability and has –as will be seen now- found ample opportunity to fill in these interpretation gaps. It is thus fair to say that whereas initially, article 228 has proven to be an "engine" for the development of a state liability doctrine, this very doctrine has in turn driven the interpretation of unclarities left in article 228.

---

[126] id. at para. 3

4.2 ECJ-Jurisdiction: Damages before National Courts: a Recourse for Individuals against Member States. The Introduction of liability of Member States under European Law.

4.2.1 Direct effect and supremacy doctrine, Van Gend&Loos

The treaties remain silent on individuals' rights of action against Member States. However, the development of the direct effect doctrine opened the way for Member State liability for breaches of European legislation.

The doctrine of direct effect is judge-made law, developed by the European Court of Justice, amongst others in its landmark Van Gend & Loos Case (1963)[127]. The concept of direct effect follows from the principle of supremacy of European law and means that if European Community law has direct effect, this law in effect grants rights to individuals which must be upheld by the national Courts.

Further, a distinction should be made between the **vertical and horizontal direct effect** of European legislation[128]. Legislation with vertical direct effect can be invoked by an individual against a Member State in national court. Legislation having horizontal direct effect can also be invoked directly by an individual against another individual in a national court. Treaties, regulations and decisions all have both these effects[129].

Directives are a special case. They do not have a horizontal direct effect since, upon timely and correct transposition by Member States, they become national legislation which is in any case applicable in national courts. As will be seen below, upon incorrect or late transposition, they have vertical direct effect, meaning that

---

[127] In this tax case, the European Court of Justice ruled that "the Community constitutes a new legal order of international law for the benefit of which the states have limited their sovereign rights, albeit within limited fields, and the subjects of which comprise not only Member States but also their nationals. Independently of the legislation of Member States, Community law therefore not only imposes obligations on individuals but is also intended to confer upon them rights which become part of their legal heritage. These rights arise not only where they are expressly granted by the Treaty, but also by reason of obligations which the Treaty imposes in a clearly defined way upon individuals as well as upon the Member States and upon the institutions of the Community." Van Gend & Loos Case, European Court of Justice (1963b)

[128] Cf. the remarks on page 4

[129] The doctrine of direct effect has been laid down by the European Court of Justice in its Case C-26/62 Van Gend & Loos / Administratie Der Belastingen European Court of Justice (1963b)

individuals[130] can invoke the directive against the Member State in question[131] in national courts.

Irrespective of this direct effect doctrine, nothing however, is said on how to deal with compensation demands when individual rights have been disrespected. The Francovich judgement described below dramatically changed this stand-still.

4.2.2 Procedural: Francovich and non-implementation of Directives

After having lost employment through bankruptcy of their private employer in the mid eighties, Mr. Francovich and thirty-four other individuals sued the Italian State in 1989 for the compensation of due wages, which their former employer was unable to pay. Mr. Francovich referred to Council Directive 80/987/EEC of October 20th 1980 on the approximation of the laws of the member states relating to the protection of employees in the event of insolvency of the employer. Leaving a large deal of discretion to the member states, this directive nevertheless foresaw in the installation of a guarantee fund (the source of funding of which was to be decided by the member state) to be used for the elimination of wage debts upon insolvency. Although the directive was to be transposed into national law by October 1983, Italy did not do so until 1992[132].

Francovich and co. reasoned that if the Italian state had transposed the directive on time, the guarantee fund would have been available to pay out the due wages and demanded the European Court of Justice to apply the (vertical) direct effect doctrine to the directive, effectively making the Italian state debtor vis-à-vis Mr. Francovich. The Court did not follow this reasoning, since the directive in article 5 arranged for the setup of an independent guarantee institutions which excludes, thus the Court, the conclusion that the Italian state is the debtor of that guarantee[133].

---

[130] In its jurisdiction, the European Court of Justice has set out conditions for individuals to hand in a liability claim against a Member State.

[131] Note that individuals do not have to be nationals of a Member State of the European Union, neither that the Member State in question should be the one where the individual is a national of.

[132] Italy finally transposed the directive by decreto legislativo Nr. 80 of January 27th 1992, after the Francovich judgement and after the Commission initiated *and finalised* a public enforcement procedure under article 226 at the European Court of Justice. In its judgement of February 2nd 1989 in Case 22/87 Commission vs. Italy, the Court judged that by not transposing the directive, Italy had failed to fulfil its obligations under the EC Treaty.

[133] See European Court of Justice (1991b) in joined cases 6/90 and 9/90, *Francovich and Bonifaci v. Italy* (hereafter: *C-6/90 Francovich*)

The Court however then had to determine *"whether a member state has an obligation to make good loss and damage suffered by individuals as a result of the failure to transpose Directive 80/987"*[134].

In answering this question, the Court ignored previous rulings on similar questions where it left the decision on this matter totally to national law[135]. Most controversially, the Court applied the general notion of legal protection and the *effet utile* doctrine as well as the general duty of a Member State to respect European legislation as formulated in article 10 of the Treaty. This duty, thus the Court, should be interpreted as a duty to lift illegal consequences of a breach of European law.

Hence, the Court ruled that *"Member States are obliged to make good loss and damage caused to individuals by breaches of Community law for which they can be held responsible"*[136] and that *"the conditions under which that liability gives rise to a right to reparation depend on the nature of the breach of Community Law giving rise to the loss and damage"*[137].

By attaching such importance to the "nature of the breach", the Court enabled itself to change or fine-tune its newly-developed state liability doctrine upon the occurrence of new cases with different facts. Indeed, as established by the Court under the *CILFIT doctrine*[138], national courts are *not* obliged to refer to the European Court of Justice questions on the interpretation of community law *only* when (a.o.) the Court has already decided on a factually similar case and no doubt persists on the proper interpretation of Community law. This decision has enabled the Court to develop and extent the scope of its state liability doctrine in consequent cases, as will be shown below.

The conditions of the nature of the breach giving rise to a right to reparation laid out in this Francovich case where the following[139]:

---

134 id. at para. 28

135 Compare with European Court of Justice (1968), C-13/68, *Salgoil vs. Italian Ministry of Foreign Trade* and European Court of Justice (1976a), C-60/75, *Camina Antonion Russo v. Azienda di Stato*

136 C-6/90, *Francovich*, at para. 3.

137 id. at paras. 4 and 38.

138 The CILFIT doctrine was established in C-283-81, C.I.L.F.I.T, Judgement of October 6th 1982

139 C-6/90, *Francovich*, at para. 40

1. The result prescribed by the directive should entail the grant of rights to individuals.
2. It should be possible to identify the content of those rights on the basis of the provisions of the directive.
3. There should be a causal link between the breach of the State's obligation and the loss and damage suffered by the injured parties.

These conditions, thus the Court, are sufficient to give rise to a right on behalf of the individual to receive reparation, a right founded directly on Community law[140].

Importantly however, the Court decided that although this right to reparation is founded on Community law, it is on the basis of the rules of national laws on state liability that the state must make reparation available[141]. This implies that similar cases will not be heard at the European Court of Justice, but that national member state's courts are to decide on compensation claims for breaches of community law. In deciding so, the Court has set minimal conditions for those rules of national law, stating that the substantive and procedural conditions of those rules should not be less favourable than those of the rules relating to similar domestic claims (for breaches of domestic law). Moreover, those rules should not be framed such as to make it virtually impossible or excessively difficult to obtain reparation.[142]

In its Francovich ruling, the Court thus established a principle of **Member State liability** for the *failure* of a Member State to transpose directives into national law. In its judgement, the Court has chosen not to go in detail on the criteria for other breaches giving rise to liability claims. This lack of guidance has caused subsequent cases to be heard before the European Court of Justice, giving the Court the possibility to slowly extend the state liability doctrine in its Brasserie du Pêcheur & Factortame cases, against the declared political will of the member states[143]. Note again that this is judge made law, the treaties remain silent on Member State Liability for breaches of EC law.

---

[140] id. at para. 41
[141] id. at para. 42
[142] id. at para. 43
[143] On numerous occasions, member states have presented their opinions against a further extension of the state liability doctrine. See for example the opinion of the German, Irish and Dutch government mentioned in the opinion of Tesauro AG in case 46/93

4.2.3 Substantive: Brasserie du Pêcheur, Factortame and liability for legislative action

Five years later, on March 5th 1996, more than two years after the German Bundesgerichtshof and the English High Court referred a number of questions in two similar cases to the European Court of Justice, the Court delivered a judgement in the joined cases Brasserie du Pêcheur and Factortame[144], effectively clarifying some questions left unanswered by the Francovich ruling.

Basing its acting on the German beer purity law, the German state effectively barred the Brasserie du Pêcheur's product from the German market between 1981 and 1987. German law prohibited the use of certain additives in the plaintiff's beer and also forbid the selling of the beverage as "beer".

In an article 226 initiative, the Commission claimed the additive clause in German law to be a breach of article 28 Treaty (article 30 at the time) foreseeing in the free movement of goods, which is –different from the secondary Francovich directive- *primary* European law. The case was brought to the European Court of Justice, which found the public health arguments for the regulation offered by Germany to be unconvincing and judged that the measure was disproportional. Hence, Germany was judged to have breached primary European law[145].

Following this judgement, Brasserie du Pêcheur initiated a suit for the compensation of foregone profits due to Germany's breach of law. As the Francovich judgement did not give any guidance on how to deal with compensatory claims following breaches of primary European law, the Bundesgerichtshof applied the CILFIT doctrine and referred the question to the European Court of Justice.

The Factortame case as well concerned acts of a member state arguably in breach of a provision of primary European law[146]. Spanish fishermen invoked article 43 of the Treaty (at that time article 52) against the United Kingdom's regulations for

---

[144] European Court of Justice European Court of Justice (1996a), joined cases 46/93 and 48/93, *Brasserie du Pêcheur v. Bundesrepublik Deutschland and The Queen v. Secretary of State for Transport, ex parte Factortame and others*

[145] European Court of Justice (1987), Case 178/84, *European Commission vs. Germany*

[146] Three different Factortame cases where brought to the European Court of Justice, the one of relevance to state liability is often labelled Factortame III. As the two other cases are not discussed here, the case will simply be referred to as Factortame.

registration of a vessel as "British", claiming those regulation were too strict and hence an infringement of the freedom of establishment[147].

In its judgement, the Court provided guidance on how to deal with breaches of primary European law.

It started with refuting the argument that the already existing direct effect of primary European law made additional liability provisions (which are not foreseen for in the treaties) superfluous[148]. The direct effect would enable individuals to defend their rights in national courts and allow them to make use of existing national reparation rights.

The Court however, claimed that the direct effect doctrine is no more than a *"minimum guarantee and is not sufficient in itself to ensure the full and complete implementation of the Treaty"*[149]. The supremacy of European law over national law does not ensure in all circumstances the effective protection of rights conferred upon individuals by European law and thus a community-law based right of reparation was made available not only for breaches of not-directly applicable law, but also for those legal provisions which were already granted direct effect.

The German government provided another critique to the extension of the state liability doctrine, claiming that a general right to reparation under Community law for breaches of European law can only be granted by the member states in legislation. Following the German reasoning, the European Court of Justice would be going beyond the treaties and its compentencies when doing so.

The Court however vigorously rejected this claim in its judgement, drawing on article 220 of the Treaty (old 164)[150]. For the Court, effectuating article 220 means that in the absence of specific rules or provisions governing consequences of breaches of community law, *"it is for the Court to rule on such a question in accordance with generally accepted methods of interpretation, in particular by reference to the*

---

[147] The background of the UK's regulation is the common fishery policy in the European Union, granting every member state's vessel fleet a quota of maximum allowable catch. By tightening registration regulations, the UK tried to prevent Spanish nationals to register their vessels as "British" and thus profiting from the UK's quota.

[148] This argument was put forward by the governments mentioned in footnote 143.

[149] Case 46/93, *Brasserie du Pêcheur*, at paras. 19-22

[150] Article 220 reads: "The Court of Justice shall ensure that in the interpretation and application of this Treaty the law is observed."

fundamental principles of the Community legal system, and, where necessary, general principles common to the legal systems of the member states." [151]
Further more, the Court argued that the general principle relevant to the treatment of breaches of Community law is to be found in article 288 (old 215), which regulates the non-contractual liability of the European Community. The Court found this regulation to be an expression of the general principle of law, common to all member states, that *"an unlawful act or omission gives rise to an obligation to make good the damage caused."*[152] Moreover, *"that provision also reflects the obligation on public authorities to make good damage caused in the performance of their duties."*[153]

The European Court of Justice has well anticipated its critics which claim the Court acts on a integrationist European agenda. More than in its Francovich ruling, where a right of reparation was derived solely on article 10 of the Treaty, in the Brasserie du Pêcheur ruling, the European Court of Justice has made an effort in proving that such right has its foundation in primary law and is based upon well-accepted principles of law. The Court also ruled that the State will be treated as unity on the horizontal level, and will hence be called responsible for breaches of its organs, regardless of the internal division of power between authorities[154]. In a later ruling on the vertical allocation of liability within member states, the Court judged that in federally organised states, reparation is not necessarily to be provided by the federal state.[155]

Besides expanding the principle of state liability for breaches of Community law, the Court has also clarified the conditions for liability more precisely as it did in its Francovich judgement.[156]

In setting these conditions, the Court took guidance of the existing primary provisions governing the non-contractual liability of the Community in article 288 and transposed

---

[151] Case 46/93, *Brasserie du Pêcheur,* at para. 27
[152] Case 46/93, *Brasserie du Pêcheur* at para. 29
[153] id.
[154] In a recent decision, the Court judged that –under certain conditions- also the national judiciary is liable for breaches of Community law. See European Court of Justice (2003b), C-224/01, *Köbler v. Republik Österreich.* Previous to the Court's judgement, Anagnostaras (2001b) has discussed liability under Community law for such issues.
[155] See European Court of Justice (1999), C-302/97, *Konle vs. Austria* at paras. 61-64 and European Court of Justice (2000c), C-424/97, Solomone *Haim vs. Kassenzahnärztliche Vereinigung Nordrhein.*
[156] For an excellent overview of these conditions see Lane (1996)

those to the acting of member states.[157,158] Two reasons can be thought of why the Court has done so. Firstly, article 288 is based upon generally accepted principles of law, which the Court has applied also in other areas of Community law[159]. Secondly, the Court found that the rules governing state liability cannot differ without proper cause, depending on whether a national authority or a Community authority committed the breach causing the damage[160].

The Court however followed this reasoning with a particular interpretation, which resulted in conditions for member state liability less strict than those for the Community[161]. In its judgement, the Court first states that in its jurisdiction on the non-contractual liability of the Community, it has taken into account the wide discretion of the Community Institutions in particular as regards legislative measures involving choices of economic policy.[162] It continues however, that *"the national legislator [...] does not systematically have a wide discretion when it acts in a field governed by community law. Community law may impose upon it obligations to achieve a particular result or obligations to act or refrain from acting which reduce its margin of discretion, sometimes to a considerable degree."*[163]

Then the Court pinpoints the duty of a member state to transpose directives into national law within a given period of time as prescribed by article 189 (now 249) of the Treaty and states that *"the fact that it is for the national legislator to take the necessary measures has no bearing on the member state's liability for failing to transpose the directive".*[164]
With this sentence, the Courts made clear that the duty to transpose directives decreases member states' margin of discretion to such degree that a classical reasonableness test is to take preference over the Schöppenstedt test, even when judging a legislator's acting. In later hearings, the Court has deemed the mere fact of

---

157 Case 46/93, *Brasserie du Pêcheur*, at para. 41
158 Drawing the analogy with Community non-contractual liability was already proposed by Advocate General Tesauro in his opinion in the Francovich Case, but not picked up by the Court at that time.
159 Case 46/93, *Brasserie du Pêcheur,* at para. 41
160 Case 46/93, Brasserie du Pêcheur, at para. 42
161 For the conditions governing Community liability, see 4.1.2 Recourse for Individuals against the EC: Damage Compensation in Primary Community law on page 81.
162 Case 46/93, *Brasserie du Pêcheur,* at para. 44
163 Case 46/93, *Brasserie du Pêcheur,* at para. 46
164 Case 46/93, *Brasserie du Pêcheur,* at para. 46

lack of non-transposition of a directive by a member states is considered a breach and needs no further investigation.[165]

In other cases, where a member state may enjoy a larger margin of discretion, *"the conditions under which it may incur liability must, in principle, be the same as those under which the Community institutions incur liability in the comparable situation"*[166], effectively judging a Schöppenstedt test preferable.

Concretely, this means that in those cases where member states enjoy wide discretion, the Court saw a right of reparation under Community law upon the fulfilment of three conditions:

1. the rule of law must be intended to confer rights upon individuals
2. the breach must be sufficiently serious
3. there must be a direct causal link between the breach of the obligation resting on the State and the damage sustained by the injured parties.[167]

Clearly, of most interest is the exact meaning of a "sufficiently serious breach". The Court precised that such is the case when a member state has *"manifestly and gravely disregarded the limits on its discretion"*.[168] Leaving the judgement of this to national courts, elements to be considered are the clarity and precision of the rule breached, the measure of discretion left by that rule to the national authority, the (un)voluntarily character of the breach and whether a position taken by a Community institution may have contributed to the (non)adoption or retention of a measure of practice contrary to Community law.[169]

However, just as the non-transposition of directives was later on[170], two more situations were identified qualifying directly in the Court's judgement as a sufficiently serious breach. Firstly, the persisting of a breach of Community law after it had been judged as such by a court of law is sufficiently serious to give rise to a right of reparation. Also, in situations where a preliminary ruling or settled case law leave little doubt that the conduct in question constitutes a infringement of law, the conduct

---

[165] European Court of Justice (1996c), Case 178/94, *Dillenkofer and others v. Bundesrepublik Deutschland*

[166] Case 46/93, *Brasserie du Pêcheur,* at para. 47

[167] Case 46/93, *Brasserie du Pêcheur,* at para. 51

[168] Case 46/93, *Brasserie du Pêcheur,* at para. 55

[169] Case 46/93, *Brasserie du Pêcheur,* at para. 56

is to be interpreted a sufficiently serious breach, and hence gives rise to a right of reparation by the victim if both other conditions mentioned above are fulfilled[171].

Summing up the jurisdiction so far, the Court has thus made clear that under European law, a right of reparation for damages caused by a breach of Community law can only exist when a member state has manifestly and gravely disregarded the limits on its discretion and such breach is causally connected to the damage if the rule of law breached was to confer rights upon individuals. Two scenario's were distinguished between. Firstly, since *Dillenkofer*, the non-transposition of a directive - per se- is seen as sufficiently serious and thus gives rise to a right of reparation since the duty to transpose heavily narrowed the member state's margin of discretion. In the second scenario, applicable to acts regulated by the treaty and regulations, the margin of discretion of member states under Community law is much larger and upon deciding whether the breach qualifies as "sufficiently serious", attention is to be given to the clarity and precision of the rule breached, the measure of discretion left by that rule to the national authority, the (un)voluntarily character of the breach and whether a position taken by a Community institution may have contributed to the (non)adoption or retention of a measure of practice contrary to Community law.

Later jurisdiction has shed light on the interpretation of the "sufficiently serious breach" condition. Many cases arose where member states did transpose directives, but arguably did so incorrectly. In *British Telecom*[172], where the UK was judged to have failed to transpose directive 90/351 correctly, the Court refused to simply apply its *Francovich* or *Dillenkofer* doctrine. It thus differentiated between not-implemented and mal-implemented directives, judging that the UK was not liable in damages for its breach since the directive was imprecise and unclear; the UK had made an interpretation of the directive which was false but in good faith and there was no available guidance for the transposition in jurisdiction.[173]
Similarly, in *Denkavit*[174], Germany's failure to transpose a directive correctly was judged to be not sufficiently serious because *"Germany's interpretation has been adopted by almost all the other member states [...]. It appears that those member*

---

[170] See footnote 165
[171] Case 46/93, *Brasserie du Pêcheur*, at para. 57
[172] European Court of Justice (1993), Case 392/93, *R v. HM Treasury, ex parte British Telecommunications plc*
[173] Case 392/93, *BT*, at paras. 43-45
[174] European Court of Justice (1996b), Case 283/94, *Denkavit Internationaal and others v. Bundesamt für Finanzen*

states took the view, following discussions within the Council, that they were entitled to adopt such an interpretation."[175]
Similar guidance on the question of sufficiently serious breaches was given by the Court in *Lomas*[176] and *Stockholm Lindöpark.*[177]

Although having given a great deal of guidance on the treatment of non-contractual liability of member states under Community law, the Court left many issues to be addressed by national law. It should be understood that the principle of state liability is truly dual in nature. The Court has established a right of reparation and its core principles and conditions under European Community law. Yet, this right must be provided by the domestic legal systems under varying procedural and substantial rules on causation, damage assessment, etc.[178,179]

The Court has observed those national efforts with its principles of ***equivalence*** (with the treatment of breaches of national law) and ***effectiveness*** (in the protection of individuals' rights) which have been the criteria for the acceptance of those national provisions.[180]
Effective protection, thus the Court, has implications for the extent of the reparation allowed for under domestic law. The reparation *"must commensurate with the loss or damage sustained".*[181] National restrictions on the size of damage compensation are allowed however, as long as the principles of effectiveness and equivalence are respected. Over the course of time, a considerable number of case have arisen which shed clarification on the interpretation of these principles[182]. Also on procedural issues, the Court has intervened on a number of occasions. In Barra vs. Belgium, the Court held unallowable a Belgian procedural rule not allowing for private

---

[175] Case 283/94, *Denkavit,* at para. 51.
[176] European Court of Justice (1996d), Case 5/94, *R. V. Ministry of Agriculture, Fisheries and Food, ex parte Hedley Lomas*
[177] European Court of Justice (2001b), Case 150/99, *Stockholm Lindöpark Aktiebolag v. Sweden*
[178] This is completely in line with prevision jurisdiction by the Court, notably its Rewe-ruling where it was stated that is the national courts which are entrusted with ensuring the legal protection which citizens derive from the direct effect of Community law. See European Court of Justice (1976b), Case 33/76, *Rewe-Zentralfinanz eG and Rewe-Zentral AG v. Landwirtschaftskammer für das Saarland.*
[179] For the devolution of authority see Ward (1995)
[180] Equivalence and effectiveness are repeatedly mentioned in the *Brasserie* ruling at paras. 67, 70, 71, 73, 83, 87 an 90.
[181] Case 46/93, Brasserie du Pêcheur, at para. 82
[182] See for example European Court of Justice (1997a), Case 94/95, *Bonifaci and Berto v. Instituto Nazionale delle Previdenza Sociale* and European Court of Justice (1997b), Case 261/95, *Palmisani v. INPS*

compensation claims anymore after the European Court of Justice had already judged that a national Belgian act was not compatible with the treaties.[183] A similar decision was taken in Deville vs. Adminstration des Impôts.[184]

Tridimas (2000) describes the influence of the Court on national rules of procedure and remedies as one of "selective deference". The Court, he claims, attempts to strike a balance "between the effectiveness of Community law and the autonomy of national procedural systems"[185] and does so by means of a dialectical process through a constant dialogue with the national courts. *"This infusion of Community standards into national legal systems by the Court of Justice may yet prove the most powerful centripetal force towards a jus communae europeum."*[186] Other authors have a different opinion. Dougan (2000) interprets this dialectical process as a retreat by the Court and sees a tendency in favour of greater domestic autonomy. Dougan warns that *"Francovich case law should not become a convenient excuse for excessive deference to the sensibilities of member states, where such caution seems to be motivated less by the legitimate desire to shield public servants from excessive liabilities (...) and more by an apparent loss of confidence by the Court in its own capacity to exercise full and effective judicial supervision over the enforcement of Community rights."*[187] Conant (2001) argues that through this decentral approach, efficient enforcement is not guaranteed. She claims that the direct effect and state liability doctrines of the European Court of Justice excessively constrain the very obligations and rights that they created. Concluding rather harshly: *"enduring restrictions and ambiguities in the EU's legal architecture generate a much weaker mechanism of enforcement and a riskier, more unpredictable system of legal recourse than is typically assumed."*[188]

Finally, attention is drawn to the fact that the *Francovich* doctrine does not exclude the legal possibility of receiving compensation for breaches of law under domestic legislation. However, even if that possibility exists, individuals could still apply a community based reasoning. The community law based claim is thus seen as an alternative to a domestic one, in case the later is not satisfactory. An interesting case

---

[183] European Court of Justice (1988a), Case 309/85, *Barra v. Belgium and City of Liège*
[184] European Court of Justice (1988b), Case 240/87, *Deville v. Administration des Impôts*
[185] Tridimas (2000) at pp. 479
[186] id.
[187] Dougan (2000) at pp. 128
[188] Conant (2001) at pp. 10

in this respect is Société Comateb[189], where traders where denied the possibility of reimbursement of charges they had to pay the State under a breach of Community law. Because traders had been obliged to pass on the costs of the charges to clients, a national law denied the reimbursement as it would constitute an unjust enrichment. In such case, the Court said, the domestic rule does not guarantee effectiveness and traders could alternatively seek reparation by applying for *compensation* under Community based law (instead of applying for *reparation* under domestic law). By saying so, the Court seems to argue that the fact that costs have been passed on already, is of no relevance to the Brasserie du Pêcheur principles for compensation. Hence, the Court would effectively by-pass national regulations.

Situations	***Type of Liability***	***Example***
Non-transposition of a Directive	Strict Liability	*Francovich, Dillenkofer*
Incorrect Transposition of a Directive	Manifest and Serious Breach (MSB)	*British Telecom*
Breach of Directly Effective Treaty Provisions	MSB	*Brasserie/Factortame, Hedley Lomas*
Non-compliance with a judgment of the (President of the) European Court of Justice	MSB	*Factortame III*

Figure 11: A Summary of Situations causing Liability and the respective Cases

4.3 The Political History of State Liability in the European Union

As mentioned before, the expansion by the European Court of Justice of Community law enforcement has often taken place against member states' declared interests. The battlefield of strengthening or weakening enforcement possibilities in the

[189] European Court of Justice (1997c), Case 191-218/95, *Société Comateb v. Directeur Général des Douanes et Droits Indirects*

European Union has received comparatively little attention by institutional or political scholarship. Most attention was focussed on the broader issue of supranational institutions' capacity to drive European integration further (see Cram (1997), Alter (1998) and Stone Sweet and Caporaso (1998)) or of member states' capacity to remain in control and halt unwanted integration (see Garrett (1992), Garrett and Weingast (1993), Moravcsik (1993) and Moravscik (1995).

Since the 1990s, the Commission and the Court have pushed the development of an Community law enforcement mechanism that is both centralised and decentralised.[190] The state liability doctrine developed by the Court presents the decentral component, the Commission's enforcement efforts through article 228 the centralised one. Both mechanisms have their own political history, which will be outlined in the following.

Prior to 1991, Community law nor national law offered the threat of financial sanctions against member states refusing to comply with European legislation. This lack of sanctions seriously impaired the Commission in playing its role of "guardian of the treaties", and on numerous occasions, the supranational institutions called for the delegation to the Community by member states of the authority to sanction non-complying member states. Proposed ideas included both the adapting of article 169 (now 226) as to include financial penalties as well as the installation of some form of state liability principle in Community law.

As early as 1975, the European Court of Justice was the first institution to present such ideas.[191] The Court criticised the omission of financial sanctioning possibilities which were present in the Treaty on the European Coal and Steel Community, but left out in the Treaty governing the European Economic Community. The Court demanded that a provision was written in the EEC-Treaty, foreseeing in financial consequences for member states refusing to comply with the Court's judgements. At the same moment, the Court claimed that, in order to protect individuals' rights, a form of state liability should be installed in Community law for member states refusing

---

[190] Tallberg (2003)
[191] European Court of Justice (1975b),

to comply with article 177 (now 234) rulings (preliminary rulings by the Court).[192] It is widely accepted that the drive towards Court of Justice regulation of damage liability (Francovich liability) arose out of a perceived need to fortify effective enforcement of Community law.[193]

In 1983, the European Parliament took side in this disagreement between member states and the Court and unambiguously stated that changes should be made to the Treaty so as to guarantee a more adequate enforcement of Community law. The Parliament clearly agreed with the Court that state liability could be an effective instrument for a better enforcement of Community law. The parliamentarians " *called upon the member states to adopt an amendment to the EEC Treaty, as suggested by the European Court of Justice, to provide effective sanctions against a member state in default of a judgement."* [194] Also, the parliament recognised that granting individuals possibilities for financial compensation of damages due to member states' failure to comply with European legislation, would be a way to strengthen enforcement.[195]

After member states clearly didn't see an interest for them to adopt these proposed changes and hence remained inactive, the Commission as well increased pressure on member states by outlining its position at the 1991 Intergovernmental Conference (IGC), where member states prepared for treaty amendments.[196]

It this document, the Commission proposed three measures to deal in a more appropriate way with the problem of non-compliance, which -due to the lengthy process of enforcement- was perceived to have reached a threatening level at the time.

- As a first alternative, the Commission proposed to install financial penalties for member states not complying with judgements of the European Court of Justice. This

---

[192] Note that such state liability didn't necessarily have to be founded in Community law. If member states were prepared to do so (which is very questionable), they could have installed such right in their domestic state liability laws. Had this happened without a provision in primary law, the European Court of Justice would not have had any control on the procedural and substantive details of these domestic state liability laws.

[193] Steiner (1993)

[194] European Parliament (1983)

[195] European Parliament (1983)

[196] See European Commission (1991)

could be done by imposing monetary sanctions upon those states, or by withholding payments from the European Union to the member state in question.

- Secondly, the Commission suggested widening the scope of article 5 of the Treaty, making more precise the rules which member states must adopt in their domestic legal systems to deal with non-compliance problems. Clearly, state liability rules based in Community law, would be part of such rules.
- Finally, the Commission put forward the idea of granting the European Court of Justice larger powers, giving it the right to strike down pieces of national legislation incompatible with Community law. Further, the Court would have authority to specify which measures member states have to take to undo harm caused by breaches and to compensate individual victims of such breaches.

Obviously, this last option was not in the interest of member states which interpreted these suggestions as serious threats to their national sovereignty. Many member states were not willing to grant (even) more powers to the Commission or the European Court of Justice. As however member states as well started to realise the dangers of non-compliance with Community law, on the initiative of the United Kingdom, they agreed on the least-intrusive measure to cope with the problem. Consequently, article 228 (then 171) was amended to include the possibility of sanctions against member states not-complying with a judgement of the European Court of Justice. Note that such sanctions can only be awarded after a second proceeding by the Commission, as was pointed out before.

Seemingly uninterested in (or unimpressed by) these top-level negotiations between the Commission and the member states, and in the midst of the intergovernmental conference, the European Court of Justice spectacularly introduced its state liability doctrine with its Francovich judgement of November 1991. Doing so, the Court in effect pursued the second option put forward by the Commission, ignoring member states' unwillingness to adopt (and their explicit repulse of) this change. Put even clearer: the Court bluntly ignored the fact that member states had decided both against stronger sanctions than those in article 228 and against the installation of a state liability principle. Clearly, the Court was skating on thin ice doing so.

Many national governments reacted strongly after the Court took this initial step in *Francovich* and later even expanded the state liability doctrine in *Brasserie* and *Dillenkofer.* In the Francovich case, three governments (besides Italy as party) submitted their observations. Both the British, German and Dutch governments rejected the Court's argument that the idea of state liability was inherent to the Treaty, and claimed that the installation of such liability would be nothing else than an attack on the institutional and procedural autonomy of national legal systems.[197]

When the Court expanded its state liability doctrine in the Brasserie du Pêcheur case five years later, still, some governments were not willing to accept this evolution. Especially the German, Dutch and Irish government contended the Court's reasoning and reminded the Court that member states had explicitly decided *against* a principle of state liability on the 1991 intergovernmental conference.[198] Illustrating the degree of protest by some member states, the German government – as plaintiff in the case – uttered its opinion rather clearly by claiming that " (...) *a general reparation for individuals could be created only be legislation and that for such a right to be recognized by judicial decision would be incompatible with the allocation of powers as between the Community institutions and the member states and with the institutional balance established by the Treaty."*[199]

In subsequent years and cases, the mentioned member states seemed to realise that the Court would not step back from its controversial doctrine. Member states did not deliver observations questioning the principle of state liability to the same extent as in Francovich or Brasserie du Pêcheur[200].

Some member states however, remained deeply disturbed by the Court's expansive activism, of which they felt the state liability doctrine was just one (well-observed) example.
In 1992, Germany's Chancellor Helmut Kohl was quoted accusing the European Court of Justice of judicial activism, saying the Court *"does not only exert its competencies in legal matters, but goes far further. We have an example of something that was not wanted in the beginning. This should be discussed so that*

---

[197] See European Court of Justice (1991b), Cases C-6/90 & 9/90, *Francovich and Bonifaci v. Italy* and Tallberg (2000)

[198] See European Court of Justice (1996a), Joined cases C-46/93 and 48/93, *Brasserie du Pêcheur v. Bundesrepublik Deutschland and The Queen v. Secretary of State for Transport, ex parte Factortame and others* at para. 18

[199] European Court of Justice (1996a), Joined cases C-46/93 and 48/93, *Brasserie du Pêcheur v. Bundesrepublik Deutschland and The Queen v. Secretary of State for Transport, ex parte Factortame and others* at para. 24

[200] See for example European Court of Justice (2001b), Case C-150/99, *Stockholm Lindöpark Aktiebolag v. Sweden*, where only the United Kingdom delivered its observation.

the necessary measures may be taken later.'[201] At the Edinburgh Summit of 1992, only one year after the Francovich judgement, Germany unsuccessfully attempted to curtail the Court's power by proposing an amendment to article 234, cutting back the necessity for national courts to refer cases to the European Court of Justice under the procedure of "preliminary rulings". Indeed, without preliminary rulings, the Court would hardly have any possibilities left to "push through" its interpretations of European law.[202]

The eurosceptic British government shared the Germans' worries and prepared for an attack on the ever expanding jurisdiction of an always more courageous Court at the 1996 Intergovernmental Conference (IGC). In a paper to a commission preparing for the IGC, the British delegation expressed its concern that certain Court judgements *"have led to significant unforeseen consequences, have been disproportionate in their effect, and have created severe practical problems.'*[203] Happily, "solutions" to these issues were offered by the British Government, which a.o. proposed that the IGC should limit member state liability for breaches of Community law, limit the retrospective character of judgements, and enable for the rapid amendment by the Council of Community legislation in cases where the European Court of Justice has "wrongly" interpreted a piece of secondary legislation.

In the stage of preparing for the IGC, none of these fierce measures stood a chance of reaching unanimity under member states in order to enable a treaty revision. Whereas France and Germany were reported to indicate a certain level of approval with some of the proposals, the smaller member states, particularly Belgium, refused to undermine the independence and compentencies of the Court.[204] As the IGC officially opened, the United Kingdom nevertheless took its chance again and officially presented its ideas on the *"risk of excessively large and unpredictable financial liabilities"*, caused by the development of the state liability doctrine by the European Court of Justice.[205]

After it became clear that this proposal would not gather the necessary support, both the German and the French Governments offered weaker alternatives to solve the

---

201 Der Spiegel (1992)
202 See Weiler (1993) at p. 444 and Tallberg (2000)
203 Davis (1995)
204 As Tallberg (2000) reports from interviews with Commission officials
205 Intergovernmental Conference (1996)

"problem". Whereas Germany argued for the splitting up of the Court's competence regarding article 234, France took up the British proposal again to grant the Council the authority to amend Community law when the Court has interpreted a provision "incorrectly".[206]

Member states could however not agree to alter primary legislation so as to exclude a possibility for state liability. Treaty revision as a method to sanction an "overactive" European Court of Justice did thus not succeed. Attempts were made however, especially by the British, German and French government to do so, but those attempts did not reach the necessary unanimity.

[206] Intergovernmental Conference (1996b) and Intergovernmental Conference (1997)

PART III: THE AIM OF STATE LIABILITY REGULATION. WHAT ARE WE REALLY LOOKING FOR?

5. Introducing Normative Law and Economics: Searching for an Aim of State Liability Law

5.1 Introduction

In the preceding parts, it was explained why, if at all, Member States might breach European legislation they voluntarily approved of. Also, existing legal remedies on both the private and the public level coping with this breaching were discussed.

Before being able to continue and to evaluate this existing legislation, utter doubts on its effectiveness or efficiency, suggest improvements or acclaim one mechanism to have comparative advantages over another one, we obviously have to be clear at the outset about the criteria against which this legislation is to be evaluated. In other words: what is the whole body of regulation on state liability made for? What is it aiming at? Or what *should* it aim at?

Law and Economics is a branch of economic science which has applied such teleologist and instrumentalist approach to different areas of law. In most cases, efficiency is set as normative aim. Moreover, it is explained what exactly this efficiency means in the concrete area of law under investigation and it is analysed whether existing legal provisions guarantee such efficient outcome.
Traditionally, law and economics scholars have confined their efficiency analysis to the main bodies of private law such as contract law, tort law or property law. However, also areas with such public law aspect as criminal law, law enforcement questions, or even questions of international public law such as international sanctions have entered the scope of law and economics[207].

State liability for breaches of European law is a topic which is not easily ranked within one of these categories, making its analysis more challenging. Aspects of almost all big bodies of law typically analysed in law and economics enter (or seem to enter) the picture, making it rather difficult to see clearly what instruments of analysis should or should not be applied in examining the topic; whether "efficiency" is a normative goal applicable to a state liability discussion and what exactly it might mean.

In this chapter, an attempt will be made to clarify in how far analogies exist between Member State liability and three main areas of the law and economics literature: contract law, tort law and criminal law. It will also be investigated whether those analogies are helpful or misleading. The normative aim at which – following law and economics- state liability should aim, will follow from that.

5.2 A First Analogy: Efficient Breaches in Contracts and Breaches of European law.

5.2.1 Terminology

Traditionally, contract theory has been one of the focal points of interest of the law and economics scholarship. The resulting literature tends to strongly advocate the freedom of contracting.[208] Assuming actors act rationally and under free will, a contractual obligation will pose a win-win situation to all contractual partners and hence to society[209,210]. That means that *all* contractual partners (and hence also society) are better of when entering the contract as compared to when not doing so. If this were not the case, the parties simply wouldn't have entered the agreement. The exact division of the contractual surplus between the parties will depend on a number of different factors (such as for example negotiation power) which are of less

---

[207] For an economic analysis of public international law, see Posner and Sykes (2004). For international sanctions, see for example Hufbauer and Oegg (2003), for criminal law and law enforcement see Shavell (2003).

[208] For an excellent overview of the Economic Theory of Contract and of Bargaining, see the Contract law chapters in Cooter and Ulen (2004) as well as Shavell (1984).

[209] In a more general way, this was already noticed by Smith (1776), which claimed the existence of an invisible hand: "By pursuing his own interest he *(men, bvr)* frequently promotes that of the society more effectually than when he really intends to promote it."

[210] Let it be mentioned that informational costs are assumed to be zero in order not to unnecessarily complicate matters at this point of time. In reality, these costs are mostly strictly positive and situations can be imagined where this can lead to the conclusion of inefficient deals or the non-realisation of would-be efficient deals.

importance here. Note also that, although the contract benefits all signing parties, there might very will exist third, non-signatory parties which can be net-losers or net-winners to the agreement. The existence of these negative, respectively positive externalities will be assumed away for the moment and will enter analysis again when discussing tort law in the next heading. Law and economics' positive view of contracting is explained by the fact that contractual freedom will lead rationally self-interested individuals to enter agreements favourable to them, and the same goes for the contractual partner(s). Contracts without negative externalities thus by definition increase welfare.

Now, once contracts have been signed, circumstances or assessments might change. Opportunity costs of respecting contractual terms might rise and the contractual parties might find it less desirable, i.e.: less profitable, to continue serving the terms of the contract. When such party decides to stop respecting contractual duties, this parties is said to *"breach a contract".*

Readers not familiar with legal wording should be aware however that the concept of *breaching* is not exclusive to the field of contract law. Also in torts for example, individuals might be found to be *breaching* standards of care, as will be seen below.

5.2.2 Dealing with Breached Contracts

Now, given that such breaches of contracts do occur in reality and given the positive attitude of law and economics to the welfare increase caused by the free establishment of contracts, how does it deal with breaches?

Surprisingly at first sight only, the law and economics doctrine takes a positive stand vis-à-vis breaches of contract, and does so basically for the same ideological reason as the one that made it such convinced proponent of contractual freedom: the strength of individual incentives.

Contracts between parties are subject to a number of conditions which are negotiated between parties upon drafting the agreement. These conditions might be summarised by the heading "price". This price indeed includes a number of factors such as quantity, delivery date and quality of a product or service contracted. How to deal with breaches of the contract is also one of those conditions incorporated in the heading "price".

Parties know that breaches of contract can and will occur, and will anticipate for their happening by providing rules along which such breach should be dealt with. Those rules are nothing else than prices, as they might make breaches more easy (cheaper) or difficult (expensive) to the breaching party. Clearly, the party insisting on easy (cheap) breaching rules might have to offer the other party a lower price for the contract to compensate for the lower level of confidence.

This claim that the provisions governing contractual breaches are an aspect of the contract price, which is in turn the reflection of the value of the contract to the parties, has considerable consequences for the way economists deal with breaches of contract.

Whereas traditional legal philosophy favoured a *"pacta sunt servanda"* approach, claiming that a word is a word and that contracts should hence be fulfilled[211], law and economics scholars see the results of negotiations under market-conditions as superior to any kind of central, regulatory rule-setting which can never take into account or estimate correctly the peculiarities of individual bargaining. Hence, contractual agreements about the manner in which to deal with breaches of contract should be respected and simply applied by courts, as they reflect the will of parties at the time of contract drafting. Every other approach by the court would be nothing else than an ex-post change of the terms of trade between parties.[212]

Over the course of time, default rules have been developed, as an answer to the acknowledgement that drafting such rules dealing with breaches of contractual duties is a costly undertaking. Hence, when parties did not include any provisions on how to treat breaches of contract, they are believed to silently agree with exactly these default rules. When these state-made rules are not mandatory however, the judge is to accept any self-made provisions as part of the deal between contracting parties, law and economics scholars claim. Failing to do so undermines the very concept of "default" rules, making their cost-saving benefit disappear.

---

[211] "Pacta sunt servanda" is a basic principle of civil and international law. In international public law, it is mentioned in the Vienna Convention on the Law of Treaties in article 26: "Every Treaty in force is binding upon the parties to it and must be performed by them in good faith".

[212] In this sense, it could even be argued that law and economics scholars favour the "pacta sunt servanda" approach. They argue that provisions on breaches which were made in the contract, should simply be applied. The contract (pact) should be followed, also in dealing with breaches.

Now, besides stressing the role of the individual in negotiating contractual provisions on breaches and other contractual matters, law and economics has expressed strong views on the content of those default rules just discussed. Law and economics scholars have argued that the normative aim of default rules should *not* be to enforce contracts made *(pacta sunt servanda)*, but to draft them thus to allow for breaches only if they are *efficient.*

The concept of efficiency applied here is the one of Kaldor-Hicks (KH) efficiency, following which a change is KH-efficient, if and only if the one(s) taking advantage of the change could potentially compensate the contractual partner(s) losing from that change. Kaldor-Hicks efficient changes thus cannot diminish total welfare.

If the goal is to draft default rules such, that they allow for efficient breaches only, the question of course remains how to do so at best. It seems very difficult for a court to judge at every single occasion whether a breach of contractual duties should be allowed from a welfare point of view. Judges simply do not have the information about both costs to the breachee and benefits to the breacher. Hence, fitting nicely in economic thinking, recourse is taken to individual incentives.

By creating a default rule obliging all breachers – in the absence of any other rule agreed upon by both parties – to make good the damage caused by the breach to the contractual partner(s), the goal of allowing only for welfare increasing contractual breaches is met. Knowing that they will have to compensate the breached party upon breach, breachers will only stop performing if their benefits resulting from breaching are larger then their costs of breaching, i.e. the amount they will have to compensate the other party/parties with.

As said before, this will only guarantee efficient outcomes upon the absence of externalities. If negative externalities of breaches exist, too many breaches will occur, since the damage of breaching to these third parties is not taken account of. If positive externalities of breaches exist, too few breaches would occur. However, if the subjects of these external effects have the financial power, they will offer the potential breachee payments in order (not) to breach. They will be willing to pay a sum of money up to the amount they will gain or lose from the breach.

Absent any budget constraints on the part of these subjects of external effects, and assuming enforceability of the deals between externals and potential breachers[213], only true welfare increasing breaches will occur.

5.2.3 Breaches of European law and lessons of contract law?

After now having shortly explained the very basics of the law and economics of contractual breaches, let's see now if some lessons can be learned from this regarding the treatment of breaches of European law by member states of the European Union.

Undeniably, some characteristics of contract law are present in the drafting of European law.

First, and most importantly: member states as contracting parties do sit together (be it during summits drafting primary law or in the council for secondary law) and negotiate European law in a setting similar to a contract-negotiating one. Unlike in the case of accidents (where parties cannot meet before the accidents to negotiate modalities), during law-negotiating, member states can form expectations about other member states' likelihood to respect the "contract" and make these expectations become part of the negotiating process.

Should this breaching of European law hence be accepted in principle and is the existence of state liability regulation foreseeing in fines or compensatory measures an attempt -as described above for more traditional topics- to allow only for *efficient* breaches?

The answer to this question is clearly negative, and is so for two reasons.

First of all, the existing legal mechanisms dealing with breaches are not suited to *filter out* "inefficient breaches" and allow only for "efficient breaches". Because of the substantial differences in the nature of the cases as compared with classical tort cases under private law, both the publicly organised enforcement proceeding (the

---

[213] The problem is pretty obvious: after paying a potential breacher for not breaching, the subject of the negative externality from breaching has no guarantee that the potential breaches will really not breach. The potential breacher might very well demand another payment the next day for not breaching. Clearly, the sum of all those payments will not exceed the value of the negative external effect.

Commission's acting under article 226-228) and the private Francovich claims lost their ability to guarantee that breaches will occur only when they are efficient. Indeed, in most cases, breaches of Community law will affect a large number of diverse individuals to a different extent. For a public body such as the Commission to correctly assess the size of the damage done, is arguably beyond the capabilities of such institute. This however is a necessary condition to set damage compensation payments or fines such that only efficient breaches take place. Given the mentioned nature of the cases, individuals themselves are much better able to correctly assess the damage done. These however, will often be confronted with relatively small per capita damages and will not have sufficient incentives to take the case to court.[214] Hence, the sum of all damage claimed for, will in most cases not nearly equal all damage done. This, in turn, cannot guarantee efficient breaches only.

Secondly, in the European Union, the respect for Community law has gained an idiosyncratic value. To understand this, one has to understand the evolution and functioning of the European Union. Surely, just as any other group of sovereign states, the member states of the European Union are involved in the act of drafting international public and private law.[215] States form agreements amongst each other regulating relations between states (as well as between states and citizens or between citizens) and write them down as treaties, regulations, directives or conventions. This is the essence of what happens in the European Union as well as in the World Trade Organisation or the United Nations Organisation. However, the unique European willingness of - to a certain degree - giving up national sovereignty and establishing the rule of law in the international arena, led Alter to assert that the *"the European Community's legal system became the most effective international legal system in the world".*[216]

Now, this willingness might not have been present to the same degree in the minds of all heads of states or citizens over the past fifty years. The European Court of Justice has however steadily proceeded in exactly that direction: member states -

[214] In this context, see the discussion on "group action" on page 169.

[215] Surely, the treaties, directives or regulations very often have implications for the domestic citizen-state relation or for intra-citizen relations and might hence not seem strictly public/private *and* international, but all these sources of law do stem from an agreement between the European Union member states and can thus be said to be public or private international law. To take account of the peculiarities of the European Union, it is more correct to speak of supra-national than of international law, but this is less important for the current discussion.

[216] Alter (2002)

although states- do not act in a lawless vacuum and are accountable for their deeds, also when those are subject to international legislation. In short: "*The King can do wrong*".[217] This legal surrounding is given by the treaties all member states agreed upon, and the European Court of Justice has attempted to truly grant those treaties the status of *law*. However straight-forward this might sound to an economic ear, it is not to a legal one.

Very few -if any- other examples exist, where a number of sovereign states have agreed upon international public law which such far-reaching consequence. These consequences include an independent, supra-national judicial body such as the European Court of Justice which has ruled the supremacy of European law over any conflicting national legal provision and went as far as to make European law directly applicable in national courtrooms.

Very few other industrialised nations have taken international law so serious by making the application of international law so available to citizens (in national courts) where they are directly concerned[218]. Since Francovich, this availability has been coupled with the right for compensation in some cases for state wrongdoing.

The role of the European Court of Justice in this process is not to be underestimated, but goes beyond the scope of this work. Reference is made again to the well-received work by Karin Alter.

Saying once again that the Court has truly attempted to make European law gain the same status as a domestic law by making it directly applicable, it becomes clear why state liability legislation cannot be thought of as a mechanism to allow only *efficient* breaches of European law. Breaches of European law simply *cannot be efficient*, from the Court's point of view. By establishing its reputation as a supranational court, the European Court of Justice truly aims at installing an environment where it is known and respected that European law, whether suitable or not, will be enforced.

Laws are not thought of as mere agreements which can be exited from at any given point, given a "rightful" compensation. On the contrary, there is extremely little room

[217] Referring to an article with that title by Betlem (1996)

in European legislation or jurisdiction for breaches of law. An interesting and almost forgotten article of European treaties however (article 297, old article 224) allows member states, to suspend some of their Treaty based duties under extreme conditions. Improper use of this provision can be challenged by member states or the Commission before the European Court of Justice[219]. Except for these extremely rare cases[220], the existing state liability regulations cannot hence not be thought of as an instrument to allow for breaches if they are efficient only.

As an example to this, take the Kouroupitos case against Greece, the first case taken to the European Court of Justice under the public enforcement article 228. Greece was convicted to pay 20.000 € a day as long as it wouldn't start implementing the court's judgement.[221] Eventually, Greece paid this daily fine for 250 days! The 20.000 € should however not be understood as Greece's price to be paid in order to be allowed to breach European law.[222]

Surely, Greek actors can be expected to have weighed benefits against costs when deciding to wait another 250 days before implementing the judgement. For them, the waiting must have offered benefits exceeding the costs of 5.000.000 € and in that sense might have been rational.

However, it is not the reasoning of the Court, nor of the Commission nor is it the philosophy behind article 228 to think accordingly. European law is and remains valid, for all member states and all subjects concerned. By no means does an article 228 judgement nor a private state liability judgement in a national court offer a member state an excuse for not acting according to European law. Member states are thus not paying, *so as* to be allowed to escape from their legal obligations. They are paying *because* they weren't respecting those obligations.

---

[218] Nevertheless, some sensitive parts of European legislation are successfully kept out of reach of the jurisdiction of the European Court of Justice. Only when directly affected, can individuals proceed for the compensation of their damages causes by state wrongdoing.

[219] This provision is discussed by Stefanou and Xanthaki (1995)

[220] In the eight cases where an article 297 case was brought before the European Court of Justice, the Court has clearly indicated its intention to limit the use of article 297, thus discouraging its potential regular exploitation by member states as a justification for violations of Community law. See for example European Court of Justice (1983), Case C-72/83, *Campus Oil v. Minister for Industry and Energy*

[221] Meant is the judgment of the Court of 7 April 1992 in Case C-45/91, Commission v Greece

[222] For the Commission's philosophy behind the penalty payments see page 190.

Concluding, from both primary legislation and the European Court of Justice's jurisdiction, it seems like there is no room in European law for efficient breaches of law. Relating this back to the traditional discussion of contractual breaches, it is fair to say that breaches are seen to have **prohibitively high negative external effects**. Respecting the law seems to have an *intrinsic value* which is always higher than the potential benefits to the member states of breaching it. This is to say nothing else than that for the European Union, perfect compensation for breaches seems impossible: there is no indifference between the situation of *"no breaches"* and the one of *"breaches followed by damage compensation"*. In simpler terms: the damage compensation cannot make up for the breach and the damage caused by it. To make clear even further that contract law considerations are of little use to this situations, one is reminded that the obligation to make good damages caused by breaches does not lead to the nullification of European legal provisions: the law has always been valid and stays valid, irrespective of this obligation on Member States to pay damage compensation. If member states really want to escape a legal obligation having its foundation in European primary or secondary law, the only acceptable way to do so is by renegotiating the provisions with other member states in the institutions designed for that purpose: the European Parliament and the Council of the European Union.

Different from these wishes for long-term changes are those for short-term breaches. One can imagine a situation where a member states doesn't contest in principle -say- the free movement of goods, but does attempt to hinder that free movement with regard to the application of it on a specific issue. These can be said to be *short-term breaches*: the member state acknowledges being bound, also in the future, by this principle, but wants to set it aside for this single case. It is clear that these case are more realistic, but cannot be analysed with the help of insights on contract law. They show some characteristics of (but are also distinctly differ from) the economics of tort law, which we will turn to now.

5.3 A Second Analogy: The Economics of Tort Law

While most legal papers on European state liability are concerned with the correct interpretation of the newly developed doctrine of state liability and with its implications for legal science, only very few economists have tried to analyse the problem. Lee (1999) applies an externalities approach, Schäfer and Van den Bergh

(2001) try to draw analogies with the economic analysis of tort law for individual behaviour. In what follows, we will look into the question as to how far this analogy with tort law can be drawn.

5.3.1 Traditional Economic Analysis of Tort Law: Reasoning and Goals

As already shortly mentioned when discussing contracts, some acts of individuals might affect others in a negative way. Whereas in a contract setting these effects are called "negative externalities", in tort law they are referred to as "damage" for which one might be "liable". Questions of liability occur after a damage has been caused to a party by the acting of another party. The well-established classical economic literature on tort law[223] analyses different legal rules (negligence rules, strict liability rules; etc.) and their effect on the main variable in human acting under consideration: the level of care chosen by the acting party or parties. This crucial concept of care possesses the characteristic that it is costly. Taking care thus costs money. This cost is typically assumed to increase linearly and is referred to as the *cost of care*. Increasing the level of care decreases the probability of a tort occurring at a diminishing rate. Taking care thus also offers benefits of damage prevention. Hence, there exists an efficient level of care where the marginal costs of taking care equal the marginal benefits of taking care; or put differently: where marginal costs of care equal marginal benefits of damage prevention. At this efficient level of care, the total costs for society -made up of costs of damage plus costs of care- are minimised[224].

In the law and economics literature, exactly this point is set forward as a normative goal which liability legislation should help achieving by giving individuals incentives to take exactly this *efficient level of care* and hence to minimise societal costs. To be able to do so, one obviously needs a theory on individual behaviour. Indeed, without understanding and being able to predict people's behaviour, it is impossible to know how to give them incentives as to change their behaviour in a way we judge preferable. Such theory on human acting exists and can be referred to by the term *Homo Economicus*. In short, this means that people will act egoistically rational in that they will minimise the costs they are faced with. Knowing this, the challenge is

---

[223] To mention just some, see Schäfer and Ott (2000) and Calabresi (1970)

[224] More precisely, these costs for society are made up of primary costs (direct costs of accidents), secondary costs of distribution of those primary costs and tertiary costs of judiciary action. The aim of liability legislation should then be to minimise the sum of those three types of costs.

thus to create the law as such, that individuals are faced with a cost function that will reach its minimum in the point where societal costs are minimised as well[225].

Thus, the economic analysis of tort law can very well be seen as an attempt to influence individual human behaviour by creating the law such that individuals are faced with circumstances giving them incentives that lead to an efficient allocation of resources. Knowing/assuming that any individual will try to minimise his/her costs (here: costs of care respectively cost of damage compensation), we can construct the rules such that the private costs for the individual reach their minimum exactly at the efficient level of care. Thus, private incentives lead to a societal optimum. Summarising, the combination of liability rules and theories on human behaviour allow us to reach an "ideal" point where societal costs are minimised[226].

In the economic analysis of tort law, damage compensation as a result of liability rules is thus seen as an alternative to a voluntarily transfer of an entitlement against an agreed price (under a property rule). If liability and damage compensation rules are set correctly, **efficient incentives**[227] are given. In tort law, this means that an efficient level of care is chosen, where marginal prevention costs equals marginal damage reduction. Applying this to the case of state liability, where only one party (the Member State) sets a level of care[228], the dependent variable is the level of regulation chosen by a Member State.

Tort law thus deals with situations where the acting of a party causes harm to another party, who seeks for compensation of this harm. Different regimes in tort law will help deciding whether the harmed party will get his loss compensated. To name the two simplest cases: a strict liability regime will make the tort-feasor compensate *all* harm caused, a negligence rule obliges compensation only upon careless, negligent behaviour of the tort-feasor. The risk of damage upon non-negligent behaviour by the tort-feasor is thus born by the victim.

---

[225] Of course, different legal rules who all meet this challenge may differ in their distributional aspects.

[226] Clearly, some might judge other points (where societal costs are not minimised) to be ideal. The setting of this point will depend on the aims of the legislator or judge. We will touch upon this controversy immediately below.

[227] In the Law and Economics literature, efficient incentives mean incentives leading to a cost minimisation. See for example Miceli (1997), p.15

[228] Some typical examples of liability cases involve situations where both parties (tort-feasor and victim) are to take care. Traffic accidents are an obvious example. The fact that both parties take their level of care makes the analysis considerably more complex.

The economic analysis of tort-law with one tort-feasor and a passive victim shows us that –given the correct defining by the Court of "negligent behaviour"[229]- both regimes possess the same ex-ante incentive effects and thus yield the identical level of care in behaviour by the tort-feasor. Note that this outcome is efficient, in that it minimises total costs. The difference between both regimes lays in its distributionary consequences. Under a strict liability rule, all costs of care in behaviour are originally born by the tort-feasor[230]. Under a negligence rule, the "tort-feasor"[231] pays precaution costs, the victim incurs damages which are not compensated for. Concluding, under the classical assumptions, the economic analysis of tort law predicts that the efficient level of regulation will be reached in any case under strict liability or; under a negligence rule when the legally required level of regulation (distinguishing between liable and not liable) equals the socially efficient level of regulation.

The efficiency goal for tort law, stipulated by law and economic scholars is not shared by all. There are two main other goals for tort law set forward by scholars analysing accident law.

Firstly, *critical legal studies* scholars have a perspective on tort law which is less centred on the individual but more on the community. They consider accidents as inevitable side-happenings of the activities that modern societies collectively supports. In their belief, the legal internalisation of accident costs by liability law does not have a significant impact on risky behaviour. Drawing on concepts of distributive justice, they believe these costs should be born collectively instead of individually, as believed by law and economic scholars.[232] To these scholars, tort systems should be judged on their ability to spread risks and to provide low-cost compensation or insurance to victims.

Secondly, in classical studies on torts, Aristoteles and Kant developed theories of *corrective justice*. Similar to law and economic scholars, these studies stress the importance of individual responsibility. Deterrence of wrongdoing is however not seen as the purpose of tort law in these theories. Rather, tort law should oblige

---

[229] "Correct defining" meaning defining it at the level minimising total cost, which are total costs of care + total costs of damage compensation.

[230] In the case of a market product, depending on the organisation of the market, these costs will to a smaller or greater extend be born by customers. This will depend on the market power of the tort-feasor, i.e.: the availability of substitutes, competitors, etc.

[231] Note that legally, this party is not a "tort-feasor", since he acted non-negligent.

[232] For distributive justice aspect of tort law, see Sugarman (1985) and Glasbeek and Hasson (1977)

persons whose "morally culpable behaviour has violated another's autonomy to restore the latter as nearly as possible to his pre-injury status"[233].

It is not aimed at here to provide a thorough analysis of these different theories on tort law, however, it should be said that the choice of the European Court of Justice to allow for liability claims against Member States breaching European law has aspects of both deterrence theories by law and economic scholars as well as of corrective justice theories.

5.3.2 Introducing the State

The literature on the economic analysis of tort law, however large and impressive, has typically neglected both the body of public law as well as the state as an acting agent and has chosen to analyse individual behaviour under private law.[234] The question dealt with here is an enrichment of this literature since it partly is a combination of both blocks. Under the state liability doctrine, rights have been conferred upon the individual, which is meant to play a role in deterring unwanted state behaviour.

Law and economics has a lot to say on liability questions. Basically however, the idea is one of ex-ante deterrence effects of damage compensation claims rather than of ex-post redistributionary justice effects. The allocation of costs (be it of "costs of care" or of "damage costs") is preferably guided by economic principles such as the minimisation of total costs, but might also be set by law or politics. This idea of ex-ante deterrence by means of damage compensation payments theoretically fits well into economic analysis with existing assumptions of the kind of a homo economicus which is utility-maximising under a budget constraint. Applying this not to the individual actor, but to the "Government" seems more difficult for a number of reasons.

1) The Government's budget constraint is not directly comparable to the ones of individuals.
2) The relative importance of a damage compensation is very small taking account of the size of the government's budget. Is there still an incentive effect?

---

[233] Dewees and Trebilcock (1992)
[234] See the literature referred to in footnote 223

3) Democratic governments are assumed to strive for re-election. A public-choice aspect which is absent to the analysis of individual behaviour enters the discussion.

In order to better understand which insight the economic analysis of torts can offer the discussion on state liability, let's consider in more detail the acting of the state subject to European state liability.

At the outset of the introduction of the State's behaviour, we should separate between contractual and non-contractual acting by the State. Contractual acts seem less problematic, since they will be taken care of with the existing private liability laws. The only peculiarity will be that one of the parties in the case will be "the State". As an example of this **contractual liability**, consider the following example. The transport ministry of Portugal decides to build a new highway connecting Lisbon with Porto and concludes a contract with a private road-building company to do so. As besides price, the contract stipulates a deadline by which the highway should be finished, the company starts preparing for the construction the day after the contract was signed. Two months after this signing however, parliamentary elections take place in Portugal, and a new government comes to power. This government is not convinced of the sensibility of the road-building project and decides to breach the contract with the private constructor. Clearly, (of course depending on the exact conditions of the contract) the private constructor will be able to sue to state of Portugal after this breach of contract for compensation of costs already incurred.

The second possibility however, is the **non-contractual liability** of the State. In this case, the acting of the state is not based upon a contractual obligation, but upon its democratic legitimacy. Indeed, the democratic state is thought of as a representative of all, acting for all.

Although acting in the name of all and for all, almost all legislation or acts by the state will inevitably harm at least some individuals' interests. Although this resembles the tort-situation where the acting of one agent harms another one, as a general principle, this harm should be seen as a legitimate consequence of the special nature of the act of government. Indeed, allowing only for Pareto-improving decisions in politics is doing nothing less than granting every individual a veto-right against decisions contrary to his personal interests. Doing this makes collective decision-making too costly. However, lowering the required level of consent to pass decisions increases the risk of not taking into account externalities inherent to collective decision taking or of increasing the influence of organised pressure groups.

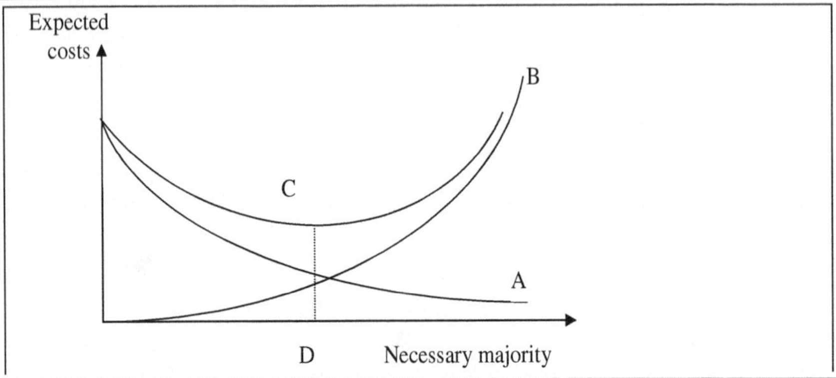

Figure 12: Costs of Voting

Figure 12 presents a graphical presentation of this challenge. Curve A shows the external costs of voting, which fall the larger the necessary majority. This external cost represents the expected loss to individuals opposed to a decision which was taken (net of resulting benefits). With a rising necessary majority, this external costs falls at the expense of a rising cost of decision-making. These costs are reflected by curve B.

Decision-time costs rise with higher necessary majorities. The sum C of both costs A and B results in the total cost of a specific voting rule. A majority of "D", necessary to pass decisions is the one minimising total costs in this figure.

As a potential solution to this problem, most representative democratic states allow for decisions being made with simple majority votes. Half of the representative plus one are thought to be big enough a group to minimise external costs of decision; and small enough to make decision-making feasible. Whether this is a sensible rule, is not the subject of discussion here.[235]

However, some of the externalities (in the form of the harm to the minority) inherent to majority decision-making are thought to be so important, that in democratic states,

---

[235] For a detailed discussion of the optimal majority, see Buchanan and Tullock (1962) at pp.63-91 or Müller (2003), Chapter 4

limits are set to the freedom of the state to take decisions with such simple majority vote.

Constitutions or a number of international treaties (e.g. on human rights) - in some cases even civil legislation- confine the power of governments or parliaments. A law forbidding women to work, also if passed by a parliamentary majority would clearly not be upheld by a higher court, and might even give rise to liability claims by women for loss of income during the period the law was in force.

Another type of confinement of regulatory power or acting by the state is given by European law. European law has directly[236] or indirectly[237] been agreed upon by Member States, and since European law is superior[238] to national legislation, it binds the signatories.

Some individual interests will be harmed by state-acting, irrespective of the fact whether this acting took place within the borders set by European law, or outside these borders. In the first case, given that the acting is not in breach with fundamental, inalienable individual rights, this harm is seen as legitimate, as an intrinsic consequence of the nature of collective, political decision-making. In the second case however, the harm inflicted is seen as illegitimate, and is considered a tort.

Citizens have a rightful expectation on their and other governments of the European Union to act within the limits set by European law. Legal science argues accordingly by means of the "rule of law" argument, saying that all legislation that passed a due, democratic decision-making process is applicable against all of its subjects, and this not only when it favours those subjects. Thus, this legal principle guarantees an individual that Member State A will act according to European Law B, also at times where the Member State would prefer breaching this piece of European legislation. Directly in European Treaties or indirectly through secondary legislation, the

---

[236] Primary European legislation, such as the treaties, has been agreed upon by all Member States. They all signed and ratified these treaties.

[237] In articles 202-210 of the consolidated Treaty, Member States agreed that some decision in the Council can be taken with a (qualified) majority vote. So, even if a specific Member State opposes a proposal of secondary legislation, a (qualified) majority of other states can suffice to pass the proposal. The state then indirectly agreed with this secondary legislation.

[238] The supremacy of European law over national law was established by the European Court of Justice in Case C-26/62 Van Gend & Loos / Administratie Der Belastingen European Court of Justice (1963b).

government willingly allowed for the narrowing of its political decision-making possibilities, and - on the basis of this rule of law principle- not acting accordingly will give rise, thus the European Court of Justice, to an obligation for the Member State to make good any damage caused.[239]

It now becomes clear that however similar to standard liability law against individuals the non-contractual state liability for breaches of European law might be, it in fact works as a law-enforcement mechanism.

The actual jurisdiction on state liability accepts that, just as car-driving, governing is a "risky" activity where some damage is unavoidable and is even not compensated for.[240] However, harm incurred by an individual because of breach (i.e.: the non-fulfilment of an obligation) by a Member State of European law should be compensated, and ever more: deterred. **The link between liability and law enforcement is thus established.**

It is apparent that, even more than is the case under classical accident law, the Court has chosen an instrumentalist approach here. The aim of the Court was to promote the enforcement of European law against Member States and not only to compensate victims for an unjust harm. To understand this, one has to see that the stress of the European Court of Justice has been more on the breach by the Member State than on the harm to the victim. Indeed, it is not even required for compensation that the Member State is the direct tort-feasor! Consider the famous Francovich case as an illustration. The Italian State failed to transpose a directive obliging employers to pay in a guarantee fund that would pay out due wages upon bankruptcy of the employer. Upon bankruptcy of his employer, Mr. Francovich didn't receive wage payments his employer was unable to pay him. For this, not the employer was held liable, but the Italian State, through the direct effect doctrine.

State liability was thus seen by the European Court of Justice as a way of convincing Member States to *care* about European law when taking national decisions. A system of liability for breaches has been set up, distinguishing between strict liability

---

[239] Joined cases 6/90 and 9/90, *Francovich and Bonifaci v. Italy*, judgement of November 19th 1991, E.C.R. I-5357

[240] The similarities between both activities of course have their limits. In fact, governing is by far riskier than car-driving because its public character almost certainly leads to damage, i.e.: harm inflicted to some individuals' interests.

(late or non-action in implementing directives) and gross negligence (*sufficiently serious breach)* in case of interpretation difficulties.

Concluding, governing causes harm, it is its nature. This however does not mean that the State can act *at will.* Limits to harm-causing behaviour are set, making some of the harm legal, some not. An prominent example of such limits to harm-causing behaviour are obligations under European law. Harmed caused to individuals by a state failing to respect obligations accruing from European law is illegitimate harm. The liability system is thought of not just as a compensatory system to the victims of such breach of European law, but also a mechanism of enforcing European law vis-à-vis Member States. **In effect, the efficiency aim set by the law and economics literature is changed for another one: law enforcement.**

5.3.3 Combining contract law with tort law to understand state liability as a law enforcement instrument.

Clearly, when making assumptions on human behaviour and incorporating those in liability rules, generalisations have to be made. As an example, take a negligence rule dealing with car accidents. For the sake of easiness, assume that the "efficient law" excludes liability for the causer of an accident on the highway when he was driving between 90 an 140 km/h and makes him liable for accidents when driving slower than 90 km/h or faster than 140 km/h.[241] The borders of liability (90 and 140 km/h) were set on the basis of estimates of the "costs of care" to the typical driver. These typical drivers will hence (when acting rationally) be incentivised to drive somewhere between 90 km/h and 140 km/h and will always be found non-liable. However, a small number of *atypical* drivers will face a "cost of care function" which is different from the typical one. They might be very much in a hurry, or might be afraid to drive any faster than 90 km/h. For those drivers, it might be very rational not to choose a speed somewhere between 90 km/h and 140 km/h. When accidents do occur, those cases will be the few ones where a driver will be found liable.[242] Referring back to what has been said before on the topic of contract law and the doctrine of efficient breaches, it becomes clear how the economics of contract and

[241] This is clearly on oversimplification: in real cases, attention will be given to the exact driving behaviour of both parties upon the accident and liability might not rest upon only one party.

[242] See Cooter (1984)

tort law are somehow interconnected. These *atypical* drivers will indeed have rational incentives to *breach* the due level of care.

Admittingly, unlike in contract law cases, there has been no prior contact between the car drivers involved in an accident. However, on an slightly more abstract level, the tort legislation regulating such accidents can be seen as a replacement for such contract. It clearly didn't leave any room for the "partners" to negotiate their preferences in a "optimal contract" with an "optimal price", but at least, even *before* the accident occurred, both knew how it would be dealt with. The contract could then be interpreted as the legislation or jurisdiction laying out the conditions for "decent driving" (here: a speed between 90 and 140 km/h) and driving "indecently" is nothing else than a breach of that duty, put upon everyone by a law, which can be seen as a societal contract.

Hence, breaches will occur only by "atypical" drivers, whose breaches are efficient.[243] Transposing this reasoning to the acting of member states allows us to combine some instinctively relevant aspects of contract law and of tort law. Also on the European level, the treaty provisions in article 226-228 as well as the European Court of Justice's state liability doctrine can be understood as the contractual provisions dealing with breaches against European law which all agreed upon.[244] As it is clear from those provisions that no breaches of European law can be accepted, this means that -on a tort law level- there can be no efficient breach of the duty to respect European law. This duty is applicable, not only between the direct contractual parties, but also -where relevant- between member states and citizens. The direct contract thus takes the form of a "rule of behaviour". Not acting along that rule exposes one to the risks of liability claims or public fines.

---

[243] This is, of course, not a charter for speeding. It was assumed that the standards of care where efficient ones, i.e.: that driving between 90 and 140 km/h minimises the benefits of driving fast minus the societal costs of accidents caused by speeding. An atypical driver attaches a higher value to speed, but it remains unanswered at this point whether society is willing to accept this higher value to speed (or time) as compared to possible costs of accidents. At least from a pure economic point of view, if damage compensation claims and/or public fines are set correctly, society should be indifferent.

[244] Although member states agreed (in)directly with every piece of European legislation, many member states did not explicitly agree with the European Court of Justice's Francovich doctrine. Many member states even disagreed openly with the development by the Court of the State liability doctrine but did not use the possibility to change primary law provisions regarding state liability. In the Francovich Case (para.15-17) and the Brasserie du Pêcheur Case (in para. 30-46), the British, Dutch, German and Irish government delivered their opinions which were arguing *against* the (further) development of the state liability doctrine.

Remains the question what exactly are those "rules of behaviour"? How can a contractual desire to respect European law be translated in a tort law setting of "optimal care for European law"? This care shares many characteristics with the traditional care of car-driving. European law has the potential of confining a national politician's choices and will potentially cost that politician support he might need. Taking account of these costs, not in a traditional welfare analysis, but rather in a realistic political balance exercise, the European Court of Justice has set a minimum level for "optimal care" for European law. This can be derived from different cases, where the Court has produced its *"Sufficiently Serious Breach"* doctrine as a condition for liability. Breaches of the European contract are thus only breaches of duty when sufficiently serious. **Staying in the language of torts, we are under a regime of liability under uncertain standards of care which is clearly used to enforce European law.**

5.3.4 Moving from Ex-post to Ex-ante, or from Enforcement to Compliance

So far, the heading "law enforcement" has been used very undefined. It was merely used to refer to a process of making the law being applied ex post. Now it is time to distinguish between the concepts of *compliance* and *enforcement.*

"Compliance" is understood to be what happens before *"enforcement"* and has a more voluntary character. When a member state complies with European law, it is said to respect it in is acting (for whatever reason) and there is no reason to bring the state to Court. More formally, Haas (1998) and Jacobson and Brown-Weiss (1995) define compliance as *"whether countries in fact adhere to the provision of the accord and to the implementing measures that they have instituted."* Compliance hence entails an actual change in the behaviour on the direction of international injunctions. The literature further distinguishes between *deliberate compliance* and *serendipitous compliance* (the latter meaning making member state actions fit international obligations without deliberate choice). The difference between both may by accomplished through enforcement mechanisms.

For the sake of simplification, in the following, deliberate compliance will be referred to as *compliance*, and serendipitous compliance as *enforcement.*

When member states do not comply, they can be brought to the Court where eventually, the law will be enforced.[245] Political reality in the European Union shows us that there are no major problems with the acceptance of the principle of enforcement of European law: although member states might not agree with the Commission's opinion in an article 226 dispute, it is difficult to imagine a member state consistently not respecting a judgement of the European Court of Justice.

It is thus fair to say that in the European Union, *some* enforcement of European law will take place anyway -on the condition that cases are detected and brought to Court - as long as the European Court of Justice moves within some borders of "political acceptance".[246] Clearly, this enforcement might be of a bad quality, or might take place only after a large time-delay.

However, it should be clear to the reader that also *without* a liability system, mechanisms exist to enforce Community law against member states. This enforcement could take the form of public enforcement with the European Commission and the European Court of Justice as main actors. Also, private enforcement in the absence of an additional liability rule (as was the case in the pre-Fancovich era) might be sufficient to guarantee this enforcement. As long as the supremacy of European law is accepted, eventually, the (re-negotiated) law will be enforced since the public enforcement mechanism cannot be interpreted as allowing payments as an exchange for breach, hence allowing only for efficient breaches.

Thus, in almost all cases, states will be "forced to comply" also without the existence of a liability possibility, since they recognise supremacy of European jurisdiction and institutional mechanisms exist to call for such jurisdiction.

Obviously, the resulting question is then what exactly the point of installing liability for breaches of Community law could be? Well, the point to be made for the tort-law supported private "enforcement" is that it attempts to <u>deter</u> from breaches actually

---

245 Chayes and Chayes (1993)

246 Note that member states do have the possibility to change primary and even secondary European law, if they were unsatisfied with the interpretation given to it by the European Court of Justice. Treaty changing however requires unanimity and in order to change secondary legislation, a qualified majority among member states needs the support of the Commission. One occasion where this has happened is the directive number 93/104 from 23.11.1993 on labour conditions. Jurisdiction by the European Court of Justice caused medical personnel's "on call duty" (Bereitschaftsdienst) to be taken into account as regular labour time, which caused considerable financial consequences to member states. After this Court judgement, member states and the Commission agreed to change secondary legislation on September 22nd 2004.

taking place. In other words: ***compliance* seems to be the aim of this private instrument, whereas other mechanisms aim at enforcement.** An example of this is the article 226 proceedings by the Commission: these do not aim at compliance. Besides minimal process costs, there is no financial reason whatsoever for member states to avoid a first conflict with the Commission over Community legislation to be brought before the European Court of Justice.[247] Member States can breach European legislation whenever they feel like, and then "comply" as late as possible after a complaint by the Commission at the European Court of Justice.

This is different in the private, tort law mechanism which seeks to promote compliance, in order to exactly avoid the necessity of an enforcement step. This seems useful since losses caused by breaches occur in the time-span between non-compliance and enforcement. Losses are really monetary to many victims, but might also take the form of pure financial losses where private loss exceeds social loss, rising difficult questions on how to compensate efficiently. An additional difficulty might be caused by the fact that per capita damages might be small, giving individuals no incentive to go to court and initiate the enforcement phase.[248]

Now, when a state liability system is to be used as to prevent member states from breaching in the first place, two additional questions remain: firstly, when should member states be held liable and secondly, can one expect any deterrence effect from liability claims?

Starting with the first question, it is important to note that the characteristics of law make things more complicated. Law is by definition vague, abstract and hence not perfectly clear. Uncertainties on the interpretation of law are inherent to it.

There is no point of holding Member States liable for unclarity and thus bona fide misinterpretation of law since this cannot be deterred. These misinterpretations will take place also when acting in good faith. However, the law itself is made by Member States and they might keep European law deliberately vague for interpretational purpose. It thus becomes difficult to distinguish between "inherent misinterpretations" and "self-caused misinterpretations".

---

[247] Remind that in this first phase, member states cannot be convicted to pay financial damage compensation.

[248] In this framework, class of group action and punitive damages will be discussed on page 169.

Some acts of member states can not be "excused" by the vagueness of law. In these cases, there seems to be a possibility of deterrence and thus a rationale for holding member states liable for breaches of Community legislation. Meant are especially cases of **late or no action** in transposing directives into national law or acts of **clear disrespect** of treaty provisions or regulations. This knowingly breaching is an act by member states which is to be deterred, hence member states should be subject to liability claims in these cases, when drawing the analogy with classical torts.

In the case of substantive breaches (as opposed to procedural breaches as in the case of late or no transposing action), borders for liability are less easily defined. Although "breaches" have no positive value and are to be hindered from occurring, "full compliance" with European law is a concept difficult to define, especially due to this vagueness of European law. It seems like Member States can respect European law to a greater or smaller extent, and limits to acceptable behaviour by states can be defined. Compliance thus seems more an *continuous* than a *discrete* variable. Generally speaking, European law often either sets a minimum or maximum level of regulation.[249] The aim of the exercise appears to be to convince Member State to move between given limits of care for European law.

Is clear that complying with European law is at times costly to member states, not only in monetary, but often also in political terms. Whereas these costs cannot be accepted as an *excuse* for breaching, their existence should be taken seriously though. The existence of these costs makes *full compliance* too costly. Meant with this is the over-deterrence problem that might exists when judging member states liable too swiftly. There is a band-with between which member states should be allowed to move with national policies, without running too high a risk of being found liable for the breach of European law. This is equivalent to tort liability under uncertain legal standards. Note that over time, the increasing volume of jurisdiction

[249] A typical example of minimum levels of regulation is consumer protection. Trade regulation is subject to maximum levels of regulation. Often, real life problems have aspects of both.

by the European Court of Justice on the interpretation of European law, has decreased uncertainty to Member States.[250]

The second question, treating the functionality of a deterrence effect in state liability, will be shortly treated in section 5.6, which will provide a general conclusion of the (non)sense of the use of state liability for breaches of Community law.

This category of deliberate non-respect for European legislation shows some analogies with the economic analysis of contract law. A main difference of course, is that in the case of Community law, the contract (the law) will stay valid. Thus, the aim cannot be to allow for efficient breaches. The concept of "breach" is simply not accepted, let alone "efficient breach". Moreover, the Court (and to a smaller extent the Commission) seem to be unwilling to accept anything like an "efficient temporary breach".

Besides an analogy with breach of contract questions, another analogy with the economics of crime or of intentional torts can be drawn. The relevancy of this analogy will be examined in the next chapter.

5.4 A Third Analogy: The Economics of Crime and Punishment

Where economic questions on the enforcement of law are posed, reference has to be made to a third big pillar of the law and economics literature: the scholarship on the economic analysis of Crime and Punishment. This research has been strongly influenced by the work of Becker (1968). More recent literature related to and heavily influenced by Becker's work has been discussing the assets of the public enforcement of law or of intentional torts as in respectively Polinsky and Shavell (2000) and Landes and Posner (1981).

---

[250] Conant (2001) however disagrees and argues that the preliminary rulings by the Court are so specific that member states feel they can give guidance only to the particular case and not to other, *similar* facts in different cases. Member states which were no party to the case often feel not bound to make any changes to existing policies. Conant's reasoning does not totally convince however. The Court has judged member states to be liable in damages against individuals for "sufficiently serious breaches" . A category of these "sufficiently serious breaches" are those breaches on which the Court has already issued judgements in similar circumstances.

Distinguishing criminal acts from tortuous acts is not always quite that easy. Some mention a list of characteristics following which crimes and torts differ. In order to rank an act as "criminal", Cooter and Ulen (2004) attach high importance to the presence of an element of *intent* upon conflicting damage.[251] Besides that, a number of more procedural elements are mentioned which however seem more useful in explaining the different way of dealing with some damaging acts already classified as *crimes*, than in really explaining differences between the acts themselves. These elements "characterising" criminal acts are: the fact that the plaintiff is the State, and not a private individual; the higher standard of proof and the fact that being found guilty will lead to punishment. Others however are less convinced of the possibility of systematically distinguishing crimes from torts. As I was told by a scholar in law and economics: "Crime is that, what we call *crime.*"[252]

As "intent" seems such an important concept to the economics of crime and punishment, some effort should be spent in analysing it. As noted by Landes and Posner at the outset of their article, *"the topic of intentional torts is, at first sight, an unpromising one for economics. "Intent" is not a normal part of the economist's vocabulary and does not appear to correspond to any concept in economics."*[253]

Three different meanings of "intent" can be thought of. Following Landes and Posner, firstly, intentional acts can refer to acts of which we possess knowledge of their (negative) consequences. These negative consequences can take the form of *foreseen* as well as of *foreseeable* damage.[254] It seems that such acts causing foreseeable damage really do not *intend* to inflict damage, since they occur as side-effects of another activity and no benefits are drawn from their occurrence. Even more, the damage might occur even though actors are acting carefully. Cooter and Ulen seem to agree with this classification, and bring it one step further, offering the example of negligent, i.e.: careless drivers. They claim that *"even careless drivers do not disregard the safety of others and do not intentionally impose excessive risk on*

[251] Cooter and Ulen (2004) at page 446

[252] This *boutade*, reproduced to the best of my knowledge, is by Maurizio Pontani.

[253] Landes and Posner (1981) at page 127

[254] Landes and Posner give the example of a railroad company of sufficient size which knows with a probability close to one that in the course of a year it is bound to kill or seriously injure at least one employee or traveller at its crossings.

them. A driver who intentionally imposes excessive risk on others is reckless. Beyond recklessness lies intentional harm.'[255]

Landes and Posner seem to aim exactly at recklessnes when discussing their second meaning of "intent", referring to it as deliberately injuring another party, whether the injurer believes the harm to be justified or to be wrongful.

Thirdly, intentional acts can be thought of as acts where the injurer deliberately inflicts damage, of which he knows it is wrongful. In this case, the injurer desires to do an unjustified, wrongful injury.

The following figure, taken from Cooter and Ulen, summarises these findings:

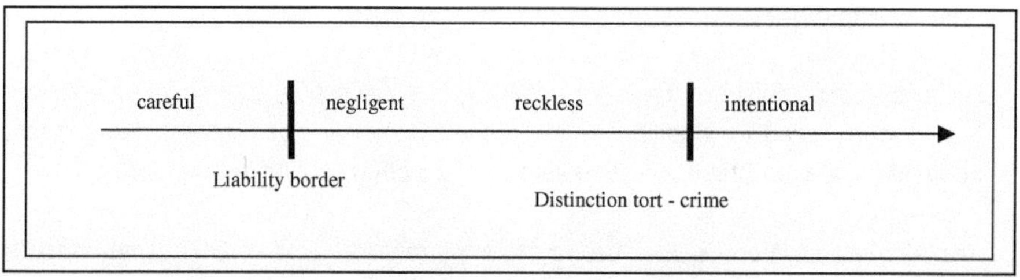

Figure 13: The Degree of Intent in Tort and Crime: A Scale of Culpability

Now, how does this all relate to the question of state liability for breaches of European law?

Well, as highlighted before, to a certain extent, the acting of a member state is a risky activity, comparable with car-driving or the running of a rail-road company. By acting as a government, some damage is bound to be inflicted, even when acting totally "careful", i.e.: in full respect of European Community law. Given the nature and intentions of the acting party, this damage should be insusceptible to neither liability law nor criminal proceedings.

Some of the breaches occurring against Community law can be attributed to negligent behaviour by the member states. If more attention or *care* were given to the question of the compatibility with Community law of some specific domestic measure,

---

[255] Cooter and Ulen (2004) at page 447.

damage could have been avoided. The member state did however not *intentionally* inflict the damage by its breach of Community law: it all might have happened *by accident.*

This is different when looking at reckless behaviour by member states. Member states might well intentionally take an excessive risk of acting in breach of Community law, and by consequence, causing unlawful damage. The separation between negligence and recklessness is not always easy to draw, and will remain subject to judicial interpretation. It the case of member states breaching Community law however, the permanent and steady refusal of a member state to install a mechanism in order to control whether domestic policy acts are compatible with Community law might be interpreted as an intention to take an excessive risk of breaching European law.

Reckless behaviour is on the verge of tort-crime distinction, and some jurisdictions have felt the need to (additionally to compensatory damages) punish the reckless actor. In the United States, punitive damages are often applied to these acts.

The element of intent is obviously more important in cases of intentional harm. In these cases, the "risk" factor is absent to the extent that the actor deliberately inflicts damage, which he knows *for certain* is wrongful. The injurer wishes to inflict the damage, as Landes and Posner say, although he does not necessarily do so for the sake of it: he might very well expect to benefit from his acts, also in a material way.[256]

Maybe surprising to some readers, this might apply to member states as well. Some acts by member states so clearly qualify as breaches of Community law, that actors must have been aware that they will inflict wrongful harm. Obvious examples of such acts are the non-compliance with judgements of the European Court of Justice or the non-transposition of directives by the foreseen deadline. Also extremely blatant acts of disrespect for treaty-provisions might qualify as such.

An important consequence of the qualification of certain acts as crimes, is the way society typically deals with it: most crimes are prosecuted publicly, and since identification of those carrying out such acts is not always given, extra penalties in

---

[256] For example: a thief stealing a lady's purse probably does so because he expects a net financial benefit from doing so, and not simply because he enjoys stealing.

financial or detention form are foreseen for. All this will be dealt with in more detail when discussing the sense of public enforcement in section 8.1.2 on page 150.

Some analogies with the economics of crime and punishment thus seem present when discussing member states breaching Community law. In some extreme cases, a sufficient intention to harm might be present, and in (those and) other cases, problems in identifying actors and breaches as well as the existence of a public enforcement mechanism make the application of some ideas of this branch of law and economics a logic conclusion.

5.5 Summarising: Is there an economic reasoning in the Private Francovich and Public Art. 226-228 Enforcement?

As a reminder, the following provides a short scheduled summary of the findings of this chapters. It firstly points out the classical aims of the three different areas of the economic analysis of law and then –for each area- mentions why these aims are (not) valid for the state liability legislation and jurisdiction.

➢ **Economic reasoning of Contract Law seems not applicable.**
- Compensate for damage done by breaches
  * such that only breaches where costs < benefits will take place
  * and societal costs are minimized

Not accepted since:
  + practically impossible to calculate damage (article 226-228)
  + letting all victims sue is not-rational and too costly (Francovich)
  + idiosyncratic value of law: buying away obligations not accepted

➢ **Economic reasoning of Tort Law**
- Setting an optimal level of care and resulting damage compensation claims
- to ensure minimisation of accident and prevention costs
- by deterrence.

This is partly found back in Francovich:
  + an "optimal" point/range of care is set by the "SSB-Doctrine"
  + not respecting this care leads to private damage compensation

+ as total damage will never be claimed by all,

+ **the aim of this is not cost-minimisation, but compliance by means of deterrence.**

+ Francovich might serve better as deterrent with a punitive damage instrument.

➢ **Economic reasoning of crime and punishment**

- Typically publicly enforced because of higher investigation costs caused by unknown identities and/or an unclear legal situation
- aspects of punishment as an attempt to make the act economically unprofitable
- stronger proof demanded than in tort cases
- deterrent aspect, but also ex-post justice

These aspects are present more strongly in articles 226-228:

+ politicised process
+ only third order deterrence
+ no punitive damages (yet, but proposed by Geelhoed)
+ SSB equivalent to stronger proof in criminal cases
+ strong ex-post enforcement stress, few ex-ante efforts

5.6 Concluding: Aim and Economic Sense of Member State Liability in Enacting Community Law.

It was made clear in the preceding that, while using tort law's instruments, the state liability doctrine does not share the cost-minimisation aim present in tort law. The member state liability doctrine does not envisage cost-minimisation, but is an instrument active on the same front as the Commissionary article 226-228 actions: the enactment of European Community law. When discussing this enactment in more detail, the distinction was made between compliance and enforcement, where compliance is the mirror-image of the ex-ante deterrence effect borrowed from tort law's instruments. The "compliance" aim was roughly defined by the "sufficiently serious breach" doctrine developed by the European Court of Justice. Given the inherent unclarity of legal provisions, a "margin of error" is set by the Court between which member states are to move. Parallels with liability under uncertain standards of care come to light.

Following, the value of compliance -as compared to enforcement- is precised and attention is given to the (un)importance of the presence of a deterrence effect.

In the European Union, credible enforcement of European law exists. Liability for breaches of European law by member states is not a necessary condition in order to guarantee this enforcement. With the use of the existing public enforcement mechanism, and the pre-Francovich private one, enforcement was more or less guaranteed. Member states did not consistently or systematically ignore European Community law. Only in very few cases, second round judgements of the European Court of Justice against member states, setting financial penalties for every further period of non-compliance, were necessary.

In the following, let's distinguish between two different scenarios:

➢ In the **first scenario**, assume that incentives to public and private enforcers are identical. There is no reason to believe that the public enforcers might be too lax or too slow in enforcing or that private parties go to Court too often.

In this scenario, what might be the gain of a private enforcement mechanism equipped with liability clauses with a functioning deterrence effect?

The gain would be the prevention of a period of time where breaches occur, but are not judged to be such. In this period of time, damage is inflicted upon diverse private parties – a damage which is deemed unlawful. Seen ex-post, a perfectly functioning liability system will redistribute all this damage to the damaged victims. This redistribution has no economic value. At the contrary, this redistribution will costs money in the form of the costs of legal action.

The interesting part of the liability exercise is the ex-ante effect.
In classical tort cases, this is interesting because the threat of financial liability will lead to the minimisation of total costs, which is the hidden aim of the liability system. Given this instrumental approach, the redistribution of damage from tort-feasor to victim is not the aim; it is merely a necessary condition to reach the aim of cost-minimisation.

In the case of European Community legislation, this has to be rephrased a little bit.

The cost minimisation aspect is totally absent in this case. Even more: cost minimisation will in many cases not be compatible with the respect for European law. The deterrence effect of the liability system in this case (if such effect exists), might lead to the hidden aim of the state liability doctrine: the prevention of breaches of Community law. Given this instrumental approach, the redistribution of damage from state to individual is not the aim here either: it is merely an necessary condition to reach the aim of respect for Community law.

This respect for European Community law can be twofold: it can occur as **enforcement** or as **compliance**. As said before, the enforcement will take place also without the liability system. When a deterrence effect is present in the liability system, this system thus adds something to the aim-setting: it reaches for *compliance*, not for *enforcement.*

The question whether deterrence exists, seems to be of importance here.
If a liability system were not to deter member states from breaching Community law, the period where member states breach might be shortened, instead of reduced to zero. This would be so because at least in some cases, bigger individuals claimants might find it worthwhile to proceed against the breaching state. Again, this shortening of breaching time should account for the costs of entertaining the state liability system.

Potential higher costs of entertaining a system of state liability vis-à-vis a system of public enforcement or pre-Francovich private enforcement can thus only be justified by the value society attaches to compliance with (as opposed to guaranteed enforcement of) law by member states. Given such value to compliance, time seems to play a big role, and the deterrence question remains important.

For a deterrence effect to exists, the threat of proceeding should be credible. Group action and punitive damages are of importance and will be treated below.[257]

<u>Thus:</u>
Liability with a functioning deterrence will lead to the prevention of breaches. This is an advantage vis-à-vis public of pre-Francovich private enforcement, where member

---

[257] For a detailed discussion of these measures, see section 8.2..

states have no incentive no to breach, as no financial sanction are immediately in sight. From an economic point of view, this is defendable only if compliance has an extra (idiosyncratic) value over enforcement. Indeed, this deterrence is costly, for both member states and individuals.

If no deterrence exists, in this scenario, private enforcement with state liability should be seriously questioned. Indeed, the (assumed perfect) public enforcers will then be as fast as the private ones in bringing a case to court.

Concluding:
In some situations, private and public enforcement mechanism are of **similar quality**. Examples for these situations might be late or non **transposition of directives**, which is an easily observable breach of Community law where the Commission has proven to be rather attentive in the recent past. In these scenarios, a private enforcement with a deterrence effect of potential state liability might be useful as it creates *compliance*; whereas the current public enforcement can only cause *enforcement*. For this deterrence to function, **group action or punitive damages** might be necessary to guarantee a sufficient threat of cases being brought to court by individuals. Uncertainty remains however, on the translation of "financial" costs to "political" costs. As a second **policy recommendation**, one might offer public enforcers the possibility of employing **financial sanctions** in the first, and not only in the second round. As there seems no reason to believe that public sanctioning has weaker or stronger deterrence effects than compensation claims from (a functioning) private system, this way, both private and public enforcers will be on equal footing with each other.
There are thus four alternatives:

1. Not granting the public enforcers a financial sanctioning possibility in the first round, but installing group action possibilities or punitive damages for private enforcers. If deterrence works, late or non-transposition of directives will be prevented. If it doesn't works, the time period of breaching will at least be shortened since the private demand for cases will increase.
2. Granting public enforcers such rights and *not* allowing for group action or punitive damages. The same result as under option 1 will be reached, as long as the public enforcer is acting "honestly". Depending on the scope of financial sanctions, deterrence might function better or worse than under the first option.

3. Granting both enforcers the rights mentioned. Both mechanisms would co-exist, and rules should be drafted to prevent both of them "going for the same case". In any case, the alternative of private action might serve as a controlling mechanism on the Commission's enforcement activities.
4. Not granting any of these rights (the current situation): the Commission proceeds at will, private enforcement remains a high-risk decision with no attractive pay-off. In many cases, victims are legally not allowed to proceed against member states. Demand for cases is low and enforcement is not effective.

Running a little bit ahead of conclusions which will be drawn in the last chapter, we can say that in environmental cases, damage seems difficult to assess and even more difficult to allocate. Unless more private rights are granted, a public enforcer might be superior to a private one. In labour law cases, where victims are easily identified and damage done is rather clear, private group actions can be thought to be good solutions.

Readers which remain **unconvinced** of the feasibility of group action or punitive damage in order to make such private enforcement threat credible, might take resort to the rather radical recommendation of **removing state liability** in this category. By allowing for **public financial penalties** in the first round, a credible threat is present in this scenario, irrespective of the question whether deterrence exists of not. All this is valid only on the important condition that public enforcers will act **objectively**, i.e.: they should take action *immediately*, *every time* a member state is late in transposing directives or does not transpose at all.

➢ In a **second scenario**, public enforcement might not guarantee the same quality as a private liability system. Incentives in a private enforcement mechanism might make cases occur, which would never have occurred under a public system. Again, the redistribution of damage is unimportant, it might even be totally incomplete. For example, only one out of one thousand victims might be compensated. This is all economically irrelevant, since it is pure re-distribution. The costs of entertaining the state liability system can only be justified by the value of a functioning enforcement of law.

So far, it was assumed that satisfactory enforcement will take place, also by the public enforcement agents. This might be too easy an assumption. Enforcement might have different qualities: the Commission might re-negotiate secondary legislation with member states, since both parties do not have an interest in meeting in Court.

If such public enforcement lacks quality, what is the advantage of a liability system? Private incentives might cause such cases to be brought to court, and the law might eventually be enforced, which might not have happened to the same extent under a mere public system or a pre-Francovich private system. Is the liability component important?

The answer is dual. The payment of damage compensation remains a mere redistribution of means from the breaching state to the private victim. Economically, this has no importance. The height or width (meaning the percentage of damage compensated for) of the damage compensation is also of no importance here.
What seems economically important is the private incentive to proceed against the member state in the first place. There should be a rational expectation for compensation in order for individuals to proceed in the first place. Group action or punitive damage might in cases be pre-conditions for such incentive to exist.

The costs of this state liability system (the costs of making the case) should be covered by the value attached to the final enforcement of European law.

Whether deterrence exists or not, is not quite that important here. If it does, the period of time of breaches will be reduced to zero. If it does not, it will be longer, but still smaller than when leaving everything to the (assumed) biased Commission.

Thus, when -because of an imperfectly functioning public enforcement mechanism- enforcement of law (and not compliance) is the main concern, the deterrence effect of state liability is not important. Important is that private incentives lead to an **sufficient demand** for court cases. In this case, the functioning or mal-functioning of the deterrence effect is of no importance. The fact that an individual right of compensation exists will lead to a demand for cases which otherwise would not occur. Again, **group action or punitive damage** provisions seem very important here to guarantee such cases being worthwhile of pursuing.

6. Are Breaches really that Bad? A Rationale not to allow Breaches.

6.1 An Elementary question and aspects of contract law: why do we need enforceability?

So far, we discussed why Member States might breach agreements they entered into and a performed a first simple analysis of state liability law in the framework of the classical law and economics literature. However, we remain with the question whether there now is a need for action upon such breaches. In other words: once an agreement (in this case, the agreement is a legal provision) exist, the elementary question will arise what one should do in case of a conflict. Should one stubbornly stick to the agreement or should one allow for breaches? This short chapter is a brief economic analysis of the preferability of breaches of European law. Due to the special nature of the agreement, we thus discuss a situation with characteristics of both contract law and law enforcement.

The European pieces of legislation are the results of negotiations creating law. I argue that these have to be enforced because of:
1. *legal/political arguments.* There are general welfare improvements resulting from the enforceability of law. This enforceability creates certainty. Also, from a political perspective, one can argue that there is an established political decision making process, and thus no reason to allow other ways of forcing decisions.
2. *economic arguments.* From an economic point of view, two options should be distinguished: either one allows for breaches of the settlement (here: legal provisions) or one does not. Any choice would needs an efficiency argument. We will distinguish between three kinds of legal provisions: Kaldor Hicks efficient ones, second (or higher) best provisions, and provisions lowering welfare.

6.1.1 Kaldor-Hicks efficient agreements

These legal provisions increase European welfare. Even more, if these agreements were Pareto efficient, there would be no possibility to change the law such that this change creates bigger net-gains. **Enforcement mechanisms might however be needed since these agreements are not necessarily self-enforcing and breaches cause a decrease in welfare.** In the European Union, the benefits of these agreements often stem from international co-operation. If incentives to free-ride were present, we cannot reach a satisfying equilibrium without enforcement mechanism[258]. The absence of such mechanism could lead to a race to the bottom. In the example of the free movement of goods, every nation would then react to another nation's attempts to partially close of its market by doing the same. The achieved level of free trade would be below optimal. The winners of such outcome would be Europe's producers, earning above competitive profits in their national markets; the losers Europe's consumers.

Clearly, this negative effect wouldn't confine itself to the freedom of movement of goods, but would affect all future international co-operation between Member States in a negative way. Many efficient co-operative acts would not take place. **Thus, even in cases of efficient legislation where every single Member State profits from the legislation, there might still be free-riding incentives. The enforceability of European legislation is a necessary condition to reach efficient outcomes in this situation.** Note again, that "efficient" is meant as "efficient for the whole European Union", and not for specific Member States. It might be very efficient for a Member State NOT to respect an obligation stemming from European law, but as long as the European Union as a whole profits from these provisions, the enforcing possibilities serve an efficiency aim. **Thus, in cases where the overall -i.e.: European wide- welfare effect of legislation is positive, single Member States might still lose from the enactment. They have an obvious incentive to breach, again making an enforcement mechanism defendable from an efficiency perspective.** Note that the enforcement mechanism cannot be seen as a guarantee for efficiency: it is thus a necessary, but not a sufficient guarantee for efficiency. If a legal provision by the Council for example were efficient, but the countries losing from it have a (qualified) majority in the Council, the proposal simply wouldn't pass the voting process.[259]

---

[258] For a discussion on the incentives for member states to free-ride, also when they benefit on the long-term benefit from an agreement, see page 38.

[259] Unless package deals are made. The losing Member States - having a blocking majority - might be compensated with another legislative proposal where they gain (more than they lost before) and the others lose (less than they gained before). There is no guarantee that this is efficient if there are more than two countries involved.

6.1.2 Second best solutions

Clearly, a great share of the provisions of European treaties, directives and regulations are not Kaldor-Hicks efficient. Many of them however are (at most) second best: they still are welfare improving. These provisions are thus not the best possible solution, but it is still better to have them than not to have them. As political reality learns us that the breaching of such obligation is mostly followed by "nothing" (the free riding argument mentioned above) rather than by a first best solution, **there is thus an economic argument, also for these provisions, to install an enforcing mechanism.**

Concluding: enforcement is welfare improving if the alternative is a collapse of the second-best treaty provision.

6.1.3 Inefficient Legislation

Finally there are those parts of European legislation who diminish European welfare. Clearly, here too, some Member States might profit from these provisions (which is why they took the initiative to pass this legislation in the first place), but these benefits might be outweighed by the costs to other Member States. What to do in this situation? At first sight, economics seems to point towards allowing for efficient breaches here. The societal cost of having this legislation is larger than not having it. Thus, a rule allowing breach that at the same time obliges the breacher to compensate all damage caused by his breach, seems to lead to a satisfactory situation: only efficient breaches will occur. This mechanism would lead to a certain competition of rules among member states and at the same time would be an argument in favour of public (and not private) enforcement of European law. Since private enforcement might not guarantee *all* victims to claim back their damage caused by a state breach, a publicly enforced fine mechanism might be a better guarantee for allowing efficient breaches only.

Economic theory thus seems to come to the conclusion that there should be room in the European Union for "efficient breaches of law". This however, is not the case. There is in fact no room at all in European primary law, nor in jurisdiction by the European Court of Justice for breaches of European law. Now, surprisingly, besides the legal/political explanation mentioned above, there is also economic arguments for this phenomenon.

Firstly, it seems very difficult, if not impossible for judges to estimate the total damage caused by a breach. The European Commission as well, which is in fact the institution suggesting a fine to the European Court of Justice in the public law-enforcement process (article 228 Nice Treaty) might be faced with considerable problems judging overall costs of a breach. The alternative law-enforcement process is the private one, following the *Francovich* doctrine of the European Court of Justice. Here, every individual or firm has the right to proceed against a Member State in national courts and should be compensated for damages caused by breaches of European legislation. Although it might be less complicated to assess the damage suffered by an affected individual, it will however hardly ever be the case that <u>all</u> damaged individuals will sue the breaching state for damages. They might act rationally in not doing so, given the absence of punitive damages and class-action in the vast majority of European legal systems. Thus, this possibility for individuals to get compensated would not deter inefficient breaches and we are back at the same point as above: we simply have great difficulties creating a system (be it public of private) safeguarding that only acts are allowed that are efficient breaches. The publicly organised systems suffers from estimate problems, whereas the private alternative suffers from participation constraints.

Another reason not to accept breaches from *primary law*, even from acts which seem inefficient is logrolling.

<u>Consider the following example as an illustration:</u>

Germany (D) and Spain (E) are discussing a bilateral co-operation in the liberalisation of trade between their countries. As a simplification, assume both countries' economy consists of two sectors: an agricultural one (where Spain holds a comparative advantage) and an industrial one (where Germany holds such advantage). Because of its competitive edge over Germany in the field of agriculture, Spain gains 90 from free trade in this area. Germany loses 50. Germany's industrialists however, will gain 60 from free trade with Spain, which industrial sector will lose 30.

	SPAIN	GERMANY	UNION
AGRICULTURE	+90	-50	+40
INDUSTRY	-30	+60	+30
NATIONAL EFFECT	+60	+10	+70

Figure 14: Log-Rolling between two Countries as a Reason not to allow for Breaches

Negotiating a liberalisation of any sector separately in a treaty setting (i.e.: with every country having a veto right) will result in no agreement. Liberalisation will take place neither in the agricultural nor in the industrial sector, although both measures would be a societal improvement. There are two solutions to this problem: side payments and package-making. In the first case, Spain would be willing to pay up to 89 to Germany to convince the Germans to vote in favour of agricultural liberalisation. Germany would demand at least 51 to do so. The second option for Spain to reach agricultural liberalisation is to bundle the issue with industrial organisation, which Germany favours. Putting forward a package-deal, including both agricultural as well as industrial organisation, allows both countries to vote in favour, since both are better of with than without the deal. In essence, this is nothing else then logrolling. Germany "gives" Spain its vote for agricultural liberalisation, only to get Spain's for industrial liberalisation. When more than two countries are involved, this bundling can go under a less formal form, and can concern very different topics.

Thus, logrolling under a two country setting or under a setting with more countries which each have a veto right, enables the conclusion of welfare-improving deals which otherwise would only have been possible through side payments between countries. The principle of both methods is of course similar: in both case, a price for giving up a veto has to be paid. However, side payments are oriented *horizontally*: there has to be a net surplus of every activity. Logrolling is oriented *vertically*: every country will only participate in logrolling if the gains from one deal offset the losses of another one. **As long as a veto remains, or as long as only two countries negotiate, efficiency is guaranteed.**

	Country 1	Country 2
Proposal A	Ga1	La2
Proposal B	Lb1	Gb2

Country 2 will agree to the package only if: $|La2| < Gb2$

Country 1 will agree to the package only if: $|Lb1| < Ga1$

Thus, the package will pass only if:

$$\begin{cases} Gb2 + La2 > 0 \\ Ga1 + Lb1 > 0 \end{cases}$$

The total welfare effect of package A&B is: $Ga1 + LA2 + Lb1 + Gb2 > 0$

A negotiating situation with more than two countries, and without voting rights, however allows also for inefficient deals to pass.

Changing the setting from a treaty negotiating situation to a (qualified) majority voting on secondary legislation, the story alters substantially. The possibility of over-voting countries makes it possible that for Spain and Germany, the package deal is an improvement, but when more countries are involved, as in the European Union, logrolling doesn't necessarily lead to welfare improving decisions. Consider for example the introduction of Belgium, making our example a three country union.

	SPAIN	GERMANY	BELGIUM	UNION
AGRICULTURE	+90	-50	-200	-160
INDUSTRY	-30	+60	-200	-170
NATIONAL EFFECT	+60	+10	-400	-330

Figure 15: Logrolling with three Countries causing Inefficiencies

Clearly, it would be better not to liberalise, given the high costs to Belgium of doing so. No single proposal would reach a majority under separate voting or under a veto-situation where Belgium would make use of its veto-right.[260] Under logrolling agreements typical to secondary legislation however, the inefficient package would pass.

[260] An critique uttered by public choice scholars is that Member State will not necessarily act in "national interest" as it seems to be assumed upon discussing logrolling processes. On the contrary, member states might have systematically advantaged or disadvantaged some groups, taking more or less account of the effect of policies on these groups. The argument that agreements should be respected because they might fit into a package (which is not necessarily welfare improving) is then weakened again.

Concluding, there are reasons not to allow breaches of inefficient legislation if that legislation passed the decision-making process in a setting of two member states (which is not the case in the European Union) or with a veto right (which is the case with primary law). This reasoning does however not apply to secondary legislation, which is passed in a multi-country setting and with a (qualified) majority voting. In this latter setting, inefficient legislation is not necessarily part of a larger, efficient package.

PART IV: INTRODUCING POSITIVE LAW AND ECONOMICS. REACHING THE AIM.

7. Evaluation of the Current Situation: Two Distinct Enforcement Mechanisms.

After having set out the function of state liability as an enforcement instrument with the use of normative analysis, the next question to be answered is how exactly this aim can be reached successfully in practice. This chapter will distinguish between two enforcement mechanisms: a *public* and *private* one. After this initial distinction we will then go on comparing both.

The *Van Gend & Loos* decision of the European Court of Justice in 1963 granted directives direct effect, enabling individuals to start court cases against Member States in national courts. However, until the Francovich judgement of 1991, individuals were unable under European law to sue Member States for compensation of damages due to breaches of European law, and could only *stop* a Member State from continuing acting contrary to European law. The Francovich judgement enabled individuals to not just halt such actions, but also to claim damage compensation for such breaches. As a reaction to the development of this private enforcement doctrine, Member States installed another regime, in which the European Commission plays a key role in making States comply with European law.

In this public enforcement mechanism, the European commission, as *guardian of the Treaties*, acts as a public enforcer of primary and secondary European legislation. The commission sends reasoned opinions to member states, finds settlements in a lot of cases, and refers a small number of cases to the European Court of Justice. This Court will judge whether the member state's act was a breach of European law but can oblige the Member State to pay fines only for a repeated disrespect of a judgement. The commission very much encourages individuals to file complaints at the commission about alleged breached of European law of Member States. With the help of this information, the commission then looks into the case and decides whether or not to start infringement proceedings against the Member State.

8. Procedural Aspects. Private and Public Enforcement: Complements or Substitutes?

It is clear from the preceding chapters that two distinct mechanisms exist who play a role in the enforcement of European law. The article 228 procedure under primary legislation is a public enforcement procedure, with the European Commission acting as some kind of *prosecutor* and the European Court of Justice as judge. The Francovich procedure functions similar to a privately initiated enforcement procedure before national judges.

In this chapter, an **institutional comparison** between this private enforcement procedure and the public one will be made, assessing the comparative advantages of both courses of action. It will be shown that arguments can be made in favour of both enforcement mechanisms and that they seem complimentary to each other rather than substitutes for each other. Secondly, it will be shown that the European Court of Justice has **consistently enlarged the role of the individual in the enforcement of European law, thus setting on private enforcement**. This will serve as an **introduction to a theoretical analysis** of the (non)-functioning of the private enforcement procedure in the next chapter.

8.1 Evaluation of public enforcement

Public enforcement of law is mostly observed in cases of tort law and especially criminal law. An example for a public enforcement of tort law is the State proceeding against a shipping company to get damages of an oil-spill compensated; for criminal law, the public prosecutor proceeding against an individual suspected of murder is publicly enforcing criminal law. Typically, fines and/or imprisonment are the instruments available in criminal law whereas the application of tort law can lead to the obligation for the tort-feasor to compensate damage to a public body. It seems fair to say that whereas tort law seeks to compensate victims[261], criminal law seeks to punish and thus *deter* specific acts considered harmful. The distinction between tort

[261] Note that law and economic scholarship would add here: "to an extent that guarantees efficiency in the level of care of both tort-feasor and victim".

and crime however, is pretty problematic. Some torts are also crimes, most crimes are also torts.

In the following, I will distinguish between two categories: the public enforcement of criminal law on the one hand and of tort law on the other hand and will provide arguments why such public enforcement might be necessary. The final task is then to argue whether these arguments are also valid to the Commission's article 226-228 public enforcement.

I will thus attempt to answer two questions:

1) Why do we need public enforcement of tort law?

2) Why do we need public enforcement of criminal law? Since almost all western States allow only for the *public* enforcement of criminal law, one can reformulate the question in more substantial terms: why do we need criminal law?

8.1.1 What is public enforcement of law and how can it work against a State? The specificity of the European Union.

Speaking generally, there are two ways for the law to be brought to application. Under private enforcement of law, an individual takes action before a court against another party (be it a civil party or a public one); public enforcement of law on the other hand is the "*use of public agents (inspectors, tax auditors, police, prosecutors) to detect and to sanction violators of legal rules*".[262]

Obvious examples of such public enforcement coming to one's mind are mostly those of criminal law (theft, murder) or administrative law (traffic fines). As will be explained below, there are good reasons for the existence of such state action, proving such *public enforcement of law* might very well be useful.

The articles 226-228 procedure explained above are a form of such public enforcement of law. The competencies of the European Commission are very broad and include not only legislative[263] and executive[264] powers, but also judicial elements

[262] Polinsky and Shavell (2000), pp.45

[263] The Commission is an "engine of integration" following its monopoly right on legislative initiative. As a general rule, the European Parliament and the Council can only decide upon legislative proposal which were handed in by the Commission. Obviously however, political pressure is exercised upon the Commission by both the Parliament and the national member states in order to (not) take legislative action in specific fields.

[264] The Commission acts as executive in its competencies to represent the European Union on the international stage, for example by negotiating agreements between the EU and other countries. Also it manages and implements EU policies and the budget.

under articles 211[265] and 226-228 where the Commission is given the task of *guardian of the treaties* in its capacity to proceed against Member States not respecting their legal obligations stemming from EC-law. The European Commission is thus the public agent detecting violators of legal rules, and the European Court of Justice is the public agent sanctioning those violators.

The acts of the State subject to the application of the Commission's article 226 public law-enforcement competence can be divided into two categories:

1. Upon acting, the State should respect primary European law as well as enacted secondary European law.
2. The State should enact secondary European legislation (directives) timely and correctly.

Upon controlling this first category, the European Commission fulfils a task very similar to the one fulfilled by a public prosecutor detecting private violators (be them individuals or companies) of legal norms.

The second category has a particular characteristic: the Commission has the authority not only to detect and bring to the European Court of Justice state-acts outside a given legal framework, but also to detect and bring to the Court the non-setting or mal-setting of this very legal framework.[266] The European Commission thus does not only make sure that state-acts non-conform to European legislation are proceeded against, but also that the very secondary European legislation *itself* comes into force in national law.[267] The article 226-228 authority of the European Commission and the European Court of Justice is thus not only a public enforcement of laws, but also has a meta - character of the public enforcement of the **in**forcement of European law. Note that from a strict legal perspective and following the jurisdiction of the European Court of Justice, the these two categories fall under the same duty of a Member State to respect European legislation as formulated in article

---

[265] Article 211 reads: "In order to ensure the proper functioning and development of the common market, the Commission shall: -- ensure that the provisions of this Treaty and the measures taken by the institutions pursuant thereto are applied (...)"

[266] Meant is secondary legislation, namely directives which Member States have to transpose timely and correctly into national legislation.

[267] Recently, not only the enacting, but also the application of secondary law in day to day "management" by Member State has drawn the attention of the European Commission. See European Court of Justice (2002), Case 304/02, *European Commission v. France*

10 of the Treaty.[268] Respecting regulations or treaty clauses fall just as well under this duty as does passing the necessary national legislation in a timely and correct manner so as to transpose directives passed in the Council.

This situation is rather peculiar, since we are analysing the acting not of individual citizens or firms, but of the State itself. There does seems to be an obvious conflict of interest: how can there be a public enforcement of law, i.e.: by a public office, against the acting of the State it is representing? Can such enforcement be effective? This peculiarity is a uniqueness of the European Union. Most legal orders do not foresee in public agents prosecuting against the State they are representing and set on private law enforcement or judicial and administrative control. In the European Union however, there is an exception.

Member States of the Union not respecting European legislation are subject to the authority of the European Court of Justice which can convict Member States to the payment of fines. This is not a uniqueness: similar constructions exist within the World Trade Organisation or the United Nations Organisation, where States have voluntarily decided to accept and respect decisions by international courts. What is unique to the European Union however, is that the European Commission takes over the role of a public prosecutor, deciding itself when to start an investigation against a State. In all other international court settings, there is no prosecutor enjoying the same degree of independence as the European Commission does. Mostly, such prosecutor can only start investigating after an individual complaint, investigate against individuals and not against a State or holds an empty treat, i.e.: there is no possibility of bringing the case to a court with holds a credible sanctioning authority.[269]

---

268 Article 10 of the consolidated treaty reads: " Member States shall take all appropriate measures, whether general or particular, to ensure fulfilment of the obligations arising out of this Treaty or resulting from action taken by the institutions of the Community. They shall facilitate the achievement of the Community's tasks. They shall abstain from any measure which could jeopardise the attainment of the objectives of this Treaty."

269 A possible example is the World Trade Organisation, where a Dispute Settlement Body fulfils the task of a superior court. This "Court" however can only take action after complaints by a member state and does not have a direct sanctioning possibility itself. When a dispute cannot be settled, a ruling will be published, after which the loosing member state will have to bring its policy back in line with international trade legislation and offer compensatory measures to the complaining member state(s). At first, the Dispute Settlement Body will not be involved in the setting of these compensatory measures. Only when no agreement on these measures can be reached or when the state is unwilling to alter its behaviour, typically, trade sanctions are imposed upon the loosing member state by the Body. The legal character of the body however, remains distinctly different from that of the European Court of Justice, which truly is a supranational Court. The United Nations International Tribunals for the former Yugoslavia and Rwanda are another example of an

Thus, the fact that European Union Member States respect the authority of the European Court of Justice in condemning them to the payment of fines under article 228, in combination with the explicit prosecutor-like task granted to the European Commission to act as a *guardian of the Treaties* under articles 211 and 226, makes it possible to enforce legal obligations against States in a public enforcement procedure. The uniqueness of this European situation has caused the issue to go largely undealt with in non-European economic scholarship.

8.1.2 Borrowing from Criminal Law. Eight Arguments in Favour of Public Enforcement.

After having explained what public enforcement of law means in the context of breaches of EC-law, let's turn to the question of its necessity. In other words: do we need public law enforcement in order to successfully enforce European Union law?
In this paragraph, partly borrowing from an existing literature, the merits of the public enforcement of law *against individuals* will be explained by means of eight arguments. I will add to this analysis by considering if the arguments offered also apply to the specific case of such public enforcement *against Member States* of the European Union.

The traditional economic literature on the public enforcement of law is largely influenced by the analysis of criminal law, which typically has been an exclusively public affair.[270] There is a large body of literature presenting economic theories on the public enforcement of law.[271] Most of this literature however, assumes public enforcement of law to be the sole means of enforcement, and thus doesn't provide a justification for the existence itself of public enforcement of law. In the following, I will initially borrow from the more limited body of literature which discusses the necessity of public enforcement of law and its comparative advantages vis-à-vis private enforcement.[272] Then, I will go on considering arguments made in favour of criminal

---

international court. These institutions, though truly Courts, can only take action against individuals, not against States.

[270] For two interesting papers on the history of the state monopoly on the public enforcement of criminal law see Friedman (1995) and Friedman (1996).

[271] See for example: Becker (1968) and Polinsky and Shavell (2000)

[272] Polinsky (1980), Landes and Posner (1975), Becker and Stigler (1974) and Shavell (1993) have written in the field. Offering most relevant arguments, Polinsky and Shavell (2000) will be relied upon most heavily to make the case for public law enforcement.

law and will argue whether those arguments are also valid in favour of public enforcement of law in the case of state liability.

8.1.2.1 Of Costly Information, Free-riders, Fishermen and Force.

Polinsky and Shavell (2000) discuss **four rationales** for the need for public enforcement of law as opposed to private suits made by victims.

A.) Firstly, they claim that in some cases, information on the identity of the injurer is unknown to the victim and might be costly to obtain.[273] Therefore, one cannot trust on private law enforcement as private parties will be reluctant to invest resources in tracing the tort-feasor and bringing the case to court. Additionally, in cases where multiple victims exist, there is a collective-action problem. The identifier of the tort-feasor would be spending private resources to create information with a public good character. Indeed, case-constellations can be thought of where the identifying by a victim of its tort-feasor might make this identity known to other victims of the same tort-feasor. This free-riding possibility could lead to a lack of incentives for any individual victim to spend resources into identifying tort-feasors, hoping in turn someone else will do so.

B.) Secondly, besides this private incentive problem, there is also a larger, social-welfare problem connected with the straight-forward strategy to overcome this information problem. The setting of financial incentives such as punitive damages, inducing private parties to spend resources into identifying tort-feasors might lead to *"wasteful efforts devoted to finding violators (akin to excessive fishing activity)".*[274] The argument is also similar to the one often made concerning patent-races. Different parties might spend a high amount of resources in order to discover something (here: the identity of the tort-feasor) and eventually, one (1) *prize* is awarded only to the first discoverer (here: the party discovering and bringing to court the tort-feasor). All other go empty-handed.[275]

---

[273] Polinsky and Shavell argue that the availability of this information in many matters of contract law explains why the enforcement of contract law is typically in private hands.

[274] Polinsky and Shavell (2000) at page 4.

[275] "Empty-handed" meaning only one party would receive the punitive damage "reward". In a typical tort-case, one could imagine all other damaged parties to receive merely a *simple* damage compensation, restituting damage done.

These arguments can be **applied to Member State liability** with minor changes. There does seem to be a problem of informational costs in cases of Member States breaching European law. Finding out the violator however, doesn't appear to be an impossible task to an individual in the European Union. Rather, individuals face uncertainty on the question whether the (non)acting of a Member State is really a violation of some norm of European law or not. It seems a distinction has to be made between **two categories of breaches**.

One kind of breaches are easily detected. If a Member State doesn't transpose a directive timely into national law, the breach is pretty obvious.[276] Of course, an affected individual or firm first has to be informed of the existence of such directive and has to be sure that he/it is personally affected. One can thus say that the breach itself is rather obvious, but that it is hidden in form, because there can be a large deal of unawareness by individuals. Staying informed on the content of directives, their deadline for transposition and the acts undertaken by governments in transposing might be quite expensive a task for an individual. For larger enterprises of for politically organised enterprises however, this seems less of a problem: they will typically be interested in a specific branch of legislation, and tend to be better informed.[277] Moreover, the fact that the European Court of Justice has considered the lack of a transposition within due time a sufficiently serious breach of European law, has led to Member State almost always transposing *something* in order to escape this direct jump to liability.[278] In reality, these cases will thus hardly ever occur.

The **second** kind of breaches are acts by governments about which there is a large share of uncertainty whether they constitute a breach of European law. These acts might be very public and a large amount of people might observe them and be affected by them, but the legal qualification of these acts as "breach" might be very uncertain. If these cases end up before a national court, it might well refer the breach-question as a pre-judicial question to the European Court of Justice, applying article 234 of the Treaty.

---

[276] Confer the jurisdiction of the European Court of Justice discussed under title 4.2.2 Procedural: Francovich and non-implementation of Directives.

[277] Lobby groups and interest groups of organised enterprises typically monitor these kind of government acts and offer information to their members. Individuals might have interest groups as well (for example: consumer interest groups), their interests are however more diverse than those of enterprises from a specific branch.

[278] See the data on the transposition of directives in European Commission (2001), European Commission (2002) and European Commission (2003).

In short, there are indeed costs to gather information *on* a breach (Member States not transposing timely), as well as costs to gather information *whether* an act is a breach. However, to claim that the height of these costs are prohibiting any effective private enforcement mechanism seems quite a risky undertaking.

The question is rather whether those costs are so high that they prohibit individuals or enterprises from collecting information on any breaches and hence make private law enforcement totally ineffective. Empirically, this question is difficult to answer as there is no collective data on the number of private law enforcement cases taking place before different member states' courts. From a theoretical point of view, one can say that these informational costs will downwardly influence the probability for a Member State of being brought to court by an individual for an alleged breach of European law. This in turn will affect the expected damage compensation payment a Member State will be faced with.

Using a well-known example which as well makes the bridge to Polinsky and Shavell's second argument, Cooter and Ulen (2004) present the consequences of the existence of such costly-information gathering. At the same time, they claim, the example illustrates the necessity of publicly enforced criminal law.

Consider the following: A thief steals a painting worth 100.000 €. When he knows that he will most certainly be caught (i.e.: the probability of being caught equals 100%), his expected net benefit of stealing equals zero.[279] The thief will thus be indifferent between stealing and not stealing. In the more realistic case where p is smaller than 1, there is a positive expected net benefit of stealing. In other words: stealing pays off.
Under a simple tort system, a lower-than-one probability of being identified, brought to court and convicted to the reimbursement of damage done will thus lead to under-deterrence. Only the instalment of a punitive aspect such as sanctions in criminal law (fines, imprisonment, etc.) or punitive damages in tort law will make the expected payoff of stealing negative, thus taking away economic incentives to steal, and will at the same time set the necessary financial incentives for investing in information gathering.

---

[279] The expected net benefit being: 100.000 – p*100.000 with p=1 is the probability of being caught.

The argument can be applied to breaches against European law. From an economic point of view, the aim of tort law should be to set compensation rules thus that efficient incentives are set and accidents occur only if the costs of avoiding them are higher than the benefit of avoiding them. The uncertainty problem described above will decrease the expected damage compensation (DC) to be paid to p * DC, where p is the probability of an individual bringing the case to court, realising that a Member State might have breached European law.

However, this **cannot be accepted as a convincing argument against private enforcement of Community law for two reasons.**

First of all: the nature of the problem is different. The aim of the state liability law is not to avoid "inefficient breaches" by perfectly compensating all victims. Rather, the aim of the liability instrument is to shorten the breaching period as much as possible, up to zero if possible. In some cases of a Member State breaching European law, the number of victims might be very large. It might be enough for only one (1) of those victims to do the effort of finding out whether he is the victim of a breach of European law. Thus, although p might be rather small for every individual, the high number of affected persons might make p approximate one (1). We note this "correction" of p as: p(COR) → 1.

Note however, that this correction of p to p(COR) can only be valid when discussing situations where the breach is pretty obvious in content. If the qualification as "breach" is uncertain in fact, and only depends on the European Court of Justice's judgement, the high number of affected individuals does not alter p(COR).[280] Moreover, this situation of "inherent structural uncertainty" cannot be treated identically with cases of breaches obvious in content, but hidden in form. The case here is one of deterrence under uncertain standards.

A second reason why Cooter and Ulen's example does not necessarily speak against private Community law enforcement is that the punitive aspects mentioned do not necessarily have to be organised publicly. Punitive damages awarded through

---

[280] In such cases, national courts will typically call upon the European Court of Justice's judgement through an article 234 procedure.

private enforcement processes might very well reach the same goal as fines and imprisonment do. Why would the tort-feasor care *who* receives his fine or damage compensation payment?

Summarising: in a private enforcement setting, costly information-gathering and inherent risks cause the probability for member states breaching Community of being caught to lower significantly. In cases of relatively mild uncertainty, the low risk combined with the large number of affected civilians or enterprises might correct for this lowering of the statistical probability. In cases of high risk and structural uncertainty on the interpretation of Community law however, individual claimants seem to be an inferior actor compared with the European Commission. This public agent might not be subject to such technical, informational and budgetary deficits and is in the whole less risk-averse than an individual complainant. Whereas Cooter and Ulen use this argument to explain for (the existence of punitive elements in) publicly enforced law, there is no obvious reason to believe this is a sufficient reason for public law enforcement.

Indeed, in the private enforcement of law as well, such punitive damage aspects are applicable and -although they might cause other problems- serve the same goals. The instalment of a punitive damage instrument is sensible from a demand-side point of view, just as collective action arrangement are. Also from a deterrence viewpoint, this punitive instrument makes sense: it makes unwanted acts (be them thefts or breaches of community law) economically unprofitable.

Before continuing with further arguments in favour of the public enforcement of law, **two final remarks** have to be made concerning Polinsky and Shavell's free-riding effect and the welfare-decreasing effect of punitive damages.

Given that the state liability doctrine is aiming rather at halting or preventing breaches altogether than at compensating victims, **free-riding** amongst victims is not a major concern here. Surely, such free-riding might exist: every individual does have an incentive to let another individual clarify a legal situation in court before taking reference himself to the resulting court-ruling and claiming damage compensation for a breach of Community law in an (almost) identical situation. As we are not interest in perfect damage compensation for all victims, this is however not the major concern. It is more important that at least one individual takes the effort of bringing the case to court.

More interesting free-riding effects might exist between the Commission and individuals. Private incentives to proceed against member state breaches could be influenced by the likelihood of the Commission proceeding against such breach. Indeed, an individual might find it profitable to wait until the Commission has taken an article 226 case to the European Court of Justice and the latter has ruled an act to be a breach of Community law. If this ruling uplifts the states' breaching, the Commission's acting might have effectively "crowded-out" individual enforcement, in as far as the individual was more interested in halting the breach than in having his damage compensated. In cases where such damage compensation is of relevance to the individual, using the ruling of the European Court of Justice, the individual might in some cases easily and cheaply get damage resulting from such breach restituted in national courts.[281] In relatively obvious breaches however, private enforcement might remain a superior strategy as it exposes plaintiffs to a moderate risk only and is simply much faster than public action: the Commission only takes cases to Court after lengthy periods of negotiations. **The free-riding effect thus seems especially relevant to cases where the Commission has a comparative advantage over individuals**, i.e.: in the discussed cases of inherent structural uncertainty, where it is not clear at all how a piece of European legislation will be interpreted by the Court.

However, also in these cases, one should warn for the overestimation of the practical relevance of this free-riding effect. Indeed, if it really is highly uncertain whether a state-act constitutes a breach, it is likely some (national) courts will find the breach not to be "sufficiently serious", therefore making the finding of state liability in these cases rather seldom.

This however, does not make the existence of this free-riding effect less problematic. If a serious, private, alternative law-enforcement instrument is to be created through the state liability doctrine, one can not exclusively rely on public acting by Commission, which is inherently confined by political considerations. **A private**

---

[281] Of course assuming the classical conditions for damage compensation are fulfilled: the rule must be intended to confer rights upon individuals, the breach must be sufficiently serious and there must be a direct causal link between the breach of the obligation resting on the State and the damage sustained by the injured parties.

***demand* for such complicated and high-risk cases is to be stimulated, for example by means of a punitive damage of group-action system.**

The more frequent occurrence of such privately initiated cases might have a twofold effect:

Firstly, breaches will be rectified much faster than under public enforcement by the Commission. There will be no letters of formal notice, reasoned opinions or two-round-hearings before the European Court of Justice. Individuals can call upon a national court to decide - possibly passing the question to the European Court of Justice by means of article 234 – whether a breach has occurred. If a breach is found and the member state does not "step back into line", the Commission should be able to use such Francovich ruling directly in an article 228 procedure (effectively shortening the public enforcement proceeding with one stage).

Secondly, if such private demand were stimulated, inevitably, member states would be found liable in (punitive) damages more often than is the case today. Predictably, political unease with this situation would rise. It seems difficult to imagine for an political initiative "turning back the clock" of state liability to be successful: the Francovich doctrine is simply too established to be amended by primary legislation. The remaining possibility for the law-maker would be to decrease its *legal production* and to make its quality better, i.e.: to make it less subject to interpretational uncertainty. It seems few legal, political or economic scholars would mind this evolution gaining ground.

The policy task just highlighted -providing private parties with financial incentives in order to make them less reluctant to invest resources in high risk cases- is a remedy to the demand-side problems of private enforcement which remains subject to Polinsky and Shavell's critique.

There remains a danger that an excessive amount of resources be spent in the "run to the punitive damage prize". On the other side, much discretion remains in the hands of the national courts. They will eventually decide whether a breach is "sufficiently serious" and hence qualifies for state liability claims. Given this hurdle, the danger of abuse, and of member states having to fear excessive random liability claims thus remains rather confined.

As a side-remark, it should be noted that, whenever a punitive aspect is foreseen for, be it in a Francovich enforcement or in an article 228 procedure, its mere existence will inevitably create possible over-investment of resources. The prospect of the European Court of Justice fining a member state might cause the Commission as well to excessively invest in specific cases.[282]

Polinsky and Shavell's **third** and **fourth** argument in favour of the public enforcement of law are less applicable to the case discussed here. They are however mentioned for the sake of completeness.

C.) Thirdly, It is argued that for private enforcement to work effectively, vast co-operation might be necessary among individuals and necessary technologies might constitute a natural monopoly because of their high costs. This might very well be understandable for criminal databases, but less so for the case of Member State liability. Even if technology were understood as knowledge of applicable law, a look at the number of European law scholars proofs that this is by no means a natural monopoly and that this argument cannot be applied against private enforcement procedures.

D.) As a last argument, Polinsky and Shavell claim that force might be needed to gather information and that the State might be very reluctant to delegate its monopoly of force to individuals, thus disabling private enforcement of law. This seems inapplicable to the nature of the cases: legal (non)acts of the State are public to everyone.

Before continuing with some more reasons offered by Cooter and Ulen (2004) why public law enforcement might be favoured over private enforcement, I will put forward **two reasons** for the existence of a public mechanism in the enforcement of European law against Member States myself.

8.1.2.2 Rational Private Ignorance and Public Goods

Fifthly, the main incentive for individuals to start proceedings against a Member State is to get compensated in damages. At the moment, no "extra-reward" in the form of punitive damages is provided for. Also, procedural difficulties might make *Francovich cases* very costly such that they do not pay off to a single individual.

---

[282] Similar to punitive damages, collective action is subject to doubts on its economic sense. For this discussion, see page 178.

Under the previous heading, the case was discussed where unavailable or expensive information made private proceeding unlikely. As a remedy, punitive damages where proposed.

The discussion here is distinctly different: even when information on breaches is readily available, it might thus simply not pay off to any single individual to privately proceed against a Member State, since the money at stake doesn't balance the costs of legal advice and litigation. Individuals thus decide to remain rationally ignorant. There would thus be sub-optimal investment by individuals in these resources, even if the sum of all individuals stakes would outweigh these costs.

In this case, the act of suing a Member State for damages would be privately non-profitable, but beneficial to society. There are thus positive externalities to the act of suing a Member State for breaches of European law. The fact that group-complaints are mostly not allowed, opens the way to free-riding by individuals: they rather have another individual bringing the case to the court (and receiving a damage compensation) if this results in the lifting-up of a (though illegal) measure than bringing the case to Court themselves. The number of court cases will thus be sub-optimally low.

As indicated before during the discussion on the gathering of costly-information, this "demand-problem" could be mitigated by means of financial incentives such as punitive damages or by the introduction of group-action claims. The main hurdles for group-action claims is the necessity of personal affection by the contented legal provision and the condition that individual rights were granted by that very source of law. At the same time however, this hurdle can be expected to prohibit many cases of abusive suing. Although group-action will be discussed in more detail in section 8.2. on page 169, below is already a short example.

In a case decided on 7 May 2002 before the Spanish Court "Audiencia Nacional" on state liability concerning non-transposition of EC Directive 94/47/EC, consumer organisations from different countries to whom an individual right was thought to have been granted by the directive were recognised locus standi.[283] Eventually, some of them received a damage compensation by the Spanish State.[284]

A **sixth** argument in favour of public enforcement concerns tort law and is of a different nature. Let's start by explaining the simple case why public enforcement in tort law might make sense. Tort law seeks to compensate victims and thus to internalise all costs of acting to parties involved. Now, if the State is one of the parties involved, namely: **if it is the victim, it is only natural for this party as well to make use of the rights it was conferred upon by tort law.**

This reason is straight-forward, it only leaves open the meaning of the "State as victim". Examples where the state can be thought of as a victim are those cases where damage is done to goods which have no private owner. In most European legal systems, individuals or organisations have no (or only a very limited) right to claim damage compensation in such cases.

There thus is a rationale for a public enforcement of tort law, especially for damage done to "non-owned goods". This enforcement procedure is actually pseudo-public, as the state is in a very similar situation as the private victim: it wants "its" damage compensated.

Now, does this argument *pro* public tort law enforcement apply as well *pro* public enforcement by the Commission? The answer to this question is mixed.

<u>Firstly</u>, it doesn't apply, since the Commission cannot be a claimant for damages to this "non-owned goods". If somebody can, it is the Member State, not the Commission. In other words: the Commission cannot apply tort law as it has no property right on the goods damaged. The tort character of the public enforcement in tort cannot be transferred to the Commission's public enforcement.

---

[283] Locus Standi can be defined as the existence of a right of an individual or group of individuals to bring an action before a court of law for adjudication.

[284] For a description of the case, see http://www.eel.nl/dossier/fran6.htm#Spain

What can be transferred to the acting of Commission however, is the residual claimant character of the State. If the Member State itself prefers not to use this power, the Commission can.

Consider the following example as clarification:

A European directive obliges oil-carriers to meet certain minimum environmental safety standards and prescribes that Member State should undertake reasonable measures in checking whether oil-carriers meet those standards. Consider a Member State transposing this European legislation in national law and doing its best to enforce it. However, a shipping company's vessel not meeting those standards slips through the mazes of the net and later causes a major oil-spill in the Member State's territorial waters, causing non-private damages worth millions of Euro by polluting the sea and killing fish and other fauna. Now, the Member State in question might claim damage compensation from the shipping-company for the cleaning-up cost, as its acting was a breach of European (and national) legislation. This is the case described above, providing an argument *pro* public enforcement of tort law. There is no need for the Commission to act, as the Member State claims damages and thus jumps in as residual claimant to the "non-owned" sea, guaranteeing that the shipping company has an incentive to respect this European directive.

However, consider the case where the same Member State did not transpose the directive, or did so, but did no effort at all to enforce it in practice by reasonable controls in ports. This might be the result either of a sort of "laziness" in respecting European law by the State or of political considerations (not weakening a harbour's economic meaning, etc). Especially in the second case, the Member State might be unwilling to start a damage compensation claim or even a criminal law claim against the shipping-company. In this case, a public enforcement mechanism by the Commission would prove useful. The European Commission could start proceeding against the Member State for its inaccuracy in transposing or enforcing the directive.[285] The fact that the damage is done to an "non-owned" good such as the environment makes it impossible in many jurisdictions for individuals or organisations to proceed against the State. The damage was not done to the individual, he is simply not "affected". The Commission could as "residual" claimant jump in, and set incentives to the Member State to respect and enforce European legislation by making the State pay damage compensation or fines.

Practice looks a bit different: following article 228, the only legal sanction available against a Member State in the public law enforcement procedure is a fine set by the European Court of Justice after the member state has ignored a ECJ-judgement. The potential positive effect of Commission acting is thus reduced to merely avoiding something similar to happen again in the future, by trying to convince the Member State to respect and correctly transpose European legislation, and threatening with the way to the European Court of Justice if the Member State doesn't do so. The ex-ante deterrence effect is not present.

We can thus conclude that the existence of damages to "non-owned goods" as a result of a Member State breaching European law offer a theoretical explanation for the existence of public enforcement of law by the Commission. In practice however, the condition that a Member State can only be fined by the European Court of Justice upon ignoring its judgement, severely weakens the deterrence effect of this enforcement.

Alternatively to public enforcement for these cases of harm to public goods, if national jurisdiction were to offer *locus standi* to environmental organisations or similar interest groups, the private enforcement mechanism could be used as an alternative.

8.1.2.3 Indifference and rights vs. interests

Concluding, Cooter and Ulen (2004) give a **seventh** and **eight** reason why we need the public enforcement of criminal law.

They argue that tort law is applicable in cases where a victim is indifferent between the situation where she doesn't suffer any harm and the situation where she suffers harm and is compensated for it. If this is not the case, criminal law finds an application. This is saying nothing else than that in these cases, perfect

[285] Not transposing a directive timely or (what the Commission holds) correctly, can lead to the Commission starting the 226 procedure against a Member State. Starting this procedure against a Member State because of insufficient measures in the application of a directive is a rather recent evolution. See European Court of Justice (2002), Case 304/02, *European Commission v. France*

compensation is not possible. Consider the case where a woman's husband was murdered. For sure (hopefully), the woman will not feel adequately compensated by a money transfer for the loss of her husband's life. This is not the aim of criminal law either. The first aim is to deter, not to compensate. Quoting Cooter and Ulen (2004): *"Rather than pricing crime, the goal of punishment is to deter it. The state prohibits people from intentionally harming others and backs this prohibition by punishment. Thus, criminal law is a necessary supplement to tort law when perfect compensation is impossible."* [286]

Now, let's consider if this argument is valid as well to explain a public enforcement procedure against European Union Member States for breaches of European law.
The idea behind this argument seems to be that these cases simply cannot be solved with a tort system, relying on compensation. Most cases where Member States breaching European law cause a harm to individuals do not fall in this category, which is the reason why the European Court of Justice has granted individuals the right to proceed against breaching Member States and claim damage compensation.

However, the issue at stake here might not only be the nature of the damage inflicted upon the victim by a state not respecting its legal obligations. The concern might rather be the supremacy and binding nature of European law. European legal provisions stand and stay standing, also after a Member State has breached this very provision. It cannot be the aim to allow for a Member State to continuously breaching a provision of European law, also if that State is compensating the damage done to the victims. Whereas there seem to be no moral problems with a party in a contract or a tort which compensates damage done, the European Court of Justice is clearly not indifferent between the situation where a Member State breaches and compensates and the one where Member States kindly respect European law.[287]

In simple terms: whereas for most victims of breaches of Community law, the damage done can be perfectly compensated; this is not the case for the European Court of Justice. The respect for European law by Member States thus has an intrinsic value, and cannot be perfectly compensated for. This is not following Cooter and Ulen completely and concluding that criminal law is a necessity to deal with this problem. Rather, it is another indication that enforcement (if possible by deterrence)

---

[286] at page 452
[287] See European Court of Justice (2000b), Case 387/97, *Commission v. Greece* at para. 90.

and not compensation is the aim of the exercise here.

Thus, if for any reason, enforcement of law/deterrence from breaching is thought of as more appropriate than compensating for it, one might apply part of Cooter/Ulen's argumentation: namely that the use of fines might well be very useful. This however, does not clarify whether such fines should be publicly enforced by the Commission of privately under some sort of *punitive damages* – procedure.

A final argument brought forward by Cooter and Ulen for the necessity of public enforcement in criminal law is the fact that rights might be worth more protecting than interests. This argument connects to the former argument, in that one might argue that every individual should have the certainty that a Member State cannot put itself above European legislation only to pay a damage compensation later on.

As explained before, the European Treaties leave no room for efficient breaches of European law. All breaches are deemed inefficient. They have to be made good for, but this obligation to pay damage compensation by no means implies that a Member State has "bought its right to break the law". The law *was*, *is*, and *stays* valid.

8.1.3 Problems of the Commission's Public Enforcement

After now having discussed some traditional arguments in favour of the public enforcement of law, we can now come back to the public enforcement of Community legislation by the European Commission and refer to a number of specific potential problems with this form of enforcement.

The public "enforcement" by the Commission, created by member states after the instalment of the Francovich doctrine, makes cases first be treated in an informal way after which, eventually, a lengthy phase of re-negotiation between Member States and Commission might follow. Although the Commission is often referred to as "guardian of the treaties", it is not clear at all that its acting against Member State under article 228 of the Treaty is indeed an enforcement of European law.

In an interesting paper, Tallberg and Jönsson (2001) offer a more practical, inside look into the Commission's article 226-228 proceedings. A number of interviews with Commission officials made them reach the conclusion that *"the structure of bargaining in post-decisional enforcement is one of bilateral negotiations between the supranational Commission and member states suspected of non-compliance. Both share a preference for amicable solutions, and the Art. 226 infringement procedure offers a formal framework for bargaining to this end."*[288]

The article 226 proceedings are described to be a process of "dialogue"[289] rather than a police-like enforcing, since neither party has an interest in letting conflicts escalate. A Commission official is quoted saying "legal proceedings are not good for anyone". Indeed, the Commission is dependent on member states' co-operation in the future as well, whereas member states are said to mostly feel highly uncomfortable with European Court of Justice judgements in favour of the Commission which harm their reputation as trustful, co-operative partners.

This political dependence of the Commission was expressed as follows by Audretsch: *"political considerations might induce the Commission to make concessions to national interests and pressure of the States. The Commission knows that the progress of integration depends to a high degree upon the willingness and the co-operation of the States."*[290]

Secondly, besides political considerations, the lack of enforcement resources plays a considerable role in the "friendly enforcement" by the Commission against member states. Referring again to a Commission official, Tallberg and Jönnson state quite boldly that *"with limited staff and an ever increasing workload, the option of informal and amicable solutions is very attractive in comparison to the resource-intensive alternative of continued infringement proceedings."*

It is thus questionable, at least in some cases, whether the commission is truly enforcing *European law*. For sure, something is agreed upon, but it might be more correct to speak about *compliance*. Although there is a threat-potential on the side of the Commission (being the ability to step to the European Court of Justice) both parties *voluntarily* agree on a certain interpretation.

The question rises to which enforcement method is more effective. On first glance, it becomes clear that the public enforcement method lacks financial sanctions for

288 Tallberg and Jönsson (2001) on page 15
289 As was quoted a Swedish government official in the same paper.
290 Audretsch (1986) on page 411

wrong-doing. If there is no political costs of loosing a conflict with the commission, this methods seems inefficient and is identical to the case of no liability rules. Indeed, a Member State has nothing to loose with non-complying and waiting until the Commission takes action. Then, it can comply at no further costs.

The risk of this is, of course, that a individual might -in the mean time- proceed against the Member State for this non-compliance. This individual has to show personal interest. If this interest is sufficiently small (because for example, it is divided over a large number of people), nobody might find it worthy to proceed against the Member State and the initiative of the Commission might be the only one guaranteeing compliance with European legislation. This problem will be dealt with in more detail later on.

8.2 Evaluation of private enforcement

8.2.1 The European Court of Justice and private enforcement.

The recent history of the state liability jurisdiction of the European Court of Justice reads like a constant strive to increase the power of individuals in enforcing European law. Before the existence of any concrete treaty provision on payments of a fine or damage compensation by Member States for breaches of European legislation, the Court shocked Member States in 1991 with its Francovich ruling. Against the declared interest of Member States, it established a state liability doctrine for failures to implement directive into national law on time.[291]

Only after this clash between the European Court of Justice and the Member States, the latter reacted by granting the European Commission a larger role in the detecting of breaches of European law in 1992. As foreseen in the Treaty of Nice in articles 226- 228, the Commission can enter in a dialogue with Member States using letters of formal notice and reasoned opinions. However, fines can only be applied by the Court after a preceding judgement of that Court has consistently not been respected by a Member State.

Contrary to this Commissionary action, the European Court of Justice's acting in a Francovich proceeding can be seen as a process of *enforcement* rather than *re-negotiation.* There is no negotiation between parties, and the European Court of Justice -which was not involved in the original legislative decision making process- will decide on the "correct" interpretation of a piece of European legislation.

It is easy to understand what consequences this might have. The European Court of Justice is granted (actually, most pointingly, it has granted *itself*) a considerable level of discretion in the interpretation of legal texts which otherwise (i.e.: under the public enforcement) is primarily given to the Commission and to the Member States. As the large number of controversial cases discussed here have made clear, the European Court of Justice has on several occasions made use of this possibility. Given its integration-friendly agenda it can very well be named a "motor of European integration" as well.

It is thus pretty straight-forward that the European Court of Justice might not only have attached importance to justice arguments (i.e.: enforcing European law and protecting the individual against failing states), but might also have promised itself a larger political influence in the interpretation, i.e.: in the enforcement of what the European Court of Justice feels is the "correct" interpretation of the legislation.

Concluding, by installing the Francovich doctrine, the Court was able to reach two goals at once. Firstly, it found a way to protect individuals' interests where other public agents might not have been willing to do so at the same extent *and* secondly, it create a possibility to establish its own interpretation of an increasing body of Community legislation.

Member States have reacted to this, *not* by disabling future Francovich rulings by means of a change of primary legislation. This might have been politically unfeasible. Member States however, are left with the possibility of simply changing secondary legislation which is subject to a controversial interpretation by the European Court of Justice. Since the Commission holds the monopoly right of legislative proposals, member states need the support of the Commission to be able to change secondary legislation. Also, such changes become more difficult the larger the necessary majority amongst Member States to pass such change.

---

[291] See the discussion on page 99

The most recent occasion where member states have succeeded in doing so, concerned secondary legislation regulating working conditions.[292] In its interpretation of the directive, the European Court decided that the time in which medical and other emergency personal is serving *on-call service*, is to be counted as working-time.[293] This in turn confronted member states with unexpected, tremendous costs in social security systems, causing the Commission and member states to quickly agree to adapt the directive in question, very much to the disagreement of medical personnel.[294] The adapted directive was expected to pass the Council and the European Parliament before the end of 2005.

8.2.2 Information as a comparative advantage of private enforcement.

Private enforcement possesses two main advantages vis-à-vis the Commission's public enforcement proceedings.

First of all, the Commission simply does not have the resources to monitor the compliance of all member states with all sources of European legislation.[295] Given the growing number of member states and the ever growing importance (and size) of Community legislation, this seems indeed a near impossible task to any institution. Individuals, which are personally affected by possible breaches of European law, seem better placed to *detect* possible breaches. If financial interests are sufficiently high and risks such as uncertainty sufficiently low, it seems reasonable to expect individuals not only to detect these potential breaches, but also to *proceed* against them in Court, and hence successfully *enforce* Community law.

The preceding paragraphs have offered ample discussion on individuals' incentives to proceed against member states' breaches in Court. In this context, it can thus suffice here to simply point out the difference of importance between simply *detecting* a breach and *enforcing* European law by successfully proceeding against it. Stated

---

[292] Meant is the Directive 93/104/EC on the protection of the safety and health of workers of 23rd November 1993.

[293] See European Court of Justice (2003c), Case 151/02, *Landeshauptstadt Kiel v Norbert Jaeger*. For legal details, which are of little concern here, this working-time would however typically not be directly payable in wages.

[294] As reported in Handelsblatt (22.09.2004) and Handelsblatt.com (22.09.04)

[295] See the discussion on page 165.

simply: it is not because individuals might be good at detecting breaches in certain situations that they are good as well in proceeding against those breaches.

Secondly, whereas individuals might have few reasons not to proceed against a breach if the stakes are sufficiently high, the Commission is a political institutions which has its own agenda. It is indeed not unreasonable to believe that the Commission might choose to proceed in a very selective manner against member states breaching Community law. The Commission needs the cooperation of those very member states in the Council to realise its political aims, and hence has an interest in not upsetting member states too much by vigorously proceeding against those allegedly breaching Community law. Quoting Rawlings: *"Commission discretion allows, and scarce resources dictate, an ordered policy of selective enforcement.'*[296]

8.2.3 The Credibility Problem of the Private Threat: on procedural hurdles, participation restrictions, group action and punitive damages.

As already mentioned in section 5.6, for a private (or any otherwise organised) law enforcement mechanism aiming at *compliance* to function, one necessary condition is the credible threat of individuals proceeding against breaching member states before a court. This credibility is preconditioned especially by remaining procedural complications as well as by the limited presence of group suits. This chapter offers an overview of this procedural critique and of some steps which have been or could be taken in order to facilitate collective action. Finally, the economic pro's and con's of collective action will be shortly analysed.

8.2.3.1 Procedural critique

Following the establishment of the Francovich doctrine, various legal scholars have remained sceptical on the credibility of this threat. They claim that a number of **procedural uncertainties and difficulties** make it very unlikely for individuals to be successful in proceeding against breaching member states.

---

[296] Rawlings (2000)

Seeing the problem from a principal-agent point of view in supranational politics, Tallberg (2000), discusses member states' strategy of sanctioning the European Court of Justice (for its perceived widening of its competencies by introducing *Francovich*) by *inaction*. Both national courts -which are to apply European Community law- and national governments –which are to enable and allow courts to do so- have proven very reluctant to facilitate the gaining ground of the state liability doctrine.

Tallberg claims that *"most national legal systems did not provide a corresponding remedy against the state in matters of national law, and where they did, this seldomly permitted actions against the legislative and judicial branches of government."*[297] Moreover, by 1997, six years after *Francovich*, no member state had made legislative efforts in order to fit in state liability actions in its domestic legislation.

Not only legislators are blamed however. The judicial branch as well could have done more. Through national case law *(de jure)* or *de facto* by hearing cases also when they didn't quite follow the correct procedural way, national courts could have lifted many of the remaining procedural difficulties and unclarities concerning state liability claims. Caranta (1993) gives the example of Italy, which deterres litigants by means of procedural incertitude: it is simply not clear which legal procedures litigants are to use in order to successfully enter a state liability claim.[298]

Stefanou and Xanthaki (2000) discuss a concurrent liability scenario as a potential solution to these procedural and substantive difficulties. They argue that such concurrent liability between member states and the Commission has been accepted by the European Court of Justice on the legal front, but that it was rejected out of practical reasons by judges, practitioners and academics alike. The reasons for this are familiar: the differences in various member states on the granting of locus standi and various substantive conditions for a successful conclusion of a state liability case. Stefanou and Xanthaki find the main flaw in the concrete application of article 234 of the Treaty: individuals are forced to rely on the knowledge and willingness of

---

[297] Tallberg (2000) on page 116.

[298] Perhaps the most striking example of this being *Francovich*. Mr. Francovich' (first) suit eventually failed because he employed the procedure designed for industrial relations, and not for civil claims.

national judges to acknowledge that a case is one of EU-law, on their awareness of the article 234 procedure and on their willingness to implement EU-law.[299]

Anagnostaras (2002) drew particular attention to difficulties in establishing ***causation*** in Francovich cases. Indeed, only very little judicial guidance has been given by the Court on the establishment of such causation. To a large extent, this fact can be explained by the lack of preliminary questions referred to the Court by national courts on this issue. Most of the preliminary questions dealt with the conditions qualifying for a "sufficiently serious breach". In this area, a certain Community-wide harmonisation has taken place, which has set the "necessary degree of seriousness" of a public act to give rise to Francovich reparation payments.

This has not been the case with the causation-condition. Although subject to the rather vague effectiveness-principle, the Court has left the determination of causality almost unconditionally to the national jurisdictions. Clearly, this delegation of power on the interpretation of "causality" to the domestic judicial systems has in turn given national judges little reason to refer preliminary questions on causality to the Court. Anagnostaras estimates the importance of this causality so high, that *"as the law stands at the moment, the community harmonisation that has been attained on the culpability standard is undermined by the application of the diverse national rules on matters of causation. This may give rise to diversities in the judicial treatment of essentially similar cases and may provide the courts with the opportunity to immunise their national governments from monetary liabilities by making recourse to questionable rules and practices".*[300]

8.2.3.2 Procedural difficulties and the role of group action in the European Union

Given these procedural difficulties associated with the private enforcement of Community law, it would be most interesting to cast an eye on the nature of some of litigators behind the privately initiated cases. Indeed, it can be expected that the difficulties mentioned would have repercussions on the cases observed. Interesting work has been performed by Marc Galanter, a prominent observer of attempts to

---

[299] Stefanou and Xanthaki (2000) at pp. 131-154
[300] Anagnostaras (2002) at page 676

realise social and economic change through the use of the legal system. Galanter (1974) categorises individual claimants into "one shotters", which seek the maximisation of tangible gain and "repeat players". Repeat players are interested in *"maximising tangible gain in a series of cases (...) and might be willing to trade of gain in any one case for rule gain. (...) It pays a repeated player to expend resources in influencing the making of relevant rules."*[301]

Looking at European law, on a number of occasions, **interest groups** have played the role of repeat players before the European Court of Justice. Craig (1995) illustrates that in the United Kingdom, particular litigants with a special interest in the development of employment law and gender equality have strategically used the greater rights granted to them under Community law than under domestic legal rules to push for changes in these fields of regulation. Other examples are offered by Harlow (1992), who describes how pressure groups have made calculated use of the possibilities offered by article 234 to query income tax assessments, to claim social security benefits, equal pay and damages for invalid administrative action and to protest against discrimination. Some of these cases were fought by such groups which concealed their identity behind a so-called front man or *-women*. A well-known example of such cases are those involving Madame Defrenne.[302] These cases established the direct effect of article 119 of the Treaty (establishing the principle of equal pay for male and female workers for equal work) and of directives on related matters. Madame Defrenne did however not take part in any of the proceedings. The cases which were fought in her name by a feminist lawyer which obviously had the financial support of interested lobby groups willing to finance these protracted cases.[303]

Mattli and Slaughter (1996) draw our attention to **large corporate actors** as another group of private repeat players which have proven to be quite active in the enforcement of Community legislation.

---

[301] Galanter (1974) at page 101

[302] European Court of Justice (1970), Case 80/70, *Defrenne v. Belgium*; European Court of Justice (1975a), Case 43/75, *Defrenne v. SABENA;* European Court of Justice (1977), Case 149/77, *Defrenne v. SABENA*

[303] Harlow (1992) mentions the *Equal Opportunities Commission* as a typical *front man* for equality cases in the United Kingdom. This Commission is endowed with statutory power to grant legal advice and assistance to individuals.

Until the beginning of the 1980s, the highest Courts of both France, Germany and Italy seemed unwilling to fully comply with the European Court of Justice's jurisdiction and were very reluctant in endorsing the supremacy and direct effect of Community law. This changed in 1984, as the Italian Constitutional Court allowed for lower domestic courts to judge Italian legislation to be incompatible with Community law without having to refer the case to the Italian Constitutional Court.[304] Little later, in its Solange II case of 1986, the German Constitutional Court decided it would no longer control the constitutionality of Community legislation, and hence effectively accepted the supremacy of European over German law.[305]

Given these evolutions in Italy and Germany, French corporate interests found themselves in a situation where they were at risk of suffering a competitive disadvantage vis-à-vis their Italian and German counterparts. Whereas the latter operated in a legal field where supremacy and direct effect of Community law were recognised, this was not the case in France. In a report on the legal situation of France from this time, Plötner (1995) notes that "*there were solid economic reasons which, in advance of the Common Market made a full integration of Community law into French law paramount. How could the Project of 1992 become effective if the almost three hundred directives intended to transform it into legal reality were not to be directly enforced by the Conseil d'État? (...) The impossibility of referring to certain Community regulations was bound to represent a serious economic disadvantage in comparison to their European competition. In the long run, this could have led to a movement of forum shopping, combined with some delocalization of head offices.*"[306]

In the light of this conviction, major French businesses active in the export and import industry started to systematically file cases against French government decisions which they felt were contrary to or incompatible with Community legislation. Their aim was to put pressure on the French government and the Conseil d'État to comply with Community law by means of a series of judgements by the European Court of Justice, finding France to be in breach of Community legislation.

---

304 Italian Constitutional Court (1984) in its Granital judgement.
305 Bundesverfassungsgericht (1986)
306 Plötner (1995) at pages 24 and 29

Eventually, after cases initiated by Philip Morris and Rothmans, the Conseil d'État confirmed the direct effect of European Community law.[307]

Some of these cases, in particular the Defrenne cases, show a certain similarity with **group actions**, where a group of persons sharing a similar interest jointly address a topic before court.

Europeans often interpret collective action possibilities as a rather recent legal practice in the United States. In reality, collective action has it earliest origins at the Chancery Court in the England of the 17th century. The "Bill of peace" allowed for a "representative suit", i.e.: for the representation of interests of concerned, but not-present parties.[308] Later, American law took over the principle of representative suits in the Federal Equity Rule no. 48 from 1842 and in the New York Field Code of 1948.

Another type of group action, the "organisational action" is less well-known, but is also by no means a recent evolution. Especially in France, and already in the first decade of the 20th century, legal rights were given to professional groups (*syndicats professionnels)* and associations to enter suits especially in the field of criminal law.[309]

More recent evolutions did take place however in the **European Union** and they clearly point at a widening of the possibilities for group or class action. The Netherlands expanded its existing group action with a general authorisation in article 3:305 of its civil code *(Burgerlijk Wetboek)* on July 3rd 1994. Under this article, "*a foundation or association may bring a claim against a party provided that such claim also protects similar interests of other persons, that the foundation or association, according to its articles of association, is committed to further these interests, and that it could not achieve the desired result through consultation with the defendant.*"[310]

---

307 Conseil d'État (1992)

308 For a history of class action in US law, see Yeazell (1980). For the first case, see Chancery Courts (1676)

309 For an overview of the French *action civile of associations,* see Puttfarken and Franke (1999)

310 See Giessen and Loos (2002)

In other European Union member states as well -but in a less general manner- similar rights were granted to specific associations. The basis for this has been European Directive 98/27/EC.

Directive 98/27/EC foresees for the installation of **organisational action (Verbandsklage)** and **suits by "qualified entities"** in a minimum of nine specified cases of consumer interests. In article 2, the directive envisions minimum standards for the protection of collective interests of individuals regulated in a number of directives. It states that in at least nine cases, Member States shall designate the courts or administrative authorities competent to rule on proceedings commenced by "qualified entities".[311] Such entities are defined in article 3 to be: *"any body or organisation which, being properly constituted according to the law of a member state, has a legitimate interest in ensuring that the provisions referred to in article 1 are complied with".*

Throughout the directive, no explicit mention is made of Francovich state liability: the foremost aim of the directive is to grant locus standi to these groups. Most interestingly, every member state is to communicate to the Commission a list of "qualified entities", i.e.: a list of bodies or organisations which is granted the locus standi. The Commission then draws up a community-wide list, and all national courts are to grant the locus standi right to *all* entities on that list, irrespective of their country of origin.[312]

The nine directives where these suits by qualified entities apply are:

1. Council Directive 84/450/EC on misleading advertisement
2. Council Directive 85/577/EEC on contracts negotiated away from business premises (Haustürgeschäfte)
3. Council Directive 87/102/EEC on consumer credit, as last amended by Directive 98/7/EC
4. Council Directive 89/552/EEC on television broadcasting activities, as amended by Directive 97/36/EC

---

[311] Note that only minimum standards are set: article 7 of the directive explicitly states that *"this Directive shall not prevent Member States from adopting or maintaining in force provisions designed to grant qualified entities and any other person concerned more extensive rights to bring action at national level."*

[312] Most remarkably, very little guidance is given in the directive as to which criteria should be applied by member states upon (not) recognising "qualified entities".

5. Council Directive 90/314/EEC on package travel, package holidays and package tours
6. Council Directive 92/28/EEC on the advertising of medicinal products for human use
7. Council Directive 93/13/EEC on unfair terms in consumer contracts
8. Directive 94/47/EC of the European Parliament and of the Council on the protection of purchasers in respect of certain aspects of contracts relating to the purchase of the right to use immovable properties on a timeshare basis[313]
9. Directive 97/7/EC of the European Parliament and of the Council of 20 May 1997 on the protection of consumers in respect of distance contracts

Interesting as these areas might be, they are just of few of those where problems with state liability due to the non or incorrect implementation of European directives might arise. Even more, there is no necessity following Directive 98/27/EC to extend this "entity action" to cases concerning breaches of *primary* European law.

Entity action bears some similarities to **class action,** which is one more way to potentially safeguard more effective protection of claimants. Indeed, through collective action, average per capita process risks -and thus costs- are divided through the number of claimants. This can overcome situations where potential claimants individually remain rationally uninterested in proceeding with their liability claim before court, even when the legal situation clearly (or even certainly) speaks in their favour. Depending on the process laws, initiating a court case might lead to fixed costs exceeding the claim at stake. Secondly, tort feasors might remain anonymous, and the victim might have to invest resources into identifying him. These costs as well might not be worth undertaking, giving the potential low value of the claim for every individual. Finally, information costs should not be underestimated. An uncertain legal framework, or the correct identification of the damage done (and whether this damage is really caused by something which can be interpreted as a "breach of duty") are all factors contributing to the fact that many cases, for every individual concerned, might simply not be worthwhile bringing to court.

---

[313] Remind the acceptance of group action in the framework of this directive by the Spanish *Audienca Nacional.* See page 159.

Finally, as a slightly different form of grouped action, different types of **bundling** should be referred to. *Procedural bundling* allows for the possibility to group pending cases based on identical or similar facts into one case which is treated at one court only. This practice does exist in US-American law, as well as in most European Union member states and offers limited possibilities to save process costs before national Courts.

The European legal system however, is ill-equipped for such doctrine. Cases are heard in national Courts first, before they can be brought to the European Court of Justice. A procedural bundling at the European Court of Justice of cases which are pending in different national courts would thus only be possible through the article 234 doctrine. One might even argue that such bundling is not really necessary since it would be enough for one (1) case to be brought to the European Court of Justice under article 234 to set a precedence for similar cases. Of course, as highlighted by Stefanou and Xanthaki (2000), for this to function, one has to rely on national judges applying the Court's opinions.

Exemplary processes (Musterverfahren) are another form of group*ed* action where courts are able to pick representative cases and continue those as exemplary processes. Other similar and pending cases are then put on hold and can be dealt with more appropriately once a judgement in these exemplary case has been issued. Here as well, the European Court of Justice would be an appropriate Court to issue this decision, as –sooner or later- it would have the final say anyway on contented questions of European Community law. Certainly, there is some resemblance with the article 234 procedure. If a preliminary question is brought to the Court by a national court, it is likely that similar, pending cases –even in other member states' courts- will be put on hold to await the Court's decision. The European Court of Justice yet does not have the power to *itself* pick out contended issues and judge in an exemplary way on the question.

Note that on the national level, this possibility is given. In Germany, so called *Musterverfahren* take place at the *Verwaltungsgericht* and allow judges to group at least 20 cases whose subject is the legality of one and the same administrative act.[314]

---

[314] See § 93a Verwaltungsgerichtsordnung

Now that the working of these three methods is explained, a question still unanswered concerns their necessity, from an economic point of view. Is there a societal benefit to making per capita costs of suing lower by allowing for case-bundling, collective action or entity-suing?

The answer to this question is dual.

Firstly, there is a strong economic argument in favour of allowing for such group actions. This argument can be best illustrated with a member state liability example.

Imagine a member state deciding to pass a domestic law in a field heavily regulated by European Community law. With a probability of 20 %, the decisions will be judged to be a "sufficiently serious breach of Community law" and will give rise to justified damage compensation claims. The total damage caused by this breach will be € 5.000.000, but since this damage is divided over a large number of individuals it will be very small per capita. As a result, many of those victims are rationally uninterested in claiming damage compensation. Assume that victims will only attempt to be compensated to an extent of €3.000.000. Now, the member state could have altered its domestic law so as to make sure that it would not constitute a "sufficiently serious breach of Community law" at a cost of €700.000. This would account for legal research costs and for foregone payments by lobbying organisations.[315]

For the responsible decision-maker, the fact that only a fraction of all victims will demand compensation has a decisive impact. Indeed, when all victims would proceed against him in the case of a breach, the expected costs of damage compensation he should anticipate are €1.000.000. As only a fraction of victims will do so, the relevant expected cost of breaching to the member state differs from its true costs and amounts to only € 600.000. On the other hand, the benefit to the decision-maker of breaching remains € 700.000. <u>It is clear that the rational disinterest of some victims will cause the member state to breach Community law, whereas this would not have been the case if all victims demanded compensation.</u>

Note that we feel unable to draw a societal welfare conclusion on the basis of these numbers. It would indeed be false to claim that from a societal point of view, the breach is unwanted as the costs of breaching (€ 5.000.000) are larger than the benefits to the decision-maker of € 700.000. Whereas in a classical tort example, one could argue that avoidance costs are smaller than expected damage costs and hence avoidance is a superior solution, this is not quite the aim of the exercise here.

As was explained before, cost minimisation is not the primary goal of state liability law. Rather, liability law attempts to convince decision-makers to move within a area bordered by minimum and maximum levels of organisation. Arguments were given to justify this aim. The fact that group or class action might increase the expected damage compensation and make it approach the true damage, might make the state liability system more effective and thus speaks in favour of it.

Borrowing from an argument brought forward by Conant (2001), group (or class) action would present defendants with a critical source of legal leverage. Bundling cases, these would loose the occasionally criticised *"highly individual value"* of the judgement. In other words, the judgements (be it of a national court or of the European Court of Justice) in group cases might be more applicable to similar facts in different cases and might thus not only lead to a higher demand of cases, but also to a wider enforcement of judgements.[316]

Secondly, an economic argument *against* such group or class actions should be mentioned as well however. The so-called booty-theory *(Beutetheorie)* is the most important argument against such actions and concerns lawyers' incentives. Representing a single client, a lawyer will be willing to pursue a tort case when his expected pay-off exceeds his fixed costs of the case. Besides the probability of winning the case, in most European member states, the expected pay-off for the lawyer will be a positive function of the height of the interest at stake. A case will thus be worthwhile for a lawyer as long as:

[315] Lobby organisations would be willing to pay for decisions by the member state offering them a financial advantage. Producers would anticipate that eventually, the act which is a serious breach of Community law would be corrected for, and would adapt their willingness to pay to the expected duration of the advantages.

$$P * V * S \succ FC$$

where
P = the probability of winning the case
V = the total value of the claim
S = the percentual participation in success for the lawyer
FC = Fixed costs of the case for the lawyer.

Now, allowing for group or class action will cause the value *V* of the claim to rise dramatically, while fixed costs will rise disproportionally slow as many similar cases are grouped into one and are dealt with by the same lawyer. Given this rise of *V*, and hence also of *V*S*, it will become financially attractive for lawyers to also pursue cases with a very low probability *P* of winning.[317] Exactly these cases would not been pursued without group or class action.

Although the net benefits of this process are per definition positive, pursuing such high-risk cases cannot be in the interest of society. As pointed out by the criterion of Calabresi (1970) and formulated by Shavell (1997), "*the social objective is simply minimization of the sum of social costs: the harm from injury to victims, plus the costs of precautions, plus the costs associated with the use of the legal system.*"[318]

The fact that class or group action might lead to cases with a low probability of success being pursued, it becomes unlikely that this criterion be fulfilled. Indeed, the threat of such cases might lead to out-of-court settlements and to an overdeterrence effect resulting in excessive standards of care.

8.2.3.3 Punitive Damages as a Demand Stimulator

Punitive damages have a considerable tradition in US-American law, and date back to the late 18th century. Already in the earliest documented case where punitive

---

[316] Conant (2001) claims that effective enforcement is prevented by so called „official obedience". Member states would very narrowly interpret existing Court judgements, and find them inapplicable to present cases, making necessary hearings on new but similar cases at the European Court of Justice.
[317] Given, of course, any (unlikely) lowering of *S* would be undone by the increase in *V*
[318] Shavell (1997) at page 8

damages were applied, little doubt was left as to their aim. In 1792, the Coryell Court made clear that punitive damages should be *"such a sum as would mark their disapprobation, and be an example to others".*[319]

Also in more recent years, deterrence and punishment remained to be the main philosophical fundaments for punitive damages. As Schlueter and Redden (2000) note in chapter two of their book: *"In almost all jurisdictions of the United States where punitive damages are available, their stated purpose is nonrenumerative. Their goal is to punish the wrongdoer and to deter others for similar conduct".*

Accepting all this, Robert Cooter nevertheless observed that throughout recent decades, punitive damages were awarded on a very unstable theoretical basis. He noted that in similar cases, very different punitive damages would be applied. Stunned by this observation, he concluded that "unpredictable damages are neither fair nor efficient" and started investigating *when* and to which *extent* punitive damages should be awarded.[320]

Laying out his arguments (especially on the reasons why punitive damage compensation might make sense) will allow us to draw some analogies with the private Francovich enforcement and will offer us some arguments in favour of installing punitive damages also in this situation.

Cooter blames the **"imperfect enforcement of the law"** for the absence of adequate incentives to conform with legal standards. Whereas a small imperfection might not make a deviation from the legal standard to pay off, a larger "enforcement error" might cause injurers to substantively fall short of complying with standards set by law.[321]

What Cooter understands under "imperfect enforcement of law" shows obvious similarities with the problems we discussed concerning the private enforcement of Community law.

---

[319] Sales and Cole (1984)
[320] Cooter (1989)
[321] id. at page 7

A typical example of such imperfect enforcement is the failure by a considerable part of victims to recover damage from the injurer. This might be because they do not know they were injured, they do not know by whom they were injured or they cannot prove it. Additionally, as discussed, the lack of financial incentives might cause victims to forego recovery of damage and might increase even further the enforcement error.

Without punitive damages, these enforcement errors make it possible for wrong-doers to externalise part of the social costs of the damage done. Compensatory damage compensation is simply not sufficient a deterrent. Punitive damages should be installed to make injurers internalise the full social costs of their acting.

As to the size of the punitive damage compensation, Cooter argues that *"the punitive multiple should equal the reciprocal of the enforcement error for the sake of deterrence."*[322]
Concretely, this means that if 2/3 of victims manages to fully recover their damage, the enforcement error equals 2/3. The punitive multiple or the ratio of total damage compensation to compensatory damage compensation should then be 1,5.

When this is done so, punitive damage compensation cost will equal expected social costs, and social efficiency will result. Without major problems, this reasoning can be applied to the case where a member states breaches Community law.

The application of this reasoning ignores a typical characteristic of state liability cases: injurers (member states) often do not know with certainty when an act will be interpreted as a breach of Community law. Especially primary European law (but to a smaller extent also the interpretation of directives) might be subject to these uncertain legal standards.

When such uncertainty exists, liability costs are continuous rather than discrete. Indeed, costs do not jump abruptly at the "negligent point" but decrease with the level of care taken.

[322] id. at page 7

Cooter argues that under such uncertainty, injurers will typically moderately exceed the (perceived) liability standard, hence granting the courts a margin of error in finding liability.[323]

If this uncertainty is combined with enforcement errors however, for some actors, a (too) low level of care might well be profitable on average. To deal with this situation, Cooter suggests that gross violations (as opposed to the moderate violations which might be attributable to the inherent legal uncertainty) should be made subject to punitive damages. The arguments brought forward above, treating the size of the punitive damages remain valid.

Such punitive damages can well be expected to function as a stimulator of the (private and corporate) demand for liability cases. Indeed, as has been discussed in detail above, because of an enforcement error in the form of complex administrative rules and a low per capita damage, the demand for cases remains rather low.

Cooter's theoretical framework also allows us to deal -at least in theory- with the excess-demand for court cases that those punitive damages might cause. Multiple litigants are not *all* entitled to receive the high punitive damages. As was laid out, the punitive multiple should equal the reciprocal of the enforcement error.

In other words, the application of this principle will cause per capita punitive damage compensation to lower with a rising percentage of victims taking judicial action. Clearly, at some point, the participation constraint will not be fulfilled anymore: for a certain victim, the punitive multiple will be too low, i.e.: her punitive damage compensation will not cover all process costs.

From a deterrence point of view, this is of no importance. The passiveness of this victim will again make the enforcement error rise and hence, the consequent increase of the punitive multiple will outbalance this inaction. The damage compensation paid out will remain the same.

---

[323] Given such moderate uncertainty and under absence of enforcement errors, Cooter claims that findings of liability can only be attributed to mistakes either on the part of the court or of the defendant.

Victims will of course not remain indifferent between both situations. As a remedy to this problem, group action remains available. Victims can claim damage compensation together, sharing process-costs and leaving the punitive multiple unchanged -compared with the situation where all proceed individually.

8.2.4 Few cases: does it work or not at all??

In the course of this work, a considerable number of famous cases were discussed in which individuals initiated liability cases against member states for breaches of Community law. Most of these cases were heard before the European Court of Justice -and not before national courts- since they were all in a way exemplary cases and referred to the Court through article 234. They were all about establishing legal principles, which were bound to have large implications for future similar cases, which were then -dixit the Court- to be heard before national courts.[324]

There is no reason to believe however, that the number of those consequent liability cases before national courts is by any means impressive. Except for the cases described on page 171 and following, the number of state liability cases is indeed rather limited.[325]

Two explanations for this observation can exist:

First of all, the lack of state liability cases might prove the well-functioning of (the deterrence of) the privately-initiated state liability mechanism. Indeed, under a negligence-regime (given the assumption of total information and a correct setting by the courts of the level of negligent care), the mere existence of a functioning tort law

[324] C-6/90 Francovich at para. 42

[325] Tallberg (2000) quotes data collected by the International Federation for European Law and the Commission dating back to 1997 & 1998. Considering only the simplest of cases (non implementation of directives) they conclude that by 1998, the bunch of member states generally saw less than five state liability cases before its national courts. In the seven years following the Francovich judgement, Austria, Denmark, Finland, Greece, Portugal, and Spain witnessed no single state liability case on these grounds. (It should be added however, that Sweden, Austria and Finland only joined the European Union in 1995.)

system will suffice to guarantee efficient, cost-minimising outcomes without any victim actually having to sue a typical tort-feasor.[326, 327]

It seems a bit too optimistic to conclude this is what we are observing. Rather, an alternative explanation is more credible: various legal obstacles as well as the scarce possibilities for group action contribute to making the private enforcement doctrine an empty treat. Diverse national rules and the large discretion left to national judges makes the way to damage compensation very long and stony. The European Court of Justice has reacted to this by demanding national courts not to make it more difficult for individuals to receive damage compensation under European law than it is under national law.[328] This however, has not proven to be sufficient a guarantee for the accessibility of the liability path.

Thus, it is fair to conclude that the aim of the European Court of Justice, as pronounced successively in its state liability rulings, to use the individual in enforcing European legislation by giving that individual a financial interest in bringing a case to court has not been successful. Practical obstructions in legal procedures as well as an insufficient financial compensation for -often high- legal risks serve as the main cause for this failure.

After having set out the problems with the implementation of the Francovich doctrine, another, more fundamental question remains. **If the private enforcement of the state liability doctrine were to be enhanced, would the state liability doctrine then reach the deterrence effect the European Court of Justice seems to hope it would?** In other words: would Member States be deterred from breaching European law by the individual's possibility to claim damages?

Empirics is of little use in answering this question in advance, since deterred actions cannot be observed (especially not before the enactment of such functioning private enforcement system). The currently available data is also not very helpful: only relatively few have managed to make a court reward them damage compensation for

---

[326] This will only be the case, of course, if the threat of being obliged to pay damage compensation when acting negligent is credible. Also, as will be treated below in section 9.4. Existing public state sanctioning: international economic sanctions, *a typical* decision-makers can explain for the occurrence of liability cases under an otherwise perfect liability system.

[327] The strict liability regime will lead to real court cases. In fact, every damage will bring about a claim against the tort-feasor, which will minimise his costs in choosing the efficient level of care.

breaches of European law. It would indeed by naive to belief this means that the deterrence effect of liability claims functions. Rather, many cases are never heard before courts because individuals fear the difficulties of such court-way or because the commission has settled the case silently with the Member State.

Thus, a theoretical answer is necessary. How does the obligation by a court upon a Member State to pay damages to individuals for breaches of European law affect States' behaviour? Is this way more efficient than a well-functioning public enforcement mechanism? These questions will be looked into through the formal approach below.

[328] See C-6/90 Francovich at para. 43

9. Substantive Aspects of Public Enforcement: Deterrence by Fines?

9.1 Details on the specificities of art. 226-228

Advocate-General Geelhoed[329] as well as Advocate-General Damaso Ruiz-Jarabo Colomer[330] recall that the fine foreseen for in article 228 is not designed to act as a penalty but to encourage the defaulting Member State to step back into line. The amount should be in proportion to the scale of the offence and enough to act as a **deterrent**.

In that respect, the Commission's information published in Official Journal OJ C63/2 of 1997 states that decisions as to the amount of a fine or penalty payment must be taken with an eye to their purpose, namely the effective enforcement of Community law. Even more, the Commission is of the opinion that a penalty payment is "the most appropriate means of securing compliance as rapidly as possible"[331].

This comment by the Commission should either be meant ironically, or is to be interpreted as an example of the difficult situation the Commission finds itself in, balancing between necessary co-operation with member states and enforcing the treaties against member states.

Describing the penalty payment as a rapid means of enforcement seems a questionable undertaking. In order for such penalty payment to be put upon non-complying member states, the Commission's case has to be heard before the European Court of Justice twice, not mentioning the long stage of formal notices and reasoned opinions, and the dialogue between member state and Commission which will take place after the first Court's judgement. All in all, the period of time elapsing

---

[329] As written in the Court's Press Release: "*the Court should apply the rules allowing it to fine member states in such a way so as to not only bring about compliance as soon as possible, but also to have a preventative effect.*" (European Court of Justice Press and Information Division (2004)

[330] As written in European Information Service (EIS) (2000): "*The Advocate-General recalls that the fine is not designed to act as a penalty but to encourage the defaulting member state to step back into line. The amount should be in proportion to the scale of the offence and enough to act as a deterrent.*"

[331] [1997] OJ C63/2 in the introduction

from the start of the breach by the member state until the setting of a penalty payment by the Court will hardly ever by shorter than 7 years. This is not exactly *rapid*. Private enforcement might well be faster.

The Commission further states that the daily penalty is calculated as follows:

- "a uniform flat-rate amount is multiplied by two coefficients, one reflection the seriousness of the infringement and the other the duration
- the result is multiplied by a special factor reflecting the ability to pay of the member state concerned and the number of votes it has in the Council."[332]

The uniform flat rate is set at 500 € by the Commission, in an attempt to "maintain pressure on whichever member state is concerned"[333].

When discussing the coefficient taking account of the **seriousness of the infringement**, the Commission looks into both the importance of the Community rules infringed and the effects of the infringement on general and particular interests.
Starting with the importance of the rules breached, the Commission interestingly distinguishes between different types of behaviour by the member states. It notes that "from a strictly legal viewpoint, of course, the infringement in such cases is always the same: non-compliance with a judgement of the Court finding that the member state has failed to fulfil an obligation and breach of article 171(1) of the Treaty"[334] but continues that attention will be given to the "nature and scope [of breaches] rather than to their standing in the hierarchy of norms"[335]. Also, the Commission will take into account the clarity of the rule breached and whether there exists established case-law on the matter of the breach. Finally, not taking any measures at all should be more expensive to the member state than taking inadequate action.
Secondly, the effect of the breach on general of particular interests is looked into. These are assessed on a case-by-case basis and include the following examples:

- the financial dimension of the infringement
- the number of people affected by the infringement

---

[332] [1997] OJ C63/2 in the introduction
[333] [1997] OJ C63/2 under title *2.Setting the Uniform Flat-rate Amount.*
[334] [1997] OJ C63/2 under title *3. The Application of the Coefficients.*
[335] Id.

- the repeat character of the infringement (repeated delays in implementing directives in a particular sector would lead to higher penalty payments)
- serious or irreparable damage to human health or environment
- financial advantages to the member state resulting from non-compliance with the Court's judgement

Combined with the importance of the Community rules infringed, this effect on general or particular interests will cause the Commission to multiply the flat-rate amount with a factor between 1 and 20.

The second coefficient with which the flat-rate is multiplied reflects the **duration of the breach**. This duration starts running from the date of the first Court judgement which made it clear that the member state's behaviour is in breach with Community law[336]. The Commission hence does not take account of the full duration of the breaching activity, which typically started at least a year before the Courts first judgement. The reason for that is that article 228 only foresees in the possibility of penalty payments in case member states do not comply with the Court's judgement. Penalty payments are not foreseen for the breaching of Community law. The Commission will apply a coefficient between 1 and 3 to the flat-rate amount, accounting for the extent the member state has failed to contribute in shortening the article 228(2) procedure. The less efforts a member state has done to keep the time period between the first Court judgement and the article 228(2) procedure short, the higher this coefficient will be. It should be mentioned here however, that in the two cases where member states have been fined under article 228(2), fines were payable only starting from the date where the second judgement was delivered[337]. Finally, in this context, it might be of interest to mention that article 228(2) cannot work retrospectively. In other words, member states cannot be fined for breaches of European law before November 1st 1993, the date on which the Maastricht Treaty entered into force.

The flat-rate amount, multiplied with both coefficient discussed, will be multiplied by a special factor once again, in order to account for the member state's ability to pay and the number of votes it has in the Council.

---

336 [1997] OJ C63/2 under title *3.2 Duration of the Infringement*
337 See the discussion of the cases on page 74 and following.

This is were the Commission most clearly considers the penalty payment as an instrument of deterrence. By taking into account the ability to pay of the member state, the Commission answers to the *"need to ensure that the penalty has a deterrent effect"*[338].

Following the Commission, this deterrent effect should safeguard that:

- *"The member state decides to regularize its position and bring the infringement to an end. The penalty must, therefore, outweigh the advantage gained by the member state from the infringement.*
- *The member state will not repeat the infringement."*[339]

The Commission has hence developed a coefficient which is a geometric mean based on the GDP of member states and their votes in the Council. The coefficient runs from 1,0 for Luxemburg to 26,4 for Germany.

Taking into account all of these coefficients, the final amount of the daily penalty payment is reached by multiplying the flat-rate amount of € 500 with the coefficients for seriousness, and duration of the breach and with the coefficient for the ability to pay.

Concluding, the setting of the penalty payment by the Commission does provide proof of some economic thinking. An attempt is made to create a deterrence effect, and care is giving not to result in overdeterrence[340]. This can be seen especially in the attempt to differentiate between different "seriousnesses" of breaches and by taking into account the ability to pay of member states.

9.2 The lack of first and second order deterrence by article 228 and proof thereof.

---

[338] [1997] OJ C63/2 under title *3.The application of the coefficients*

[339] [1997] OJ C63/2 under title *4. Taking the member state's ability to pay into account*

[340] Clearly this attention to avoid overdeterrence will have more than only economic motives. It can be reasonably expected that the Commission does not want to provoke member state with exorbitant fines and will hence consider political motives as well. Legal motives are not totally absent either: the Court will only upheld penalty payments which are reasonable and proportional.

Also when economic reasoning seems present in the concrete application of article 228 fines by the European Commission, the procedure cannot be said to be powerful or effective when looked at more closely. If at all, a deterrence effect cannot be said to be present in the *first* order or even in the *second* order.

With is meant with a "first order deterrence effect" is the prevention of breaches occurring in the first place. On the basis of its interpretation of a member state's behaviour, the Commission will introduce its initiatives based upon article 226. Clearly, when just considering the public enforcement mechanism, a member state doesn't run any risk by knowingly breaching European law up to this point (and even further as will be explained immediately). Indeed, at this point the Commission is obliged to enter the lengthy procedure of issuing "letters of formal notice" and "reasoned opinions" and the Commission is not in the position to use any financial "sticks" to hit non-complying member states with. Member states can thus breach Community law at no cost, a first order deterrence effect can hence *not* be identified.

This is even more so the case since the length of this period of "risk-free breaching" extends beyond these introductory actions by the Commission. Even when the Commission –after a considerable period of time has elapsed- sees no improvement in the member states behaviour and decides to bring the alleged breach to the European Court of Justice for the first time, besides minimal process costs, a member state has very little to lose financially. Indeed, the Court will only decide *whether* a breach of Community law has taken place, but will not have the possibility to set any financial sanctions for the time-period of breach so far, nor for the period of time starting with its judgement. A second order deterrence effect is thus also not identifiable.

At this point of time however, breaching member states *do* know that their behaviour is judged by the European Court of Justice to be contradictory to Community law, but – given the current jurisdiction by the Court in these matters- still might not be given sufficient incentives to halt the breaching. Indeed, in the cases where the Commission has seen the necessity to bring member states to the European Court of Justice *again* for repeated disrespect of a judgement, that Court has decided to set (daily or yearly) sanctions <u>only for the further</u> non-respect for the judgement starting from the day of judgement in this second case, and <u>not</u> for the time-period between the first and the second judgement. In other words: the sanctioning is not for breaches of Community law, but is for the non-respect of a Court judgement. The sanction itself can only be imposed upon member states by a second judgement and could only function as a third-order effect.

Summarising, under the current application by the Court of the sanctioning regime under articles 226-228, no first or second order deterrence against breaches of Community law can be identified. A deterrence effect might exist only starting from the day of the second Court's judgement, typically after many years of unsanctioned breaching. In some cases, depending on the nature of the breach, this effect can hence hardly be called a *deterrence* effect, it would be more appropriate to speak of an estoppel effect.[341]

The dissatisfaction with this situation seems to mount however, as illustrated by the changes recently proposed by Advocate General Geelhoed documented on page 77. Much of the credibility of the public enforcement mechanism will depend on the outcome of the judgement in case 304/02. Will the Court accept Geelhoed's proposals and accept a financial punishment for member states unwilling to alter their breaching behaviour directly after such finding by the Court, or will it continue to punish member states only in second instance?

A first order deterrence would be present only if the Commission or the Court would be able to fine a member state *immediately* after the finding of a breach of Community law. For example, a change in articles 226-228 might enable the Court to impose a lump-sum penalty payment upon member states directly after the first finding of a breach of European law, or enable the Commission to do so upon cases of very obvious breaches such as the non transposition of directives[342]. If such penalty were sufficiently high, a deterrent effect against breaches might exist.

From a realistic political point of view, quite obviously, member states will not be over-enthusiastic to install such changes in primary law and the proposal will hardly

---

[341] In some cases, compliance with Community law will demand some preparation by the member state. In those cases, it might well be that member states will start *pre*paring their compliance already before this second judgement is delivered by the Court to avoid too many daily sanctions. A possible illustration of such case in the UK is given below on page 193.

[342] Clearly, legal accountability would have to foresee a possibility for member states to appeal against such decision before an authorised court.

find the necessary unanimity amongst member states. From an economic point of view, the proposal seems to make sense under some conditions only.

European Community law is a rather young and at the same time complex body of law. More than in domestic legal systems, uncertainties prevail in the interpretation of certain legal provisions. Under such situation, comparable to the one of liability under uncertain legal standards, the installation of first-order financial punishments against member states for breaches of Community law might create an over-deterrence problem. Member states should be able to adjust their behaviour such, as to avoid breaches of Community law. When the exact conditions demanded by Community law are uncertain, the imposition of potentially horrendous penalty payments for unpredictable breaches might paralyse domestic political activity. This again would not promote the long-term willingness of member states to commit to European legislation. Expressed to economic terms, the opportunity costs of acting within the European legal framework might grow increasingly high when the exact demands of European law are unclear. As these opportunity costs seem to play a role in the existing mechanisms of state liability, it would seem more appropriate to install such first-order deterrence only in cases of sufficiently serious breaches.

When trying to apply this theory to empirical observations, the most obvious remark is that over the years since 1992, extremely few cases have occurred where article 228(2) has been applied by the European Court of Justice. In part, this might be explainable by the long period of time necessary for case to be "ready" to be taken to the Court a second time and more cases might still be to come. A counter-indication for this argument however, can be found in the fact that also before the instalment of a financial sanctioning possibility in article 228 in 1992, the Commission proceeded against non-complying member states and cases were brought to the European Court of Justice. At that time article 169 was the basis for such enforcement action, and the Commission could have brought unsolved cases to the Court on the basis of the new article 228 after 1992.

Two other explanation exist to account for the low number of article 228(2) cases before the Court: the sanction possibility might really deter member states from a continuous breaching or, alternatively, the Commission is enforcing incompletely.

An indication of such possible third-order deterrence effect is given by the British government in its comment in the House of Commons on the Commission's 18th

annual report on monitoring the application of Community Law (European Commission (2001)). Making reference to an article 228 conflict between the UK and the Commission, in his comments, Mr. Peter Hain, the Minister of State at the Foreign and Commonwealth Office stated that *"the (British, bvr) Government is taking every step to ensure that the bathing waters at Blackpool and Southport comply with the required water quality standards before a financial penalty is imposed by the European Court of Justice".*[343]

9.3 Law and Economics of crime

In the analysis of the potential deterrence effect of publicly enforced penalty payments upon member states, this chapter has until now looked into both the likelihood of such penalty payments being imposed upon non-complying member states (**see 9.2)** and into the size of potential penalty payments (**see** 9.1). Where such issues are discussed, a short reference has to be made to Becker (1968), the modern pioneer in the economic analysis of public and private policies to combat illegal behaviour. When discussing the optimal location of scarce resources, Becker identifies exactly these two variables: the probability *p* of discovery of an offence and the size *q* of the punishment for the convicted. Optimal decisions on both are defined to be those which minimise societal damage, which is defined by Becker as "the sum of damages, costs of apprehension and conviction, and costs of carrying out the punishments imposed".

It should be made clear now that from a pure legal point of view, breaches of Community law by member states cannot be said to be *criminal* acts. The fact that they are (at least partly) publicly enforced, enables the comparison with Becker's analysis of crime, though.

A first problem occurring with this comparison is the difficulty of estimating the costs of "crimes", or is this case: of breaches. Material costs to victims of such breaches are already very difficult to approximate, but what to do with the intrinsic value of the respect *for* and the enforcement *of* the law? As long as such value cannot be identified, it will remain impossible to minimise costs as defined by Becker.

---

[343] See United Kingdom Parliament-House of Commons (2001)

A second best aim to take resort to, is to accept the scarcity of both the investigation-funds available to the public enforcer[344] and the limit to the height of the penalty this enforcer can politically afford to set. Given these limitations, the optimal combination, i.e.: the one causing the highest impact, of both variables should be found.

Since –as was described above- under the current public enforcement mechanisms of article 228, the probability for breaching member states of being detected *and* punished is extremely small, fines should be set higher, to reach a sufficient deterrence effect. In the light of this reasoning, advocate general Geelhoed's proposal can be supported as a sensible way to allocate scarce resources.

Alternatively, one should take into account the existence of a second enforcement mechanism: the private one. The existence of this mechanism has repercussions for the allocation of resources by the Commission. The informational advantage that private Francovich enforcement might have over public enforcement which was described below in title 8.2.2, should cause the Commission to invest its scarce financial resources in those case where it (the Commission) has a competitive advantage. Thus, it might increase the probability p of detection of member states' breaches at no costs, since individual claimants would take over the cases which are cheaply detectable.

In all, the *Beckerian* analysis is not easily applied to the public enforcement activities of the Commission, especially since it seems difficult to set financial values on the consequences of breaches. The efficiency argument remains applicable however to the question on how to best divide scarce resources of enforcement both within the Commission and between the Commission and individuals.

9.4. Existing public state sanctioning: international economic sanctions

In the preceeding, some analogies with the existing economic literature on crime and punishment were found, and although those analogies have proved to be helpful in

---

[344] As reported by Tallberg (2003), interviews with Commission officials have revealed that the identification of breaches by member states is a very time-intensive task, given scarcity of time and financial resources in the Commission.

part, some aspects remain rather difficult to compare. When analysing enforcement against states, be it through the Francovich state liability or through the Commission's public enforcement mechanism following articles 226-228, the economic analysis of international sanctions as well shows some remarkable similarities.

In both cases, the subject dealt with is a state which is facing financial incentives to change its behaviour. Whereas -at least to law and economics scholars- in the European Court of Justice's state liability doctrine, the ex-ante deterrence idea of being held liable is clear, it might not be so when thinking of economic sanctions.

International economic sanctions are defined by Hufbauer, Schott et al. (1990) as "*the deliberate government-inspired withdrawal, or threat of withdrawal, of 'customary' trade or financial relations, where 'customary' means levels that would probably have occurred in the absence of sanctions.*" When reviewing the literature on sanctions, one is often confronted with some of the famous cases such as the US sanctions against Cuba or UN sanctions against Rhodesia, South-Africa or Iraq. Attention is almost exclusively given to the evaluation of cases, creating an impression that -if at all- sanctions can only stop something from continuing in the future.

This is of course untrue. Sanctions can very well have a deterrence effect. The ex-ante *treath of using* sanctions can be enough of a deterrence making their use superfluous. Secondly however, they can indeed be installed in order to *prevent* something from happening or from continuing. In this case however, the ex-ante deterrence effect cannot have been sufficiently strong. As argued by Eaton and Engers (1999): *"If sanctions are used, something must have gone horribly wrong."*

In his book on "The Sanctions Paradox", Drezner (1999) offers a general critique on most of the sanctions literature[345]: *"Almost all of the arguments use an inductive approach; theories about economic statecraft are developed only after an examination of case studies. (...) The concern is not with theory, but with explaining the specific event. (...) Certainly, these sanctions cases are well known, but they do*

---

[345] Drezner (1999) at pp.20-21

not necessarily represent the universe of observations. Their very celebrity suggests they are atypical; they are important because they stand out in some unusual way."

Thus, international economic sanctions and the Community law enforcement practices against member states share one idea: in both cases, there is an attempt to convince an actor to act in a specific way, not just in the present, but also in the future. A deterrence effect is thus present in both instruments. However, what has been deterred is unobservable and thus not measurable by case-watching. The concentration in the literature on cases where sanctions have been used or liability has been found, flaws the ex-ante deterrence idea and cannot provide us with a full picture of the working of neither public or international sanctions nor state liability law.[346]

Despite common elements such as the deterrence effect, some **differences** remain in the economic analysis of international sanctions and Community law enforcement against member states.

Typically, international economic sanctions will be used more often with respect to less democratic states, whereas the state liability instrument is a tool atypical for such states. It seems thus fair to say that the analogy between international economic sanctions and the European law enforcement practices lays in the prospected deterrence effect on state behaviour. State liability legislation is the more civilised tool of deterrence for democratic states, and international economic sanctions the brute one more frequently used between or with respect to less democratic states.

Another difference between both issues is that in the Community enforcement analysis, the *sender* of the sanction is not necessarily a State, but will in most cases be an institution such as the European Commission or the European Court of Justice. In the case of Francovich liability, the sender might even be an individual.

[346] Note that this is not necessarily the case for other phenomena. The influence of tort law on car-accidents or on other "traditional torts" can be reasonably well measured by observing the number of accidents, correcting for a.o. increased car use and stricter law enforcement. This is very difficult to do in the case of state liability and economic sanctions. In both cases, the highly political nature of enforcement makes data on the frequency of use of the instruments subject to a bias difficult to correct for.

International economic sanctions are clearly a political instrument which aims at realising an own aim abroad, irrespective of the fact whether these aims are legally sound or not. Tort liability is a legal instrument which will grant victims a compensation to undo the harm done to them. It thus also has a justice perspective in it, since victims are compensated. The sender of an international economic sanction will mostly also claim that protecting victims in a foreign country is exactly the aim of the sanction in place. Whether this is correct is often matter of political debate.[347] It would however be over-simplistic to pretend that the European state liability story is merely one of deterrence and justice to the victims, without political aims. Indeed, the State liability doctrine, as developed by the European Court of Justice, is a tool not just, or even not primarily for reaching justice, but aims at reaching the political aim of a stronger, stabile European Union, where Member States are obliged to respect obligations, also when these are against there own, national interests. One can thus say that the liability tool here has been thought of by the European Court of Justice as a law enforcement mechanism which fitted well in the philosophy of the Court.

Eaton and Engers (1999) analyse international sanctions where a *sender* sanctions a *target* country with the tools of repeated game theory and bargaining under incomplete information. The result of their analysis can be summarised as follows: sanctions tend to be successful the smaller the loss of sanctioning to the sender compared to the gain to this sender of sanctioning. Also, the greater the damage to the target of not complying compared to the cost of complying, the more successful the sanctioning will be. Partly overlapping results were found by Van Bergeijk (1989), who concluded that economic sanctions tend to be more of a success the larger is the pre-sanction trade linkage between sender and target.

Whereas Van Bergeijk concludes that sanctions can be effective instruments in international politics, also Hufbauer, Schott and Elliott (1990) and Elliott and Hufbauer (1999) have empirically tested the effectiveness of sanctions and

---

[347] Consider for example the controversy over U.S. sanctions and embargos on Cuba. For a long time, the European Union did not impose sanctions on Cuba. In general, the European Union has been more reluctant than the United Sates in imposing sanctions on states. For an overview of European sanctions, see the Delegation of the European Commission to the United States at http://www.eurunion.org/legislat/sanctions.htm. For data on U.S. initiated sanctions, see Elliott and Hufbauer (1999)

concluded rather sceptically. It is generally pointed out that severe sanctions can induce perverse political responses in the target country, in that its citizens **"rally around the flag"**, and politically support the decision which is targeted against. This view however, is premised on the instrumental theory that imposing the hardest possible economic harm on the target country is the best way to bring about a policy change. The remarks mentioned above might explain why this is not necessarily so. Using a public choice approach, sanctions with a minimal economic effect might still bring about a political change, since they communicate signals, information or threats.

Nevertheless, the large majority of scholars in the field remain very sceptical as to the effectiveness of international sanctions.[348] In their influential study, Hufbauer, Schott and Elliott (1990) identified 103 cases of economic sanctions in the period of 1914-1990, of which they found 34 percent to be successful. Pape (1997) criticised the resulting tendency to see economic sanctions in a better light by claiming that the result are not representative, and that modern states are better able to resist external economic pressures, for a longer time. This reasoning, again, is criticised by a number of other scholars, claiming that globalisation will cause states to be more -not less- vulnerable to external influence.[349]

Given a scenario where a single Sender faces a single Target, Eaton and Engers (1999) distinct between the case of complete and incomplete information. Given complete information, that is, both parties having full information about the existing rules, the costs of complying for the target, the cost of the sanction (i.e.: of not-complying) to the target and the seriousness of the sender (i.e.: the sender's costs and gains of sanctioning), sanctions should actually never be applied, since the threat to use them should suffice. **If sanctions were used, something most have gone wrong.** As possible explanation for this might be found in Cooter (1984), whose tort-reasoning can easily be interpreted to be valid for states (as opposed to individuals) as well: *"Unlike the typical decision maker, some individuals will be in a situation where nonconformity with the legal standard is cheaper than conformity. Consider someone whose compliance costs are extraordinarily high (...), deterring such unusual person requires a severe sanction."*

---

[348] See the work of Pape (1997) for the "rally around the flag" argument, White (1994) for the negative side-effects on innocent civilians of sanctions, Renwick (1981) and Galtung (1967) for an analysis of the sanctions against Rhodesia and Doxey (1972) and Hoffmann (1967) for a general analysis.

In this context, Eaton and Engers as well, criticise the existing empirical analysis of the effectiveness of sanctions. Indeed, these studies only look at sanctions when they were actually really used, and thus miss a considerable part of the story in that they do not consider the situations where sanctions where being threatened with but never actually used since the target complied "voluntarily".

The second scenario in Eaton and Engers analysis is the case of incomplete information, where things grow more complex. In this case, sanctions might eventually be applied since the costs to targets of a sanction were overestimated by the sender or the cost to the sender was underestimated by the target.

With these two scenario's, the similarity with Community law enforcement becomes clearer: the case of **complete information** can be compared to the one where member states fail to transpose directives or do so too late. The **incomplete information** case resembles questions of uncertainty over legal interpretation. If sanctions (penalty fines under article 228) were more credible and realistic than they are now, Eaton and Engers thus suggest that under complete information, and correct setting of sanctions, deterrence against late or lack of transposition of directives should function.[350]

The literature on sanctions attaches high importance to the expected future conflict potential and to reputation setting. If many more conflicts between *sender* and *target* are expected, the target will be careful to get a "though" image, making sanctions rather unlikely to have much of a success. This argument seems less appropriate to the discussion of state liability, the deeper reason for which being the fact that there are no two competing nations confronted on a single issue. In contrary, there is one respected Court and one respecting member state which in the end will have no

---

[349] See Haas (1998) and Evangelista (1997)

[350] Note however, that article 228 sanctions might be more subject to judicial and political control than international sanctions. Clearly, setting a tremendously high sanction for late transposition might deter member states from doing so. It remains very questionable however, that such sanction would pass the treaty changing process. Also, if European legislation were judged to be excessively stringent by European politicians or the population, it cannot be excluded that the supremacy of European legislation will be questioned. In short: public sanctioning of member states in the European Union is subject to tighter conditions than international economic sanctioning.

choice than to respect the Court's ruling. Image questions are not of interest exactly because the Court is sufficiently established now.

In fact, the ex-post discussion typical to the literature on sanctions is rather uninteresting to state liability from an economic point of view. There is little doubt that a member state eventually will pay damage compensation, if ruled so by the European Court of Justice or a national court. The question is rather whether the *threat* of being held liable or of being convicted under article 228 by the Court is likely and impressive enough not to breach European law in the first place.

PART V: STATE LIABILITY IN TORTS AS A LAW ENFORCEMENT INSTRUMENT. DOES IT WORK?

10. Substantive Aspects of Private Enforcement: Deterrence by Damage Compensation?

10.1 Introduction

In part III, we analysed the real aim of the European Court of Justice's doctrine of allowing for private tort claims against member states for breaching European law. Part IV discussed the usefulness of this approach vis-à-vis a more public approach and some practical, procedural problems that do arise with it. This chapter moves one step further in examining exactly how deterrence with monetary means could (not) function against democratic states.

The standard law and economics literature, dealing with firms or individuals as economic agents, to a large extent avoids an in-depth discussion of the deterrence effect of monetary claims. Firms are assumed to be cost-minimising, which is a fairly accepted assumption given fierce competition on both consumer and capital markets. Individuals are –also commonly accepted- assumed to be utility-maximisers, but as utility is not observable, monetary income is taken as the closest proxy. Equating money to utility is however problematic: the same monetary damage claim of € 1.000 surely causes a different change in utility when distinguishing between a rich and a poor person. In other words: the marginal disutility of that claim will be different as those individuals will have different utility functions. Equating monetary effects to utilitarian effects incorrectly makes this difference disappear and estimates deterrence wrongly[351, 352].

---

[351] Realising this, some countries such as Finland have adapted their traffic laws, making the height of speeding fines a percentage of net income.

[352] Some literature has focussed on the role of "image" instead of financial sanctions for board-members when being litigated against for mismanagement, giving a more correct understanding of the deterrence effect.

The standard reply that there is no true, better alternative of measuring utility and thus also anticipated disutility (deterrence), cannot be accepted without debate when discussing the behaviour of states represented by democratically elected politicians. Those are subject, not only to (different) monetary restrictions as individuals are as well, but also to a democratic restriction: they have to get (re)elected.

In the following, some characteristics of states will be discussed which make them distinctly different from individual actors and which might influence the (mal)functioning of monetary deterrence. States will be treated as rational, unitary actors. After that, in an attempt to analyse possible deterrence effects in a more analytical manner, similarities with the literature on international trade will be uncovered and applied to analyse state liability.

10.2 Distinct features

Just as individuals, politicians are rational in that they will maximise revenue and minimise costs. Distinctly however, politicians' costs are more of a political kind than of a monetary one. Surely, politicians are subject to monetary constraints as well, but eventually, their "market" will be the one for political support. The challenge at hand is to establish a link between these monetary and political constraints.

10.2.1 Different budget restraints

In one of the first of few economic articles on liability of States, Spitzer concludes that *"governments should be suable in tort"*[353]. A contrary position is held by Cohen, who claims that the optimal liability rule is one of no-liability.[354] It should be mentioned though that Cohen does not discuss state liability in an European Union institutional context. He is not considering breaches of European law, but is more concerned with acts of state officials such as for example the police. Also, the law in-/enforcement aspect of tort liability as introduced by the European Court of Justice is absent in his

[353] An Economic Analysis of Sovereign Immunity in Tort, 1977, 50 So. Cal.LR 515
[354] Cohen (1990)

considerations. He is merely "*evaluating the role of liability rules in reducing primary accident costs*"[355].

Cohen distinguishes between two possible types of state behaviour:
Firstly, if a state acted efficiently ("*whatever that means*"), liability would be a superfluous instrument to reach efficiency.
Secondly, if a state acted inefficient, any argument in favour of a state liability system should be made dependent of a satisfying answer to the two following questions:

1. Is the liability system cost-justified?
2. Does the state respond to liability?

Concerning the first question, Cohen is sceptical on the marginal net-benefits of a set of liability rules, as their establishment and application of court and non-court institutions might give rise to considerable transaction and error costs.

Understandable as this remark might be in considering the cases Cohen does, it seems to be less convincing when considering the case of state liability for breaches of European law.
This is so since the normative aim of the two cases discussed are distinctly different. In the case of European law breaches, the role of liability rules is not to minimise primary accident costs, but to convince Member State to respect European law. This enforcement of European law is subject to cost-justification arguments in a limited sense only. It can not be accepted that European law remains non-enforced because its enforcement is more costly than the law is worth itself. The fact that a legislative proposals passes the law making process is an indication that this proposal is wanted by a necessary majority. From that moment on, it deserves protection against an unwilling minority. This gives the law an intrinsic value absent to contract agreements.

This is not to say that system costs are totally irrelevant to the case of law enforcement. Enforcement of European law will probably always be necessary, the question will be which institutional arrangement is performing most efficiently in enforcing European law: a private liability system under national

[355] Cohen (1990), pp. 214

courts or a public enforcement system initialised by the Commission under the European Court of Justice.

The second question is of no less importance. Even if private liability were a more efficient enforcement system than public enforcement, it still has to possess a deterrence effect. I share Cohen basic argument that it is unlikely that the state will react in the same manner as an individual: *"the State cannot be assimilated to the position of a private firm."*[356]

Cohen however goes further and claims that *"the response of the government to legal liability risks will not generate a reduction in accident costs".*[357] Besides the absence of empirical proof, theoretical arguments for this claim are rather thin.
Cohen relevantly highlights that the proportional impact of the costs of liability on a governmental decision maker's budget are minimal[358]. Although Canadian and European state liability law are definitely different and although there is no empirical data available on the percentage impact of non-contractual liability claims on European Union Member States' budgets, it is safe to expect similar conclusions in the European Union.

Cohen however makes this argument superfluous by further arguing that liability cannot have an incentive effect as states are not subject to (especially capital) market constraints in the same manner as individuals are.

However true this might be, also for governments money is a scarce resource the use of which for the payment of damage compensation claims has its opportunity costs. Money paid to settle liability claims cannot be used by government anymore to pursue political aims which might have granted this government public political support. Alternatively, taxes have to be raised or debts made in order to still be able to pursue these aims. Both alternatives influence political support, in which positive, negative or marginal way ever. The fact that the liability expenditures might be included as "general costs" in the yearly state budget, as Cohen claims, does not change the fact that they prevent the realisation of other plans and thus cost or cause

---

[356] Cohen, pp. 246
[357] Cohen, pp.246

political support.[359] It thus follows that the state is indeed not subject to the same market constraints as individuals are, but that it is confined by a competition for political support. This competition is not primarily one between States (as Cohen suggests) but one between political competitors within a country. These institutional factors will decide whether this *market constraint in votes* will confine governments' acts thus that liability for breaches of European law can be said to have an incentive effect.

10.2.2 The Efficacy of Tort Systems in deterrence

Whereas most scholars would agree that efficient deterrence is one of the most important aims of tort law, testing this phenomenon is however not that easy. Everything that is deterred is, of course, not directly observable. Dewees and Trebilcock[360] have evaluated the efficacy of tort systems against three normative criteria: corrective justice, distributive justice, and deterrence. The subject of the study were five classical types of accidents: car accidents, medical malpractice, product related accidents, environmental injuries and workplace injuries. They found that the deterrence effect is strongest with respect to car accidents and weakest with respect to environmental injuries. The other cases gave a mixed image.

More interesting perhaps than these results, is the method used by both authors to measure deterrence. Dewees and Trebilcock distinct between an *input evaluation* and an *output evaluation.*

The latter tries to observe behavioural changes in levels of care or activity under different tort rules. Everything else being equal, a lack of such changes in the behaviour observed, must lead to the conclusion of the tort system being ineffective. When such changes do occur, it remains rather difficult to easily draw conclusions on the *efficiency* of the deterrence induced by tort law.

---

[358] Using data from the *Public Accounts of Canada*, Cohen concludes that those costs of legal liability never exceed 0,2 percent of a departments budget.

[359] Liability costs may cost political support because of opportunity costs, but might also create political support as voters might share the decision-maker's preference of breaching European law and paying damage compensation over complying with the law.

[360] Dewees and Trebilcock (1992)

The application of this output evaluation to state liability in the European Community suffers from some serious problems. Most importantly, the data is biased. It is questionable whether it makes sense to compare data on breaches before and after the instalment of the Francovich doctrine. The decisive variable (the occurrence of breaches) has been constantly "polluted" over time by the public enforcement activities of the Commission. It seems very difficult to correct for the activity of the Commission in this analysis.

The alternative, mirror-imaged method applied by Dewees and Trebilcock to analyse deterrence is the so called input evaluation. *"The deterrence goal is likely to be well served if empirical evidence suggests that most victims of wrongdoing <u>have ready access to the legal system</u> without <u>excessive barriers to suit</u>; that <u>legal standards are certain and well understood</u> by the parties subject to them; and that the damage principles confront the defendant with <u>the full social costs</u> of wrongoing without abandoning incentives."*

Neither of the three last underlined criteria are fulfilled in the majority of member state breaches of Community law. Ready access to the legal system is the criterion most often fulfilled, although groups of victims are not always granted locus standi.

This approach summarises many of the (sceptical) thoughts expressed above on the (mal)functioning of deterrence against state breaches. The more formal approach following now attempts to make our predict a bit more precise.

10.3 A formal Public Choice Approach

Public Choice literature on interest groups and political decision-making distinguishes between models of *political competition* and *political support.*[361] In the former, the political competition between different candidates is modelled. Lobby groups favour those parties whose programmes and policies favour their interests and offer them contributions so as to convince uninformed or easily impressed voters and win the election.[362]

---

[361] For a survey on these differences see Hillman (1989)
[362] See the work of Magee (1989) and Hillman and Unsprung (1988)

The latter models of *political support*, which will be used here, model incumbent governments setting policies while being aware that these choices might affect their re-election chances. Lobby groups have an apparent interests in some of those decisions and offer contributions to ensure decisions on *"pliable topics"* (i.e.: topics on which no fixed, well-known party line exists) being made in their favour. Interest groups do not offer contributions to increase chances of candidates at the ballot. In short, contributions are offered to influence policy decisions, not vote results. The incumbent government can have an interest in these contributions for various reasons: past campaign debts may be paid off with them, or the ability of a politician to raise campaign funds might strengthen his position in the party, deterring competitors from running for office. Clearly, accepting contributions might go at the cost of alienating voters or simply of general welfare. Since incumbents are assumed to care about re-election, these models typically make the politician maximise a weighted welfare function[363, 364].

European law can be said to be of particular importance in two areas. The first one is the area of trade, where regulation of the common European market has attempted to lift barriers to trade within the European Union. Secondly, a great deal of European regulation concerns producer-consumer or employer-employee relations. In the first instance, European law typically attempts to set a maximum level of national regulation; in the second case, minimum rules are aimed at.
Certainly, many other areas exist in which European regulation plays an important role. Environmental issues for example, have been heavily influenced by European legislation. However, these issues are not directly subject to a functioning market and hence to a market price, making their analysis more complex from an economic perspective. They will therefore not be considered here.

For the two main areas mentioned - trade and consumer or employee rights, this market is readily available in the form of product and labour markets. In the following, policy decisions by the member states will be analysed with regard to their repercussions on European markets. In particular, the policy decisions are instrumentalised by the level of regulation R, set by every member state. This level of regulation R is subject to European legislation. The analysis is that of a small, open

---

[363] This approach was first applied by Stigler (1971)

[364] Although it is mainstream opinion in economic literature that legislators will be influenced by special interest groups, Farber and Frickey (1987) remain sceptical about the size of that influence.

European economy. It will be argued that choices of R by member states might affect domestic prices to a different extent than world prices. As the actors under investigation are the European Union member states, what is actually meant by "world market" or "world prices" are "European market" and "European prices." Because of the conventionality of referring to "world markets" in the international economics literature, this will be done here as well.

Before entering into more formal analysis, two exemplary situations will be discussed, taking account of both trade and consumer/employee affairs as main areas of regulation and at the same time acknowledging analytical differences between directives and regulations/treaties as sources of European law. This is done to show how the true problems can be "translated" into an economic framework, as well as to show the reasonability of some of the assumptions made later on.

10.3.1 Treaty provisions and regulations: Nontariff Barriers and Free Trade Regulation

Member states can set a level of regulation R on foreign-produced products in order to protect the public health of the domestic population. This is allowed for by European regulation in article 30 of the Treaty, which however also foresees free movement of goods in the European Union and does not allow for unfounded discrimination between domestic products and imports[365]. This example reflects at best the discretion left to national member states when trying to act in accordance with <u>treaty provisions</u> and European <u>regulations</u> which might affect domestic and foreign producers in different ways. It is most relevant to situations where doubts might arise as to whether the <u>substance</u> of an act is a breach of European law (as opposed to the procedure as under 10.3.2 below).

---

[365] Article 30 foresees that "The provisions of Articles 28 and 29 *(on free movement of goods, bvr)* shall not preclude prohibitions or restrictions on imports, exports or goods in transit justified on grounds of public morality, public policy or public security; the protection of health and life of humans, animals or plants; the protection of national treasures possessing artistic, historic or archaeological value; or the protection of industrial and commercial property. Such prohibitions or restrictions shall not, however, constitute a means of arbitrary discrimination or a disguised restriction on trade between Member States

Now, concretely, national regulators might demand foreign producers to provide their products with manuals in the local language(s), translate package-details, set up call-centres with operators able to address customers in the national language, require them to acquire a license, make them subject to inspections before allowing them to become active on the local market or any other requirements the domestic regulator seems necessary in order to safeguard public health[366].

Clearly, all of this makes foreign producers face higher costs than their domestic counterparts which do not export or which are not subject to the same regulation. The following figure shows the effects of this regulation R.

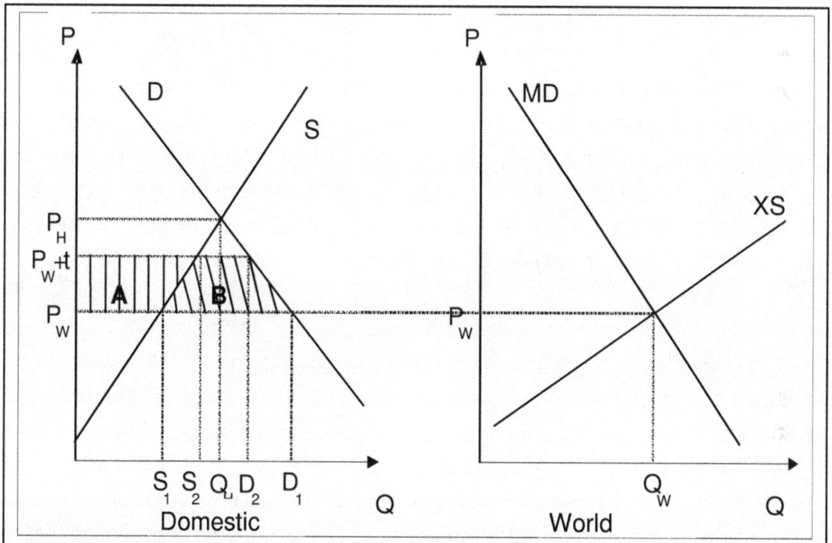

Figure 16: Market Effects of Regulation

As can be seen, the price level P_W on the World market (which in this case is the European market) is lower than prices P_H domestically. If this were not the case, trade would of course not take place. Note that P_W is set by the Import Demand (MD) and Export Supply (XS) on the world market (MD).

---

[366] Think for example of Germany not allowing for French and Belgian beer to be sold under the label "beer" in Germany because it wasn't brew in the way the German Purity Law (1516) prescribes. The German government mentioned health concerns as main argument for doing so.

Now, the policy decision R by the government at Home causes extra costs t for importers alone. As the country under analysis is small, the increased price on the Home market does not lead to price decreases on foreign markets, leaving the world market price P_W unchanged and passing all costs of the importers' costs to consumers in the domestic market. The market price of relevance to this domestic market alone is thus P_W+t. Clearly, the burden t put on importers increases with the level of regulation R.

The effect of this regulation is thus clearly to raise the domestic price above world prices. This makes some of the imports unprofitable, and hence imports will decrease from D_1-S_1 to D_2-S_2. Domestic producers' surplus will rise with A, consumer surplus decreases with (A+B), but consumers will also gain through a better protection of their health, leaving the exact effect on welfare unclear for the moment. More exact formulations of these gains and losses will be provided for below. Note the special case where P_W+t exceeds P_H. Here, the level of imports falls to zero. In this scenario of prohibitively high non-tariff costs, consumer surplus also decreases by more than producer surplus rises, but again this might be welfare-increasing when taking into account public health losses imports might have caused.

Concluding, it is clear that the regulatory policy of the member states will in this case work in the same way as a tariff does. There are however no tariff revenues to be collected by the government. The gains to public health (assuming that the regulation does at least partially serve that purpose) are to consumers directly. Interestingly and importantly, the choice of R made by the member state influences prices, which –as will be seen later- will cause interest groups to try to influence that choice. Domestic producer interest groups are evidently interested in a domestic price exceeding world prices and since more regulation leads to higher prices, contributions offered by interest groups will increase in R.

10.3.2 Transposing Directives: Francovich and the effect on producers' costs

The situation offered by the transposition -whether correct or not- of European directives is distinctly different from the question whether the substance of a governmental act is in accordance with European treaties and regulations. The analytical difference lays in the outside option for the domestic government. When all other member states do transpose a directive and the domestic government chooses not to do so, it will find itself in a situation with similar effects than that under a non-tariff barrier. (The difference being that it is the transposition of the directive by foreign governments that has shifted upwards supply curves and hence also world prices, and not an act of the domestic government. Its non-acting caused domestic prices P_H to remain unchanged though.) The outside option of the domestic government is to take action itself as well and "transpose" the directive. Assuming that all other member states have done so correctly, if the domestic government transposed the directive correctly as well, cost curves at home would shift up by the same amount as on world markets, increasing domestic prices to P_{HT}.[367]

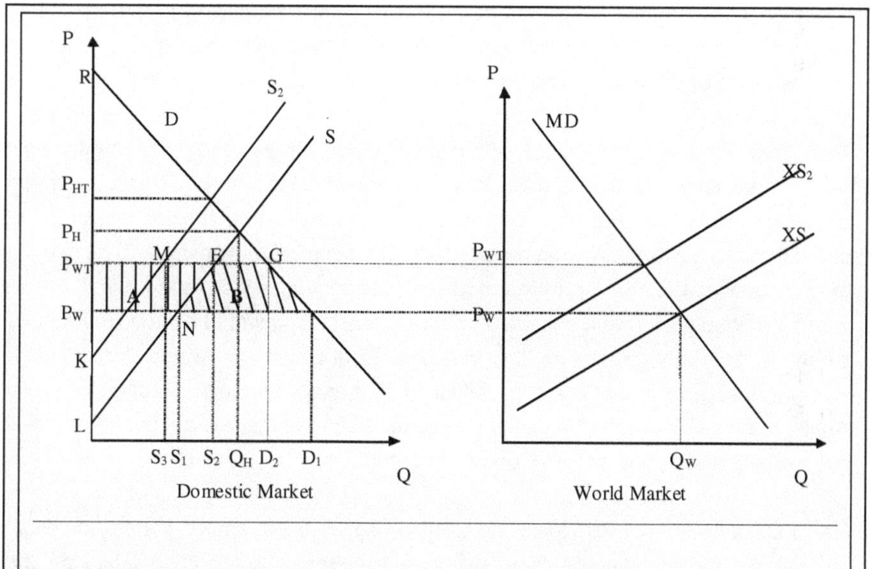

Figure 17: Directives increasing domestic Producers' Costs on the Market

Now, let's look at the welfare effects of both options to the domestic government. Three situations can be distinguished.

---

[367] Note that this is a silent assumption that all producers are affected by the content of the directive to an identical extent.

In a first scenario, no member states transposes the directive in question. Domestic producers' surplus amounts to $P_W NL$, consumers' surplus to $P_W FR$.

As a second scenario, all other member states do comply with the directive, but out domestic government does not transpose the directive. Producers' surplus rises with A and reaches $P_{WT} EL$. Consumers' surplus decreases with (A+B) to $P_{WT} GR$.

Thirdly, choosing to transpose the directive, producers' surplus will lower from $P_W NL$ under free, unregulated trade without directives to $P_{WT} MK$ when the domestic government transposes the directives correctly, just as all other member states. Compared with this free trade, the consumers' surplus will diminish with (A+B), the same amount as in the second scenario, which is due to the fact that the country under analysis is small. Like this, transposing or not transposing is merely shifting production from importers to domestic producers. Importantly, note that any benefits to consumers/employees are not taken into account yet.

The directive transposition scenario is not solely discrete, i.e.: the act of the domestic government is not just of a dual nature of "transposing" or "not transposing" the directive. The problematic becomes substantive as well when considering an act by the domestic government that would shift the supply function from S to S_1 (not drawn), between S and S_2. In that situation, consumer as well as producer surplus would be affected as well, and the benefit of transposing would accrue to a smaller extent to the beneficiaries of the directive. Doubt however would persist as to whether the government's act is sufficient in transposing the directive correctly. Again, the difference with the cases mentioned before is that the act by the domestic government also raises costs for domestic producers.

Concluding, here as well, the regulatory policy of the member states influences interest groups' stakes and they will have an interest in trying to influence that regulatory choice. Regulation by the domestic member state does however not influence prices as it did under the previous example: it merely increases costs for domestic producers (and hence also influences their surplus) to a smaller or bigger extent. Since the country under consideration is small, these costs changes do not influence prices. However, more regulation by the domestic government will leads to higher costs for domestic producers, so the attempt this time will be to convince decision makers to choose a level of R as low as possible. Contributions offered by interest groups will hence decrease in R.

10.3.3. The Formal Framework for non-tariff barriers[368]

A. Decisions under the absence of liability

Assuming the member state in question is a small and open economy unable to influence world prices, the governmental actions described above will lead to domestic prices exceeding those world prices with a factor *t* (tax) or will apportion production to domestic producers rather than to foreign ones. In any case, the level of regulation R will influence producers' surplus, be it through its impact on prices or on domestic production costs.

In the following, a formal framework is set up to deal with non-tariff barrier cases as explained under title 10.3.1, where *substantial* discussions on the compatibility of government acts with treaty provisions or regulations arise.

Assume a small, open economy with *n* different and independent economic sectors, each of those sectors producing one type of good. Domestic prices for those goods are noted p_i, world prices are noted p_i^w. The government sets a regulatory policy R_i for every economic sector *i*, and R_i is a continuous variable between 0 and 1. The vector **R** denotes all regulatory choices by the government for all sectors i.

As explained under title A, the burden placed upon importers is assumed to increase linearly in R_i. Hence, domestic prices are a function of R_i and increase in R_i. More precisely, $t = a_i R_i$ with $a_i > 0$. Thus:

(1) $p_i = p_i^w + a_i R_i$ with $a_i \geq 0$. $\forall i = 1, 2, \ldots, n$

Differences in the value of a_i over various economic sectors can reflect differences in the intensity of competition in those industries or in the relative size of the domestic economy in those sectors.

The inhabitants of our small and open economy are assumed to have identical preferences, but different factor endowments. These endowments can also be understood to be property rights in one of the i industries. For the sake of simplicity,

---

[368] The basics of the model set-up are inspired from Grossman and Helpman (1994).

individuals are assumed to have property rights in not more than one sector at a time.

Every single individual is assumed to maximise a simplified utility function given by

$$(2) \qquad u = \sum_{1}^{n} u_i(x_i)$$

where x_i is the consumption of the good of sector i with i = 1, 2, ... , n.[369]
For all utility functions u_i : $u_i^{'} > 0$ and $u_i^{''} < 0$.
For every good i, an individual demand function $x_i = d_i(p_i)$ is defined, which is the inverse of $u'(x_i)$, Since domestic prices p_i are determined by a fixed world price p_w and by a variable regulatory choice R_i, we will denote this individual demand function as $x_i = d_i(R_i)$

Just as vector **R** expresses all regulatory policies R_i, vector **p** denotes all prices p_i, given which the individual consumer surplus CS(**p**) takes the form:

$$(3) \qquad CS(\mathbf{p}) = \sum_{i}^{n} u_i[d_i(p_i)] - \sum_{i}^{n} p_i d_i(p_i) = \sum_{i}^{n} u_i[d_i(R_i)] - \sum_{i}^{n} u_i[p_i d_i(R_i)] = CS(\mathbf{R})$$

For the owners of factor endowments, the rewards to these are noted by $\prod_i(p_i)$ and are thus only dependent on the price of good i, given that wages are assumed constant. Again, as the single variable influencing prices is R_i, we can also note this factor reward as $\prod_i(R_i)$.

It is important to realise now that the enactment of government regulation does not necessarily lead to an increase of domestic prices at zero benefit. Indeed, regulating the availability of customer information might very well have a positive value. The net value on a per capita basis of such regulation, is given by:

$$(4) \qquad V(p_i) = \sum_{i} b_i(p_i - p_i^w)\left[d_i(p_i) - \frac{1}{N} H_i(p_i) \right]$$

[369] Clearly, this utility function will be a simplification: hardly any individual will attach equal weight to all *n* consumed goods.

where N equals total population and $H_i(p_i) = \prod_i^{'}(p_i)$ equals the domestic production of good i [370]. Per unit of consumption of imported good i, the value of the benefit resulting from the government's regulation R_i is said to be $b_i(p_i - p_i^w)$, with $0 \leq b_i \leq 1$. The different coefficients for b_i reflect the different degrees to which products can cause dangers as well as the general "true effect" of regulation in reducing unsafety - i.e.: the efficacy of regulation.

Given (1), this expression (4) can be re-written as

(5) $$V(\mathbf{R}) = \sum_i a_i b_i R_i \left[d_i(R_i) - \frac{1}{N} H_i(R_i) \right] \qquad \forall i = 1, 2, ..., n$$

Given that preferences were assumed to be identical among individuals, this net value is distributed equally over the total population.

Clearly, those individuals with factor endowments in sector *i* will have an interest in regulations concerning that sector which exceeds their interest as a consumer in the same sector. They will be concerned about the effect of regulation on the specific factor reward $\prod_i(R_i)$, as this will affect their income.

In some of the sectors, individuals will manage to organise in lobby groups, overcoming the free-riding incentive every of those individuals faces. [371] Hence, different groups i are taken as given in a sector $i \in L$, which will offer politicians payments in exchange for regulatory policies maximising these groups' members' net welfare. Contributions by every sector's producers are written as $C_i(R_i)$ which increase in R_i since p_i increases in R_i.

Hence, group i's joint net welfare can be written as:

(6) $$W_i(\mathbf{R}) - C_i(R_i) = \prod_i(R_i) + \alpha_i N\left[CS(\mathbf{R}) + V(\mathbf{R})\right] - C_i(R_i)$$

with $i \in L$ and α_i being the percentage of population this group i represents.

---

[370] Hotelling's Lemma

[371] Everyone with producer interests in a specific sector will hope that other producers of his sector will engage in costly lobbying, which has the character of a public good for those producers. Producers will hence hope to reap the benefits of others' activities while staying idle themselves.

Individuals holding factor endowments in sectors which did not manage to organise in lobby groups refrain from attempting to influence decision-makers as they feel their influence is too small.

The government from its side, will accept contributions $C_i(R_i)$ for a number of different reasons. First of all, contributions can be used in election campaigns to convince undecided, uninformed or easily-impressed voters. Secondly, contributions might be used to pay off debts incurred in previous elections or might serve as an instrument to establish power within the party and deter others from becoming direct competitors.

This is not to say that government will care about contributions solely. As most governments will strive for re-election, it is assumed they care about aggregated welfare as well, believing they will be credited for a rise in welfare at the next ballot. Governments are thus said to maximise the following function,

(7) $$G(\mathbf{R}) = \sum_i C_i(R_i) + cW(\mathbf{R}) \text{ with } c \geq 0 \text{ and } i \in L$$

and where W(**R**) equals aggregate welfare equal to

(8) $$W(\mathbf{R}) = \sum_i^n \Pi_i(R_i) + N\left[V(\mathbf{R}) + CS(\mathbf{R})\right]$$

What is of interest now is the equilibrium which will be reached. This equilibrium exists of a set of contributions $C_i(R_i)$ and regulatory choices **R** resulting from them, which in turn determine domestic prices at which each interest group -given other groups' contributions and anticipating politicians' maximising efforts- maximises its own welfare and which maximise the government's utility function specified under (7).

Following Bernheim (1986), such equilibrium $\left(\{C_i^0\}_{i\in L};\mathbf{R}^0\right)$ is a sub-game perfect Nash-Equilibrium if and only if:

1) C_i° is possible for all interest groups $i\in L$

2) $\mathbf{R}^0$ maximises $G(\mathbf{R}): \sum_{i\in L} C_i^0(\mathbf{R})+cW(\mathbf{R})$

3) $\mathbf{R}^0$ maximises the sum of the government's welfare function G(**R**) and the welfare of any interest group j, given the contributions of all interest groups $i\neq j$.

Thus, for $i\neq j$, $\mathbf{R}^0$ maximises $W_j(\mathbf{R})-C_j^0(\mathbf{R})+\sum_{i\in L} C_i^0(\mathbf{R})+cW(\mathbf{R});\forall i,j\in L;i\neq j$

When assuming that the contribution functions $C_i(R)$ are differentiable, the first order condition following from this third condition to be met at an equilibrium regulatory choice R° reads:

(9) $$\Delta W_j(\mathbf{R^0})-\Delta C_j^0(\mathbf{R^0})+\sum_{i\in L}\Delta C_i^0(\mathbf{R^0})+c\Delta W(\mathbf{R^0})=0 \qquad \forall i,j\in L$$

However, in order to fulfil condition 2) in equilibrium:

(10) $$\sum_{i\in L}\Delta C_i^0(\mathbf{R^0})+c\Delta W(\mathbf{R^0})=0$$

Hence, combining (9) and (10) we reach

(11) $$\Delta W_i(\mathbf{R^0})=\Delta C_i^0(\mathbf{R^0}),\forall i\in L$$

This means nothing else than that in equilibrium, a marginal change in the contribution of interest group i will cause an identical marginal change in that group's welfare. Said differently, in equilibrium, one extra euro in contributions will yield one extra euro in welfare to that interest group.

Summing (11) over all interest groups $i\in L$ and substituting the result back into (10), we get

(12) $$\sum_{i\in L}\Delta W_i(\mathbf{R^0})+c\Delta W(\mathbf{R^0})=0$$

which is a first order condition for

(13) $\mathbf{R^0}$ to maximise B(**R**) : $\sum_{i\in L} W_i(\mathbf{R})+cW(\mathbf{R})$ in **R**

Interestingly, this expression shows that in equilibrium, contribution schemes will make the government maximise a weighted welfare function B(R), attaching a weight of *(1+c)* to the interests of all voters which are members of an interest group; and of *c* to the interest of all those who are not.

Now, we still have to find out the equilibrium level $\mathbf{R}^0$ of regulation. With the use of equation (12), we deduct the effect that a small change in the choice of regulation **R** will have on both *general* welfare *W* and *interest group* i's welfare W_i.

Starting with the effect on ***interest group welfare***, departing from (6) and again making use of Roy's Identity we find that:

$$\frac{\partial W_i(p_i)}{\partial R_j} = \frac{\partial W_i(p_i)}{\partial p_j} \cdot \frac{\partial p_j}{\partial R_j} = a_j \frac{\partial \prod_i(p_i)}{\partial p_j} + \alpha_i N \left[a_j b_j \left(\frac{1}{N} M_j(p_j) + \frac{1}{N}(p_j - p_w) M_j'(p_j) \right) - a_j d_j(p_j) \right]$$

where $M_j(p_j) \equiv N d_j(p_j) - H_j(p_j)$ represents the import demand function $\forall i, j \in L$.

So, when i=j: $\frac{\partial W_i(p_i)}{\partial R_j} = a_j H_j(p_j) + \alpha_j a_j b_j M_j(p_j) + \alpha_j a_j b_j (p_j - p_w) M_j'(p_j) - \alpha_j a_j D_j(p_j)$

Alternatively, for cases where i is not equal to j:

$$\frac{\partial W_i(p_i)}{\partial R_j} = \alpha_i a_j b_j M_j(p_j) + \alpha_i a_j b_j (p_j - p_w) M_j'(p_j) - \alpha_i a_j D_j(p_j)$$

Formulating for both cases, we get

$$(14) \qquad \frac{\partial W_i(p_i)}{\partial R_j} = \partial_{ij} a_j H_j(p_j) + \alpha_i a_j b_j M_j(p_j) + \alpha_i a_j b_j (p_j - p_w) M_j'(p_j) - \alpha_i a_j D_j(p_j)$$

with $\partial_{ij} = 1$ for i=j and 0 otherwise.

Summing over all $i \in L$ to find out the influence of a policy change R_j on all interest groups' welfare, we find $\forall i, j \in L$:

$$(15) \qquad \sum_{i \in L} \frac{\partial W_i(p_i)}{\partial R_j} = a_j I_j H_j(p_j) + \alpha_L a_j b_j M_j(p_j) + \alpha_L a_j^2 b_j R_j M_j'(p_j) - \alpha_L a_j D_j(p_j)$$

with $I_j \equiv \sum_{i \in L} \partial_{ij}$ being a measure for the organisation of industry j which is 1 if the industry is organised and 0 otherwise. $\alpha_L \equiv \sum_{i \in L} \alpha_i$ and denotes the fraction of the population which is organised in interest groups.

Turning our attention now to changes in ***general welfare*** resulting from minimal policy changes, we find that:

$$\frac{\partial W(p_i)}{\partial R_j} = \frac{\partial W(p_i)}{\partial p_j} \cdot \frac{\partial p_j}{\partial R_j} = a_j \frac{\partial \Pi(p_i)}{\partial p_j} + N\left[a_j b_j\left(\frac{1}{N} M_j(p_j) + \frac{1}{N}(p_j - p_w) M_j'(p_j)\right) - a_j d_j(p_j)\right]$$

Which can be re-written as

$$\text{(16)} \qquad \frac{\partial W(p_i)}{\partial R_j} = a_j^2 b_j R_j M_j'(p_j) + a_j b_j M_j(p_j) - a_j\left(D_j(p_j) - H(p_j)\right)$$

To find equilibrium levels of regulation now, insert equation (15) and (16) into (12) to find:

$$a_j(I_j + c) H_j(p_j) + (\alpha_L + c) a_j b_j M_j(p_j) + (\alpha_L + c) a_j^2 b_j R_j^0 M_j'(p_j) - (\alpha_L + c) a_j D_j(p_j) = 0$$

$$\Leftrightarrow a_j(I_j + c) H_j(p_j) + (\alpha_L + c) a_j\left[b_j M_j(p_j) + a_j b_j R_j^0 M_j'(p_j) - D_j(p_j)\right] = 0$$

From which follows:

$$\text{(17)} \qquad R^0 = -\frac{(I_j + c) H_j(p_j)}{a_j b_j (\alpha_L + c) M_j'(p_j)} - \frac{M_j(p_j)}{a_j M_j'(p_j)} + \frac{D_j(p_j)}{a_j b_j M_j'(p_j)}$$

This R^0 reflects the level of regulation a government will set respect to problems such as non-tariff barriers in the absence of state liability.

Now, when attempting to express this R^0 a bit more clear, take $F \equiv \frac{\partial \Pi_j(p_j)}{\partial p_j} / \frac{\partial M_j(p_j)}{\partial p_j} = \frac{d \Pi_j(p_j)}{d M_j(p_j)}$ is the impact of price driven import changes on domestic producers' capital rewards. Then, using Hotelling's Lemma and Roy's Identity again, we reach:

$$\text{(18)} \qquad \mathbf{R}^0 = \frac{F}{a}\left(1 - \frac{I_j + c}{b(\alpha_L + c)}\right) + \frac{b-1}{ab}\frac{d(CS)}{dM}$$

The level of regulation **R** thus changes in the light of F and d(CS)/dM.

- The more changes in the levels of imports affect domestic producers' profits in a positive way, the more decision-makers will attempt to regulate imports.
- A high alfa value reflects a powerful lobby group. If alfa is high, the level of protection R will be high as well. Formula (18) somewhat hides this reasoning. However, such high alfa will typically go hand in hand with a high level of organisation I. Then, given that $0 \leq b_i \leq 1$, the product of the first factor in the sum will be positive and will result in a high level of regulation.
- No general conclusions can be drawn from the welfare weighting of governments. The effect of the relative weight attached to general welfare vis-à-vis producers' welfare is unclear. This is a consequence of the introduction of the usefulness *b* of regulation in this model.
- Levels of regulation will increase with the influence of changes in the volumes of imports on consumers' surplus.

B. Introducing member state liability

Now, assume liability exists and a finding of liability is subject to uncertainty.[372] In cases of international trade discussed here, the main concern of European law is to prevent levels of national regulation being set too high. Hence, when setting **R** higher than a uncertain level $\mathbf{R}_H$, member states will certainly be held liable for the breach. When setting **R** lower than a known level $\mathbf{R}_L$, member states will certainly escape liability.

If $\mathbf{R}_L < \mathbf{R} < \mathbf{R}_H$, the likelihood of a member state being held liable is given by a distribution function P.

P=P(**R**), with $P(\mathbf{R}_L) = 0$, $P(\mathbf{R}_H) = 1$, 0< P(**R**)<1 if $\mathbf{R}_L < \mathbf{R} < \mathbf{R}_H$, and P´(**R**)>0.

---

[372] This assumptions seems realistic since European law is subject to a large deal of interpretational uncertainty.

P´(**R**) is the probability density function.
Private parties' damage compensation will then amount to the difference between the profits of foreign producers if they had not been discriminated and the profits they actually made under the discriminating regulation. Accounting for the uncertainty however, the expected damage compensation (DC) of foreign exporters is then equal to the difference of their profits at the expected maximum regulatory value which the European Court of Justice is anticipated to tolerate and their profits at the chosen regulatory level multiplied with the probability of being liable at this level.[373]

$$(19) \qquad DC = \int_{R_L}^{R_H} P'(\sigma)\prod_F(\sigma)d\sigma - P(\mathbf{R})\prod_F(\mathbf{R}) \text{ for } \mathbf{R_L} < \mathbf{R} < \mathbf{R_H}$$

If the chosen regulatory level is equal or higher than the upper threshold $\mathbf{R_H}$, the expected compensation is:

$$(20) \qquad DC = \int_{R_L}^{R_H} P'(\sigma)\prod_F(\sigma)d\sigma - \prod_F(\mathbf{R})$$

Now, let us see how these damage compensation costs, which were anticipated for ex-ante, alter the decision-making process. Damage compensation to foreign producers is not seen as mere redistribution, but as a cost to be paid for by the domestic citizens (and thus also interest groups).

Besides a monetary effect which, in most cases, will be rather small on a per capita basis, the obligation for a member state to pay damage compensation can earn a political dimension as well. This non-monetary dimension is taken into account by introducing a variable A which expresses the general public's political dissatisfaction or agitation.

We assume individuals have political preferences on N issues. Parliamentary elections are seen as "block votes", in which voters' opinion is asked on a package deal consisting of ideas on N different issues. When one considers an election as such a *block* or *package vote*, the applicability of the median voter theory becomes problematic. Indeed, the median voter theory can only give information on voters' position on one (*closed* block of) specific issue(s). The question at hand here is

[373] See Schäfer and van den Bergh, 2001 at page 16

however in how far a (i.e.: *one*) topic might influence the outcome of a package vote. As is illustrated by the following simplified example, for politicians to *obey* the median voter in every topic of the package does not guarantee a majority, since voters may have different preferences over the N topics.

Consider a parliamentary vote where only two issues play a role: police presence on the streets*(PP)* and the height of company tax *(CT)*. Two political parties L(eft) and R(ight) compete for the voters' support and offer decisions on both issues ranging from 1 *(very low)* to 5 *(very high)*. The voting population consists of three individuals V1, V2 and V3. The table below documents their crude preference on both issues. Note that crude preferences are normally distributed. Not all voters care equally for both issues (V1 does). Every voter attaches a relative weight to the issues at stake and cumulative individual weights equal 1. Whereas voter 2 cares greatly about company taxes, he can't really be bothered about police presence. Voter 3 is his mirror image.

Preferences&action → on Issues ↓	1	2	3	4	5	Winner of a 1 issue vote
PP **Party position**	0,5V1		0,1V2 **party L**		0,9V3 **party R**	**Party L** (2votes) over Party R (1 vote)
CT **Party position**	0,5V1		0,1V3 **party L**		0,9V2 **party R**	**Party L** (2votes) over Party R (1 vote)

When voting on both issues separately, party L, which took the median voter position, earns a majority on both issues over party R which represents the opinion of voters at the right side of the political spectrum. In these "one-issue-votes", the relative importance of issues to voters doesn't play a role. Given that the topic is important enough for voters to participate in the vote, they will choose the party closest to their opinion.

When considering a *block vote* on {PP; CT}, the outcome of the voting process changes.

Clearly, voter V1 will prefer party L, which on both issues is closest to his preferences.
For Voter V2, the decision is not quite that easy. Party L represents exactly his opinion on police presence, but party R expresses his ideas in corporate taxation problems. Since voter V2's interest in the tax issue is nine times as high as his preoccupation with police presence, he will give his vote to party R. For similar reasons, voter V3 will vote for party R as well.

Concluding, **party R** wins the package vote, although it did not follow the median voter theory as party L did. The introduction of the intensity of preferences illustrates the problems of a median voter approach in block votes. For these reasons, this approach will not be applied here.

Coming back to the model now, the political preferences every individual i has on the N different issues translate into a preferred, *ideal* level of care for European legislation concerning topic t by voter i : ID_{it}. R_{eut} is the level of regulation for topic t which would be compatible with European law. R_{nat} is the national level chosen for topic t. The divergence between both gives rises to a function of individual political unhappiness a_{it}

$$(21) \quad a_{it} = \frac{R_{eut} + R_{nat} - 2ID_{it}}{R_{eut}} \quad , \forall\, t \in [1,N]$$

This function is valid for the case of trade issues dealt with in this model. In the issues, the European level of regulation will typically be lower than the one member states attempt to set. Graphically:

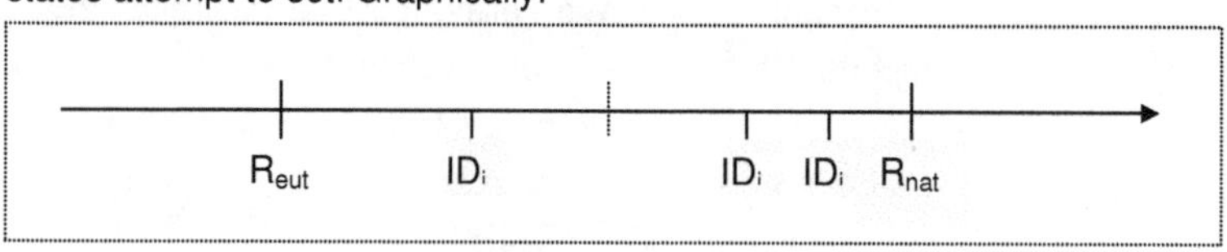

This construction of political unhappiness allows us to take into account a possible enlarged or diminished effect of a state liability judgement. Voters have different ideal levels of care ID_t for every topic t. Roughly however, we can distinguish between those voters to the left and those the right of the middle of the position between R_{eut} and R_{nat}. If voters are nationalist or prefer stricter (more protective) legislation than what is foreseen for in the treaties, this variable a_{it} will be negative and -as will be shown below- will lead to a lower weighting of the damage compensation than when considering only its monetary consequences. Thus, **the rally around the flag** phenomenon will be simulated.

For voters who are more on the European side, the obligation for their government to pay damage compensation will serve as a **signal for bad government**. They will attach a higher weight to the damage compensation.

Additionally, to make this model more realistic, consider a weight φ_{it} which reflects the relative importance of topic t to voter i. $\sum_{t=1}^{n} \varphi_{it} = 1, \forall i$. The total political agitation for an individual i is then: $a_i = \varphi_i \frac{R_{eut} + R_{nat} - 2ID_{it}}{R_{eut}}$. This refinement seems to make sense, since a clear disagreement with a political choice [meaning $\frac{R_{eut} + R_{nat} - 2ID_{it}}{R_{eut}}$ is large] does not necessarily lead to a change in voting behaviour. Of importance is also the significance to the voter of the issue at stake, the increased media attention devoted to the topic caused by a possible state liability judgement or the possible lack of personal interest, given low per capita cost of a damage compensation payment.

Aggregating individual ideals and political agitation for the whole voting population, we get

$$(22) \quad A = \varphi \frac{R_{eu} + R_{na} - 2ID}{R_{eu}}$$

Finally, we now introduce a discount factor r. We believe political frustration in the voting population is more important the closer to an election it occurs. Assume a government period of four years and y being the time left to the next election (y ∈ [1,4].) We thus identify $A^{y=1}$, $A^{y=2}$, $A^{y=3}$ and $A^{y=4}$. The present value A_θ of A is then

$$(23) \quad A_\theta = \frac{A^{y=1}}{1+r} + \frac{A^{y=2}}{(1+r)^2} + \frac{A^{y=3}}{(1+r)^3} + \frac{A^{y=4}}{(1+r)^4}$$

These damage costs change the decision process. In the same way as under the absence of state liability rules, we calculate the equilibrium.

$$(24)\quad \frac{\partial W_i(p_i)}{\partial R_j} = \partial_{ij} a_j H_j(p_j) + \alpha_i a_j b_j M_j(p_j) + \alpha_i a_j b_j (p_j - p_w) M_j^{'}(p_j) - \alpha_i a_j D_j(p_j) - \alpha(1+A_\theta) DC'(R_j)$$

where $\partial_{ij} = 1$ for i=j and 0 otherwise and

$DC'(R_j) = P'(R_j)\prod_F(R_j) - P'(Rj)\prod_F(R_j) - P(R_j)\prod_F^{'}(R_j) = -P(R_j)\prod_F^{'}(R_j) > 0$

Summing over all i

(25)

$$\sum_{i\in L} \frac{\partial W_i(p_i)}{\partial R_j} = a_j I_j H_j(p_j) + \alpha_L a_j b_j M_j(p_j) + \alpha_L a_j^2 b_j R_j M_j^{'}(p_j) - \alpha_L a_j D_j(p_j) + \alpha_L(1+A_\theta) P(R_j)\prod_F^{'}(R_j)$$

with $I_j = \sum_{i\in L} \partial_{ij}$ being a measure for the organisation of industry j which is 1 if the industry is organised and 0 otherwise. $\alpha_L \equiv \sum_{i\in L} \alpha_i$ and denotes the fraction of population organised in interest groups.

Similarly,

$$(26)\quad \frac{\partial W(p_j)}{\partial R_j} = a_j^2 b_j R_j M_j^{'}(p_j) + a_j b_j M_j(p_j) - a_j\left[D_j(p_j) - H(p_j)\right] + (1+A_\theta) P(R_j)\prod_F^{'}(R_j)$$

Using equation (12) as equilibrium condition, (25) and (26) give:

$$a_j(I_j + c)H_j(p_j) + (\alpha_L + c) a_j b_j M_j(p_j) + (\alpha_L + c) a_j^2 b_j R_j^0 M_j^{'}(p_j) -$$
$$(\alpha_L + c) a_j D_j(p_j) + (\alpha_L + c)(1+A_\theta) P(R_j)\prod_F^{'}(R_j) = 0$$

$$\Leftrightarrow a_j(I_j + c)H_j(p_j) + (\alpha_L + c)\left[a_j b_j M_j(p_j) + a_j^2 b_j R_j^0 M_j^{'}(p_j) - a_j D_j(p_j) + (1+A_\theta) P(R_j)\prod_F^{'}(R_j)\right] = 0$$

which results in

$$(27)\quad \mathbf{R}_{\mathbf{SL}}^{\mathbf{0}} = -\frac{(I_j + c) H_j(p_j)}{a_j b_j (\alpha_L + c) M_j^{'}(p_j)} - \frac{M_j(p_j)}{a_j M_j^{'}(p_j)} + \frac{D_j(p_j)}{a_j b_j M_j^{'}(p_j)} - \frac{(1+A_\theta) P(R_j)\prod_F^{'}(R_j)}{a_j^2 b_j M_j^{'}(p_j)}$$

Using the same notation as above:

$$(28) \qquad \mathbf{R}^0_{\mathbf{SL}} = \frac{F}{a}\left(1-\frac{I_j+c}{b\left(\alpha_L+c\right)}\right)+\frac{b-1}{ab}\frac{d(CS)}{dM}-\frac{(1+A_\theta)P(R_j)\prod_F^{'}(R_j)}{a_j^2 b_j M_j^{'}(p_j)}$$

As explained in previous chapters, the state liability legislation is not installed with the aim to minimise costs as is the case in private tort law; but aims at a goal of compliance with European law.

As enforcement will inevitably take place when private individuals proceed against member states, the goal of a breaching member state is to reap the benefits of breaching as long as possible. State Liability law can be said to be effective when it manages to deter national governments to set a level of **R** above $\mathbf{R}_\mathbf{H}$. Indeed, pure ex-post law enforcement can be dealt with without liability, as is demonstrated by the Court's and the Commission's public enforcement efforts. The aim of European legislation in the area under discussion here is however to *prevent* (and not just to cure) a level of national regulation too high, as was summarised in section 5.5.

As can be seen when comparing formulas (18) and (28), the ex-ante anticipation of possible liability leads to a change in the chosen level of regulation of $\mathbf{R}^0\text{-}\mathbf{R}^0_{\mathbf{SL}} = \frac{(1+A_\theta)P(R_j)\prod_F^{'}(R_j)}{a_j^2 b_j M_j^{'}(p_j)} = \frac{(1+A_\theta)}{a_j b_j}P(R_j)\frac{d\prod_F}{dM}$ when $\mathbf{R}_\mathbf{L} < \mathbf{R} < \mathbf{R}_\mathbf{H}$.

As this expression exceeds zero, this results in a lower level of regulation. Deterrence hence works, but what remains to be seen is to which extent it does. In other words, does this factor make $\mathbf{R}_\mathbf{0}^{\mathbf{SL}} < \mathbf{R}_\mathbf{H}$?

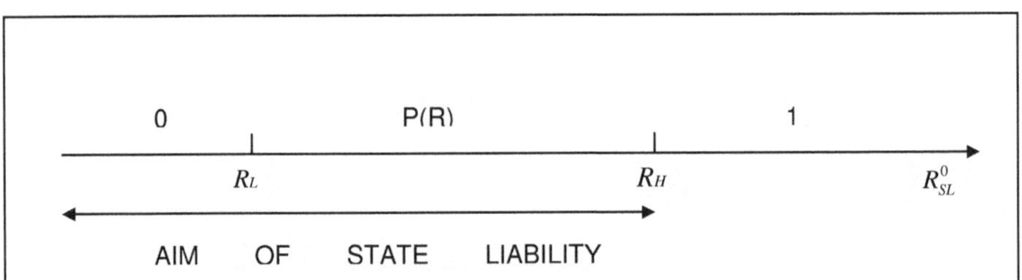

Of interest now is to express the level $\mathbf{R}_\mathbf{H}$ which the European Court of Justice might claim to be the upper level of regulation still compatible with European legislation.

Considering that the area of regulation under analysis is prone to be subject to economic thinking, also by the Court; it is assumed that the European Court of Justice will compare the safety benefits of national regulatory measures hindering free movement of goods with their costs to foreign producers. Costs to foreign producers will be measured as foregone profits.

Hence, national impediments of free trade will be allowed as long as:

$$-\frac{\partial \Pi_F}{\partial \mathbf{R}} < \frac{\partial V(\mathbf{R})}{\partial \mathbf{R}} z$$

Where z is larger or equal to 1 reflects the uncertainty inherent to the interpretation of European law and the preparedness of the European Court of Justice to act against member states. The Court has decided to hold member states liable only in cases where the breach has been sufficiently serious. In other words, it has applied a value of z, which is rather high. One could imagine this uncertainty (the z) becoming smaller as the number of judgements as well as the experience with and acceptance of European law grows.

Note that this is by no means a guarantee for economically efficient outcomes. Typically, the discrimination of foreign producers will cause benefits to domestic producers: a case of pure financial losses. The ever dominating interpretation of the free movement of goods provisions under European law however, has focussed solely on losses caused to foreign producers, and on how those relate to potential gains which are recognised under article 30 of the Treaty. Following this interpretation, gains to domestic producers are not to be considered. In economic terms, the welfare effect of protective measures on domestic and foreign markets is analysed incompletely. By excluding the gains those measures cause to domestic producers, the European Court of Justice's interpretation will be too strict, from a pure economic point of view.[374]

This is another example where economic reasoning and legal doctrine clash. However connected free trade regulation and economic welfare theory might be, current legal interpretation in the European Union is not aimed at welfare maximisation. Mirroring the political idea behind realising a common European market, the stress is laid on enforcing non-discriminatory ideas.

---

[374] Note that changes in foreign and domestic producers' surpluses caused by protective measures are more than mere redistributions between producers. Both groups of producers are subject to different cost functions, which is the reason why trade occurred in the first place.

Having said this, at $\mathbf{R_H}: -\frac{\partial \Pi_F}{\partial \mathbf{R}} = \frac{\partial V(\mathbf{R})}{\partial \mathbf{R}} z$

Applying Roy's Identity and Hotelling's Lemma, we reach:

$$-\frac{\partial \Pi_F}{\partial R_j} = z a_j b_j \left(M(Rj) + \mathbf{R_H} \frac{dM}{dR_j} \right)$$

$$\Leftrightarrow \mathbf{R_H} = -\frac{1}{a_j b_j z} \left(\frac{\partial \Pi_F}{\partial M} \right) - \frac{M(R_j)}{M_j^{'}(R_j)}$$

Meaning that

$$\text{(29)} \qquad \mathbf{R_H} = -\frac{1}{a_j b_j z} \frac{d\Pi_F}{dM} + \frac{1}{a_j} \left(\frac{dCS}{dM} + F \right)$$

Now that the aim of state liability is formalised, let's see under which conditions deterrence can be expected to be successful.

Given a certain value z, a deterrence effect can be said to be present if and only if :

$$\mathbf{R_{SL}^0} < \mathbf{R_H}$$

$$\Leftrightarrow \frac{F}{a}\left(1 - \frac{I_j + c}{b(\alpha_L + c)}\right) + \frac{b-1}{ab}\frac{d(CS)}{dM} - (1 + A_\theta)\frac{P(Rj)}{ab}\frac{d\Pi_F}{dM} - \frac{1}{a}\left(\frac{dCS}{dM} + F\right) + \frac{1}{abz}\frac{d\Pi_F}{dM} < 0$$

$$\Leftrightarrow \frac{F}{a}\left(-\frac{I_j + c}{b(\alpha_L + c)}\right) - \frac{1}{ab}\frac{d(CS)}{dM} - \frac{1}{ab}\frac{d\Pi_F}{dM}\left((1 + A_\theta)P(Rj) - \frac{1}{z}\right) < 0$$

$$\Leftrightarrow -\frac{I_j + c}{(\alpha_L + c)}F - \frac{d(CS)}{dM} - \frac{d\Pi_F}{dM}\left((1 + A_\theta)P(Rj) - \frac{1}{z}\right) < 0$$

$$\text{(30)} \qquad \mathbf{R_{SL}^0} < \mathbf{R_H} \Leftrightarrow -\frac{I_j + c}{(\alpha_L + c)}F - \frac{d(CS)}{dM} < \frac{d\Pi_F}{dM}\left((1 + A_\theta)P(Rj) - \frac{1}{z}\right)$$

Obviously, a deterrence effect is obtained easier when *z (i.e.: the reluctance of the Court to hold a breach of sufficiently serious) is higher.*[375] This doesn't necessarily imply any changes in the member state's behaviour however, it merely means that

---

[375] If z is higher, R_H will be higher as well. This z expresses the willingness of the Court to allow higher levels of regulation. Whether one can still consider the effect on states to be "deterrence" remains a matter of personal opinion.

being found liable is more difficult since the Court has set the allowed level of regulation rather high.

Finally, let's now have a closer look at the final conclusion from the model: the conditions under which deterrence against member states can function. The condition for this function was:

$$-\frac{I_j + c}{(\alpha_L + c)}F - \frac{d(CS)}{dM} < \frac{d\Pi_F}{dM}\left((1 + A_\theta)P(Rj) - \frac{1}{z}\right)$$

Note that both factors at the left side of the inequality are positive.

- The better industry is organised, the more likely the variable I_j will take on value 1 instead of 0. Ceteris paribus, In these cases, $-\frac{I_j + c}{(\alpha_L + c)}F$ will be higher (and positive) and compliance with European law is more difficult to obtain.

- The fraction of population an interest group represents is noted by α_L. Interestingly, the larger the relative size of an interest group, the smaller the likelihood that this will make a member states ignore state liability and breach Community law. Clearly, this is the result of the construction of the model. The "organisation" will be more and more similar to the consumers it represents and these consumer interests are weighted as well when calculating this group's welfare.

- F is the impact of import changes on domestic producers' capital rewards. This effect is negative. When these capital rewards are only moderately influenced by changes in imports, c.p. the left side on the inequality will be smaller and the conditions for deterrence against breaches will be reached easier. This sounds acceptable, since in this situation one might expect producers to have less incentives to push for import discrimination through a higher level of regulation.

The right hand side of formula (30) expresses the expected damage compensation for a breaching member state. The basis of such damage compensation is the loss of foreign producers: $\frac{d\prod_F}{dM}$.

- The introduction of punitive damages would make this right hand side higher, creating (ceteris paribus!) easier deterrence. In the current scenario, the expected damage compensation is influenced by two uncommon factors: A_θ and z.

- The variable z exceeds 1 and reflects the uncertainty inherent to the interpretation of European law and the preparedness of the European Court of Justice to act against member states. In any case, this z will decrease the expected damage compensation. The Court has decided to hold member states liable only in cases where the breach has been sufficiently serious. In other words, it has applied a value of z, which is rather high. The higher z, the larger the right-hand side of (30) and the sooner $\mathbf{R}_{SL}^{0} < \mathbf{R}_{H}$. Deterrence will be reached. The problematic character of this conclusion has been explained. Note that a high z, in combination with a low probability P(Rj) for member states of being held liable at a regulatory level Rj, makes deterrence highly unlikely.

- The political agitation A_θ as well influences the expected damage compensation. When the weighted opinion of the general public reflects a wish for a significantly higher level of regulation than European legislation foresees, the variable $(1+A_\theta)$, taking account of both monetary and political effects, will turn below one and will cause decision-makers to take account only of a part of the financial cost of a damage compensation payment. For such voting public, a higher damage compensation might be necessary. For a European friendly public, the conviction to pay damage compensation might signal them bad governance by their national government. The damage compensation will receive extra political attention.

The concept of *political opinion* (ID) should be understood widely. As was noted in the empirical chapter, the length of membership in the European Union was significant in explaining for breaches. The size of a member state might however explain for a higher reluctance of the public to accept European decisions and sanctions. In such nations, the weighted position ID might be more to the right and $(1+A_\theta)$ thus smaller than one.

Also, the high relative importance of an issue can explain for the lack of deterrence. In fact, a great deal of the cases observed where a member state was found liable (and deterrence hence didn't function) concerned such situations of symbols of "national pride", which might carry a high relative weight to voters. In such cases as well, only a fraction of the damage compensation will be internalised by decision-makers.

Clearly, the political discount rate will play a role as well. If voters tend to "forget" conflicts with their government rather fast (a high discount rate), the present value A_θ of political dissatisfaction will turn out less extreme. The political punishing or supportive (from the point of view of the breaching government) correction of the damage compensation effect will be smaller. This as well might be supported by the empirical data. The fact that larger member states breach more might mean than they have a higher discount rate. The damage compensation payment would lose a lot of its political dimension and only the -arguably rather weak- monetary effect would remain. Why then, would voters in larger countries have higher discount rates? One possible explanation could be that, in larger countries, there simply occurs more. Media attention to breaches might well be smaller and the number of political "bads" and "goods" is larger, which might result in voters forgetting faster.

- Finally, P(Rj) expresses the probability of being held liable at a level of regulation Rj. When it is more likely for member states *-given a certain strictness z of Courts-* to be forced by a Court to pay damage compensation at a given level of regulation, we can expect them to be deterred faster. This might not be surprising, but has great consequences for the comparative evaluation of private and public enforcement mechanisms. In past chapters, the current relative (dis)advantages of both mechanisms have been discussed and a mixed image resulted. In the absence of punitive damages or credible group action threats and even given solutions for numerous procedural difficulties, private enforcement can only occasionally deliver a reasonable threat, i.e.: a high P(Rj). Action by the Commission is more of a threat to member states, but the lack of a first-order deterrence manifestly decreases P(R). In the current situation, member states are exposed to an extremely low probability of being held liable.

10.3.4 Policy Conclusions

In the remaining part of this last chapter, we can now apply the current reality of state liability in the European Union to the conclusions of this model. In other words: do the existing rules facilitate compliance or do they make it less likely?

A. The Status Quo

The condition for compliance (Formula 30) contains exogenous variables on the left side of the inequality and (partly) policy variables on its right side. Whereas the exogenous fact remain identical, the policy variables might be set differently in the two legal remedies discussed in this work. Three such policy variables can be identified: P(Rj), z and $\frac{d\Pi_F}{dM}$. The analysis of their working is interdependent.

Starting with the latter, $\frac{d\Pi_F}{dM}$ is the basis for setting damage compensation in the Francovich state liability cases. When the Commission takes a member states to Court for a breach of Community law, the sanction is calculated on a different basis. (See section 9.1)

It is difficult to compare the height, and hence the deterrence effect of both damage compensations. Commissionary action can indeed lead to high sanctions (even higher ones if the discussed case against France is decided in the line of Advocate General Geelhoed's proposals), but as will be repeated below, through a low probability of being held liable, this potential deterrence effect most often disappears. On the other hand, the damage compensation $\frac{d\Pi_F}{dM}$, resulting from private action will in most cases be too small to have a serious deterrence effect. Individual victims' damages will in most cases hardly be large enough to cause a member state to think twice about breaching.

Concluding, only the height of the public enforcement action can in theory be high enough to impress a breaching member state. It is unlikely that individual victims' harm is large enough to impress member states.

This is of course not a sufficient reason to judge public enforcement superior to private action. The nominal height of a damage compensation should be seen together with its probability of occurring: **$P(R_j)$.**

For the public enforcement by the Commission, the effect of introducing this probability-weighting is quite clear. The expected damage compensation of a temporary breach (*temporary* meaning a member states is willing to eventually agree with the Commission on a compromise) is zero and there simply **exists no ex-ante deterrence against breaching.**

The reasons for this have been discussed in detail, the main one however is the necessity for the case to be heard before the European Court of Justice **twice**, before a fine can be set. This fine is thus in effect set for the breach of a Court judgement, not for the initial breach of Community law.

In these cases, the right side of the inequality in (30) will be so small that an effective deterrence against breaches of Community law does not take place. For such deterrence to occur, it is essential to higher the expected fine. Increasing the fine -as suggested by Advocate General Geelhoed- is one way to reach this aim. Another one is to higher the probability $P(R_j)$ of being fined, for example, by allowing the European Court of Justice to fine member states for the breach of Community law and not only for the non-respect for its judgement.

For reasons which we will clarify shortly below, we believe that Geelhoed's approach is a superior one.

Before that, let's first treat the expected damage compensation costs of private action. In this case, the picture is mixed. As just argued, the nominal damage of most single individual claimants will be rather low, given the rather special character of a state's budget constraint. Moreover, as explained on page 169, the probability $P(R_j)$

for member states to be held liable will be rather small, given that a number of legal and procedural limits exists before individuals can successfully sue a state. However, in a small number of cases, group action has been facilitated and the expected damage cost might grow to deter member states.

The conclusions below will suggest changes to increase the expected damage compensation and make deterrence more likely. We believe changes to both variables $P(R_j)$ and $\frac{d\prod_F}{dM}$ are necessary in this case.

The third and final policy variable is the factor z, taking into account the relative reluctance of judges to make member states liable in damages for breaches of community law. This is formalised in the condition of a finding of a "sufficiently serious breach", before liability is established. Over time, judges have interpreted the non-transposition of directives as a sufficient breach per se, and have thus successfully differentiated between cases.

B. Recommendations

For the sake of clarity, we distinguish between four different breach scenarios. This distinction is based on the one first made in Chapter 3.1 on page 15.

We identify:

1. Non-transposition or late transposition of a directive
2. Non-proper incorporation of a directive in domestic law
3. Non-proper application of a directive (concerns national law)
4. Violations of Treaty provisions, Regulations and Decisions

For the **first group** of cases, the Court has already lowered barriers for member states to being found liable. The non-transposition or late transposition of a directive counts as a "sufficiently serious breach" and thus fulfils by definition one of the three liability conditions (in the following: the *Brasserie Conditions*) set by the Court in its Brasserie Case. (see page 92)

This, together with the duty for member states to inform the Commission on transposition measures has led to impressively positive numbers of compliance. As argued on page 24, these positive numbers deceive. Member states will transpose "something", in order to escape the direct qualification as "sufficiently serious breach" and scenario 2 will be more of a problem.

Despite this "unwanted side-effect", we support the Court's jurisdiction to immediately qualify the lack of transposition as a sufficiently serious breach.

Nevertheless, this process is not finished. The *Brasserie Conditions* also stipulate that the rule or law must be intended to confer rights upon individuals and that there must be a direct causal link between the breach and the damage of the injured parties. Many directives may not satisfy these conditions and the Francovich doctrine hence remains unavailable upon breaches of such directives.

Since the non-transposition or late transposition of directives is such a clear and obvious breach of Community law, we suggest to widen the application of the Francovich liability also to directives not granting rights to individuals. In these cases, qualified entities should be allowed to proceed against member states and should receive a sufficiently high punitive damage. Concerning directives which do grant individuals certain rights, we suggest granting locus standing to all individuals (i.e.: also those not fulfilling the third Brasserie Condition) for the initial proceeding only. The first successful claimant should receive a deterring punitive damage.[376] *All consequent proceedings concerning the same directive can then only be initiated by affected individuals, which should be compensated in simple damages. Given the first cases, legal costs to the individuals should remain small.*

It is most important that a credible sanction exists for member states which breach community law so obviously as by not or late transposing a directive. The breach is easily observable and there is no legal uncertainty: hence private enforcement is an adequate instrument that should be equipped with convincing tools. Given such functioning private tool, we see no reason for the Commission to become active here. Ideally, private enforcement would be a fast working mechanism to ascertain that the

---

[376] We believe the costs of the resulting "patent race" phenomenon will be neutralized by the informational benefit of this case to all other "true" victims.

probability function $P(R_j)$ expresses the chance for an elected executive of being held liable while still in office.

The creation of this conditioned strict liability for non or late transposition of a directive has without doubt caused member states to transpose "something" timely, in order to avert this liability. The **second group** of breaches, those of directives badly transposed into domestic law, has hence gained importance.

It is important that this group of cases does not escape a credible enforcement mechanism. Once these directives have been transposed, they become national law. Conflicts on state acts allegedly breaching such badly transposed directive would then be treated in national law, making the threat of damage compensation (and thus deterrence against badly transposing directives) considerably smaller.

Similar to group 1 cases, the existing legal arrangements do not guarantee such credible threat. Differently to non or late transposed directives, cases of badly transposed directives are subject to a higher level of legal uncertainty. However, the member state can be said to be better informed on inherent risks than its citizens. Hence, for directives which grant individual rights and where the claimant's own damage is caused by the breach (Brasserie Conditions 1 & 3), we would <u>introduce and massively facilitate group action</u> to compensate for the costs of this uncertainty. Of course, the uncertainty goes for the transposing legislator as well. Therefore, US-style <u>class action seems to create overdeterrence.</u> <u>Punitive damages</u> should be reserved for cases of <u>severe breaches.</u>[377]

Similarly as in group 1 cases, the bad transposition of directives failing a granting of individual rights should be left to <u>qualified entities</u> to proceed against. A <u>punitive damage</u> is more appropriate here since the number of victims will be smaller and a market-based damage will only occur in very few cases.

For cases where this private mechanism would not function (especially the group action might be dependent on national rules and circumstances), the <u>European</u>

---

[377] Severe breaches are not to be confused with sufficiently serious breaches. We believe the sufficiently serious breaches doctrine to be meaningful, given the inherent uncertainty about compliance with European law.

Commission might take action against states as well. However -and differently as in the case of breaches against the treaties or regulations- , upon a sufficiently serious breach, fines should be made available to the Commission already in the first Court hearing.

There is undoubtedly a level of legal uncertainty in the act of transposing directives into national law. The Court –through its factor z and the sufficiently serious breach doctrine - has sufficient instruments at its disposal to take this into account and to guarantee that member states are not exposed to a liability risk too high.

In the interest of member states as well as of legal interest (and thus also of individuals) it seems appropriate to install a time constraint to act against a bad transposition of a directive.

The **third** group of cases concerns directives which are not properly applied. Through their transposition, these directives have become national law and any breaches against these provisions will be treated by national law. The Court has set minimum standards to this national state liability law. Although there is no data readily available on the number of cases applying these national procedures, there is little reason to assume that breaches of this category would occur less frequently than other ones. At the same time, one can doubt that national state liability rules are stricter than the ones put into place by the Court. When hurdles to effective private enforcement would occur, and given the possibility to identify European born national legislation, one might consider applying the stricter, European state liability law to these breaches.

Also for the **final group** of cases including breaches of treaty provisions, regulations and decisions, changes can be formulated. For these cases, a distinction has to be made between cases subject to a relatively high and low level of legal uncertainty. Judges seem the only authority able to do this.[378] Cases with a relatively low level of legal uncertainty are well suited to be treated by individuals. We propose a mixture of the instruments discussed above.

---

[378] In effect, they already partly include this considerations through the sufficiently serious breach doctrine.

Starting with cases of relatively low legal uncertainty which concern breaches of provisions granting individual rights, breaches should give rise to simple damage compensation. As before with the transposition of directives, group action should be enabled and promoted. In cases of severe breaches under low legal uncertainty, judges should be able to award the first individually affected claimant punitive damages, all following ones should be awarded simple damage compensation.

Similarly as in group 1 and 2 cases, provisions subject to low legal uncertainty failing a granting of individual rights should be left to qualified entities to proceed against. For the same reasons as above, a punitive damage is appropriate here also in cases of non-severe breaches.

A final novelty is reserved for cases with a relatively high legal uncertainty. These cases should become the core task of the Commission's public enforcement activities. Resources spent on different sources of law should be concentrated here. We believe some cases show an uncertainty which is so high that member states could not avoid breaching community law. Exposing member states to liability in these cases will not result in compliance.

The commission should actively, and much faster than is the case now, use the notices of the general public about alleged breaches to take contact with member states. Also, judgements of the European Court of Justice should be sought much faster than is the case now, since these offer a final clarification of the legal situation.

Given this clarification, the case of relatively low legal uncertainty applies and individuals as well can take action. Upon a continuing breach, the advice of Advocate-General Geelhoed should be followed and member states should be fined starting from the first day of the breach following this first judgement. This way, the commission serves as an enforcer of last resort and would better serve its role as guardian of the treaties.

Summary

This economic discussion of the non-contractual liability of Member States of the European Union started with some thoughts on the importance of the enforcement of law. In fact, over the course of the whole argument, different aspects of law-enforcement played a major role.

However surprising the use of liability - a classical law and economics instrument for the minimisation of accident costs - might be to reach such an unusual aim as law-enforcement, throughout this study, it was attempted to illustrate the sound theoretical basis for such goal.

The problem dealt with here was found to have various experimental features.

Firstly, only very rarely, the topic of supranational law enforcement in the European Union has been treated in an economic fashion. Scholars in legal and political science have written extensively in the field, but in lack of an adequate method, economists have long ignored the topic. In this work, the framework and findings of the relatively new law and economics literature was applied to the topic of law enforcement through state liability.

Secondly, however helpful, the standard answers emerging from this law and economics scheme could not satisfy. Indeed, it was at first rather unclear how the facts under analysis were to fit in this scheme. Member states' breaching and the following reaction show elements of both *contract law*, *tort law* and -of course- *law enforcement*. Legal rules are similar to those products analysed by contract law, the instruments applied are those of tort law, but the aim -as was found out- is similar to the one of law enforcement.

Additionally, in the fields of contract law and especially tort law, the well-established findings and methods of the law and economics literature were to be *applied to* an actor which has typically been left out of law and economic textbooks: the state. In the field of law enforcement, the complication was found in the *applying* actor: instead of public enforcement by the state, the role of the individual as enforcer was shed light upon.
The special nature of the European context was acknowledged by an introductory chapter presenting the basic European institutions and the essentials of the

Community's legal framework. After that, we started with a thorough analysis of breaches of European Community law: to which extent do they occur; how do we explain them, given that member states agreed with the rules concerning breaches and what is the legal answer to those breaches?

On the first question, we introduced and discussed in detail the data on breaches from the Commission's annual reports. Unfortunately, the quality and the one-sightedness of this data did not allow us to form ourselves a clear impression of the dimension of the breaching problem. In fact, more questions than answers arose. We concluded that the optimist data offered by the Commission does not necessarily reflect a high implementation of European law. The data could not provide us with any information on the role of private enforcement and -fiercely opposed to mainstream scholarship's opinion- implies that the European Union does not suffer from a severe non-compliance problem.

Following, we attempted to better understand breaching states by means of empirical analysis. Understanding why member states act as they do is indeed a necessary condition to being able to influence this very acting. The identification of independent variables was followed by extensive data gathering. The limits of the available data - only public enforcement data is available- was used to gain insights over the effect of the Commission's enforcement efforts.

The results of this empirical analysis made it possible to explain member states' breaches by means of different explanatory variables. Most interestingly, a high number of variables was found to be of no statistical significance in explaining for breaches. Whether a state is governed centrally or in a federal way, its level of corporatism as well as the instability of its political system (frequency of governmental changes or the number of parties in government) proved to be of no statistical relevance.

On the other hand, the size of a member state's economy as well as its (correlating) voting power in the Council relate positively with the number of infringement proceedings initiated against a member state. A considerable part of this relation can be explained only with the willingness of member states to breach and the lack of fear to search the conflict with the Commission. This confirms the critique that the

Commission's article 226 action is really rather a political negotiation process than a law enforcement one.
Confirming political research in the field of international public law, corruption and the correlating effectiveness of states' bureaucracy is found to be the most important factor explaining infringements of Community law. We interpret this as an illustration of the importance of "lower executive powers" in applying community law.

Older member states have more serious conflicts on infringements with the Commission than younger member states do. Historical reasons might explain for this. It cannot be excluded however, that older member states fear the conflict with the Commission less than younger ones do.

As a final finding, the number of no-votes in the Council negatively explains the number of breaches detected. We read this as a demonstration of the existence of logrolling in the Council which leads to problems with the ex-post enforcement of deals made. It is indeed rather shocking and surprising to observe that the incentives to breach Community law are bigger after voting *in favour* as part of vote-trading than after voting *against*.

On a general level, we were able to conclude that intentional decisions play a considerable role in explaining for breaches. In the following, we then looked into the possibilities to influence exactly these intentional decisions.

These possibilities were extensively dealt with by setting out the current legal possibilities to deal with breaches as well as the historical path that led to these rules. Some of the ongoing changes and expected evolutions were highlighted.

This descriptive legal chapter brought up the question what all this really aims at. In this critical chapter, we sought the connection with the law and economics literature. The methods and ideas of the three main branches of law and economics were analysed and it was then tested whether they could be applied to the non-contractual liability of member states.

After a detailed discussion, we were able to profoundly imbed the topic of member states' non-contractual liability in the law and economics field. We concluded that contract law is of no help in dealing with problems arising in the post-negotiation period. There is no such thing as an efficient breach of law. Most importantly, tort law proved to be a major guidance. Borrowing from the deterrence concept, we introduced the idea of ex-ante *compliance* with the law instead of mere ex-post *enforcement*. The relevance and -under some conditions- necessity of public enforcement were illustrated through the comparison with the economics of crime and punishment.

Resulting from this analysis, a number of policy recommendations were made to better deal with three different cases of breaches against Community legislation.

In a first scenario, the non-transposition or late transposition of directives granting individual rights, locus standi is initially to be given to all individuals, and punitive damages should not be excluded. After a first judgement, only affected individuals are to be awarded simple damage compensation. In the case of directives not granting individual rights, qualified entities are to be awarded punitive damages.

In the second scenario, the non-proper incorporation of directives in domestic law, group action should be introduced and/or facilitated where individual rights were granted by the directive in question. In case of severe breaches, punitive damages should be awarded. In case the directive did not concern individual rights qualified entities are to be heard before Court. Punitive damages are appropriate here since the number of victims will be smaller and a market-based damage will only occur in very few cases.

Were this private enforcement mechanism found not to function appropriately, upon a sufficiently serious breach, fines should be made available to the Commission already in the first Court hearing.

Finally, in the scenario of violations of treaty provisions, regulations and decisions; high legal uncertainty offers another reason for public enforcement by the Commission. The Court should be involved earlier than is the case now, in order to enable further private enforcement. Also, upon continuing breaches, fines should be awarded starting from the first day from first judgement.

Under low legal uncertainty, private enforcement should be facilitated by group action and initial punitive damages when individual rights are breached against in a severe way. In the alternative case, qualified entities should be awarded punitive damages.

LIST OF CASES

Chancery Courts (1676), 1 Ch. Cas 272, Brown *v.* Vermuden, judgement of 1676

European Court of Justice (1963a), Case C-25/62, Plaumann v. Commission, [1963] E.C.R. 95, judgement of 15/07/1963

European Court of Justice (1963b), Case C-26/62, Van Gend & Loos / Administratie der Belastingen, [1963] E.C.R. 1, judgement of 05/02/1963

European Court of Justice (1968), Case C-13/68, Salgoil *v.* Italian Ministry of Foreign Trade, [1968] E.C.R. p. 661, judgement of 19/12/1968

European Court of Justice (1970), Case 80/70, Gabrielle Defrenne v. Belgium, [1971] E.C.R. 445, judgement of 25/05/1971

European Court of Justice (1971), Case 5/71, Aktien-Zuckerfabrik Schöppenstedt *v.* Council, [1971] E.C.R. 975, judgement of 2/12/1971

European Court of Justice (1975a), Case 43/75, Gabrielle Defrenne *v.* SABENA, [1976] E.C.R. 455, judgement of 08/04/1976

European Court of Justice (1976a), Case C-60/75, Camina Antonion Russo *v.* Azienda di Stato, [1976] E.C.R. p. 45, judgement of 22/01/1976

European Court of Justice (1976b), case C-33/76, Rewe-Zentralfinanz eG and Rewe-Zentral AG *v.* Landwirtschaftskammer für das Saarland, [1976] E.C.R. o, 1989, judgement of 16/12/1976

European Court of Justice (1977), Case 149/77, Gabrielle Defrenne *v.* SABENA, [1978] E.C.R. 1365, judgement of 15/06/1978

European Court of Justice (1978), Case 83/76, Bayerische HNL et al. *v.* Council and Commission, [1978] E.C.R. 1209, judgement of 25/05/1978

European Court of Justice (1979), Case 141/78, French Republic *v.* United Kingdom of Great Britain and Northern Ireland, [1979] E.C.R. 02923, judgement of 4/10/1979

European Court of Justice (1983), Case C-72/83, Campus Oil Limited and others v. Minister for Industry and Energy and others. Reference for a preliminary ruling: High Court - Ireland, [1984] E.C.R. 2727, judgement of 10/07/1984

Italian Constitutional Court (1984), Case 170/84, Granital, [1984] CMLRev 756, judgement of 08/06/1984

Bundesverfassungsgericht (1986), BVerfGe 73, 339, Solange II, judgement of 22/10/1986

European Court of Justice (1987), Case C-178/84, European Commission *v.* Germany,, [1987] E.C.R. p.1227, judgement of 12/3/1987

European Court of Justice (1988a), Case 309/85, Barra v. Belgium and City of Liège, E.C.R. [1988] p. 355, judgement of 02/02/1988

European Court of Justice (1988b), Case 240/87, Deville v. Administration des Impôts, E.C.R. [1988] p.3513, judgement of 29/06/1988

European Court of Justice (1991a), Case C-64/88, European Commission *v.* France, judgement of 11/06/1991

European Court of Justice (1991b), Cases C-6/90 & 9/90, Francovich and Bonifaci *v.* Italy, [1991] E.C.R. I-5357, judgement of 19/11/1991

European Court of Justice (1992), Case C-45/91, Commission v. Greece, [1992] E.C.R. I-2509, judgement of 07/04/1992

Conseil d'État (1992), Contentieux 56776 et 56777, S.A. Rothmans International France et S.A. Philip Morris France, judgement of 28/02/1992

European Court of Justice (1993), Case C-392/93, R *v.* HM Treasury, ex parte British Telecommunications plc, [1993] E.C.R. I-1631, judgement of 26/03/1993

European Court of Justice (1996a), Joined cases C-46/93 and 48/93, Brasserie du Pêcheur *v.* Bundesrepublik Deutschland and The Queen *v.* Secretary of State for Transport, ex parte Factortame and others, [1996] E.C.R. I-1029, judgement of 5/3/1996

European Court of Justice (1996b), Case C-283/94, Denkavit Internationaal and others v. Bundesamt für Finanzen, [1996] E.C.R. I-5063, judgement of 17/10/1996

European Court of Justice (1996c), Dillenkofer and others *v.* Bundesrepublik Deutschland, [1996] E.C.R. I-4845, judgement of 08/10/1996

European Court of Justice (1996d), Case C-5/94, R. *v.* Ministry of Agriculture, Fisheries and Food, ex parte Hedley Lomas, [1996] E.C.R. I-2553, judgement of 23/05/1996

European Court of Justice (1997a), Case C-94/95, Bonifaci and Berto *v.* Instituto Nazionale delle Previdenza Sociale, [1997] E.C.R. I-03969, judgement of 10/07/1997

European Court of Justice (1997b), Case C-261/95, Palmisani v. INPS, [1997] E.C.R. I-4025, judgement of 10/07/1997

European Court of Justice (1997c), Case C-192-218/95, Société Comateb v. Directeur Géneral des Douanes et Droits Indirects, [1997] E.C.R. I-165, judgement of 14/01/1997

European Court of Justice (1998), Case C-92/96, Commission v. Spain, [1998] E.C.R. I-505, judgement of 12/02/1998

European Court of Justice (1999), Konle *v.* Austria, [1999] E.C.R. I-03099, judgement of 01/06/1999

European Court of Justice (2000a), Case C-388/95, Belgium v. Spain, [2000] E.C.R. I-3121, judgement of Judgement of 16/05/2000

European Court of Justice (2000b), Case C-387/97, Commission *v.* Greece, [2000] E.C.R. I-5047, judgement of 04/07/2000

European Court of Justice (2000c), Case C-424/97, Salomone Haim v. Kassenzahnärztliche Vereinigung Nordrhein, [2000] E.C.R. I-05123, judgement of 04/07/2000

European Court of Justice (2001a), Case T-191/99, Petrie and others *v.* Commission, [2001] E.C.R. II-3677, judgement of 12/12/2001

European Court of Justice (2001b), Case C-150/99, Stockholm Lindöpark Aktiebolag v. Sweden, E.C.R. I-493, judgement of 18/01/2001

European Court of Justice (2002), Case 304/02, European Commission *v.* France, judgement of (Pending Case)

European Court of Justice (2003a), Case C-278/01, Commission v. Spain, judgement of 25/11/2003

European Court of Justice (2003b), Case C-224/01, Gerhard Köbler v. Republik Österreich, judgement of 30.09.2003

European Court of Justice (2003c), Case C-151/02, Landeshauptstadt Kiel v Norbert Jaeger, [2003] E.C.R. I-8389, judgement of 09/09/2003

European Court of Justice (2003d), Case C-112/00, Schmidberger *v.* Republik Österreich, [2003] E.C.R. I-5659, judgement of 12/06/03

BIBLIOGRAPHY

Alter, Karen J. (1998) "Who are the "Masters of the Treaty"?: European Governments and the European Court of Justice." International Organisation *52*(1), pp. 121-47.

Alter, Karin (2002) *Establishing the Supremacy of European Law - The Making of an International Rule of Law in Europe.* Oxford University Press

Anagnostaras, Georgios (2001a) "The Allocation of Responsability in State Liability Actions for Breach of Community Law: A Modern Gordian Knot." European Law Review *26*(2), pp. 139-58.

____ (2001b) "The Principle of State Liability for Judicial Breaches: The Impact of European Community Law." European Public Law *7*(2), pp. 281-305.

____ (2002) "Not As Unproblematic As You Might Think: The Establishment Of Causation In Governmental Liability Actions." European Law Review *27*(6), pp. 663-76.

Audretsch, H.A (1986) *Supervision in European Community Law.* Amsterdam: North-Holland

Baltagi, Badi (2001), *Econometric Analysis of Panel Data.* Second Edition, John Wiley, Chichester

Becker, Garry S. (1968) "Crime and Punishment: An Economic Approach." Journal of Political Economy *76*(2), pp. 169-217.

Becker, Garry S. and Stigler, George J. (1974) "Law Enforcement, Malfeasance, and Compensation of Enforcers." Journal of Legal Studies *3*(1), pp. 1-18.

Bernheim, B. Douglas and Whinston, Michael (1986) "Menu Auctions, Resource Allocation, and Economic Influence." Quarterly Journal of Economics *101*(1), pp. 1-31.

Betlem, Gerrit (1996) "The King Can Do Wrong: State liability for Breach of European Community Law in the Post-Francovich Era." Web Journal of Current Legal Issues *4*(1996).

Börzel, Tanja (2001) "Non-Compliance in the European Union: Pathology or Statistical Artifact?" Journal of European Public Policy *8*(5), pp. 803-24.

Buchanan, James and Tullock, Gorden (1962) *The Calculus of Consent.* Ann Arbor: University of Michigan Press

Calabresi, Guido (1970) *The Costs of Accidents, A Legal and Economic Analysis.* 3rd Edition, New Haven and London: Yale University Press

Caranta, Roberto (1993) "Governmental Liability after Francovich." Cambridge Law Journal *52*(2), pp. 273-97.

Chayes, Abram and Chayes, Antonia (1991) "Compliance without Enforcement: State Behavior under Regulatory Treaties." Negotiation Journal *7*(3), pp. 311-30.

____ (1993) "On Compliance." International Organisation *47*(2), pp. 175-205.

Cohen, David S. (1990) "Regulating Regulators: The Legal Environment of the State." University of Toronto Law Journal *40*.

Coleman, James (1966) "The Possibility of a Social Welfare Function." American Economic Review *56*, pp. 1105-22.

Conant, Lisa (2001) "Official Obedience as Enduring Evasion? National Governments and the European Court of Justice." Paper delivered at the 2001 Annual Meeting of the American Political Science Association, 30 August - 2 September 2001, San Francisco.

Cooter, Robert (1984) "Prices and Sanctions." Columbia Law Review *84*, pp. 1523.

____ (1989) "Punitive Damages for Deterrence: When and how much?" Alabama Law Review *40*(3), pp. 1144.

Cooter, Robert and Ulen, Thomas (2004) *Law and Economics*. Boston: Pearson Addison-Wesley

Craig, Paul (1995) "The European Court and National Courts - Doctrine and Jurisprudence: Legal Change in its Social Context (Report on the United Kingdom)," *European University Institute Working Paper RSC 1995/29,* Florence.

Craig, Paul and de Burca, Grainne (2003) *EU Law: Text, Cases and Materials.* Third Edition, Oxford University Press

Craig, Paul P. (1997) "Once more Unto the Breach: the Community, the State and Damages Liability." Law Quarterly Review *113*, pp. 67.

Cram, Laura (1997) *Policy-making in the EU.* London: Routledge

Davis, David (1995) "Inter-governmental Conference: European Court of Justice," *Paper distributed in the Reflection Group.*

Der Spiegel (1992) "Die Leise Übermacht," Nr. 49, pp. 102.

Dewees, Don and Trebilcock, Michael (1992) "The efficacy of the Tort System and its alternatives: a review of empirical evidence." Osgoode Hall Law Journal *30*(1), pp. 57-138.

Dougan, Micheal (2000) "The Francovich Right to Reparation: Reshaping the Contours of Community Remedial Competence." European Public Law *6*(1), pp. 103-27.

Doxey, Margareth (1972) "International Sanctions." International Organisation *26*, pp. 527-50.

Drezner, D. (1999) *The Sanctions Paradox. Economic Statecraft and International Relations*. Cambridge University Press

Eaton, Jonathan and Engers, Maxim (1999) "Sanctions: Some Simple Analysis." American Economic Review *89*(2), pp. 409-14.

Elliott, Kimberly A. and Hufbauer, Gary C. (1999) "Same Song, Same Refrain? Economic Sanctions in the 1990's." The American Economic Review *89*(2), pp. 403-08.

European Commission (1991) "Intergovernmental conferences: contributions by the Commission." Bulletin of the European Communities *Supplement 2/91*.

European Commission (1996) "13th Annual Report on monitoring the application of Community Law.",

European Commission (2001) "18th Annual Report on Monitoring the Application of Community Law (2000).",

European Commission (2002) "19th Report on monitoring the application of Community Law(2001).",

European Commission (2003) "20th Report on monitoring the application of Community Law(2002).",

European Court of Justice (1975b) "Suggestions of the Court of Justice on the European Union." Bulletin of the European Communities *Supplement 9/75*, pp. pp.17-21.

European Court of Justice Press and Information Division (2004) "Press Release No 34/04 of 29/04/2004."

European Information Service (EIS), (2000) "Environment: EU Court expected to fine Greece in Waste Case.", 09/06/2000

European Parliament, (1983) "Report drawn up on behalf of the Legal Affairs Committee on the responsibility of member states for the application of Community law.", Document 1-1052/82,

European Parliament-Commissie juridische zaken en interne markt, (2002) "Werkdocument over de bijeenkomst met de voorzitters van de bevoegde commissies van de nationale parlementen: Omzetting in nationaal recht door de parlementen van de lidstaten.", PE 316.181/A/def., 13 June 2002

Evangelista, Matthew (1997) "Domestic Structure and International Change," M. Doyle and G. J. Ikenberry, *New Thinking in International Relations Theory.* Boulder, Colorado: Westview Press

Farber, Daniel A. and Frickey, Philip P. (1987) "The Jurisprudence of Public Choice." Texal Law Review (5), pp. 873-928.

Friedman, David (1995) "Making Sense of English Law Enforcement in the Eighteenth Century," University of Chicago Law School Roundtable. online at:

____ (1996) "Beyond the tort/crime distinction." Boston University Law Review *76*, pp. 103.

Galanter, Marc (1974) "Why the "Haves" Come Out Ahead: speculations on the limits of legal change." Law and Society Review *9*, pp. 950-97.

Galtung, J. (1967) "On the Effects of International Economic Sanctions, with Examples of the Case of Rhodesia." World Politics *19*, pp. 378-416.

Garrett, Geoffrey (1992) "International Cooperation and Institutional Choice: the European Community's Internal Market." International Organisation *46*(2), pp. 533-60.

Garrett, Geoffrey and Tsebelis, George (1999) "Why resist the tempation to apply power indices to the European Union." Journal of Theoretical Politics *11*(3), pp. 291-308.

Garrett, Geoffrey and Weingast, Barry (1993) "Ideas, Interests and Institutions: constructing the EC's Internal Market," J. Goldstein and R. O. Keohane, *Ideas and Foreign Policy.* Ithaca: Cornell University Press

Giessen, Ivo and Loos, Marco (2002) "Liability for Defective Products and Services: the Netherlands." Electronic Journal of Comparative Law *6-4*(December 2002).

Giuliani, Marco (2003) 'Europeanization in Comparative Perspective: Institutional Fit and

National Adaptation' in Kevin Featherstone and Claudio Radaelli (eds.) The Politics of Europeanization. Oxford: Oxford U.P.

Glasbeek, H. and Hasson, Reuben (1977) "Fault: The Great Hoax," Klar and L. N., *Studies in Canadian Tort Law.* Toronto: Butterworths,395-424.

Grossman, Gene and Helpman, Elhanan (1994) "Protection for Sale." American Economic Review *84*(4), pp. 833-50.

Gujarati, Damodar N. (2003) *Basic Econometrics.* 4th edition, New York: McGraw-Hill

Haas, Peter M. (1998) "Compliance with EU Directives: insights from international relations and comparative politics." Journal of European Public Policy *5*(1), pp. 17-37.

Handelsblatt.com, "EU: Vorschriften für Bereitschaftsdienst gelockert", 22.09.04,

Handelsblatt, "Ärzte lehnen EU-Vorschlag zu Bereitschaftsdienst ab", Nr. 184, p. 6, 22.09.04

Harlow, Carol (1992) "Toward a Theory of Access for the European Court of Justice." Yearbook of European Law *12*, pp. 218.

____ (1996) "Francovich and the Problem of the Disobedient State." European Law Journal *2*, pp. 199.

Hillman, Arye (1989) *The political economy of protectionism.* Chur: Harwood

Hillman, Ayre and Unsprung, Heinrich (1988) "Domestic Politics, Foreign Interests, and International Trade Policy." American Economic Review *78*(4), pp. 729-45.

Hoffmann, F. (1967) "The Functions of Economic Sanctions: A Comparative Analysis." Journal of Peace Research *3*, pp. 140-59.

Holler, Manfred (1984) "A public good power index," M. Holler, *Coalitions and collective action.* Würzburg: Physica Verlag,51-59.

Hooghe, Lisbet and Marks, Gary (2000) *Multi-level governance and European Integration.* Lanham: Rowman and Littlefield

Hufbauer, Gary C. and Oegg, Barbara (2003) "Economic Sanctions: Public Goals and Private Compensation." Chicago Journal of International Law *4*(2), pp. 305-28.

Hufbauer, Gary C.; Schott, Jeffrey J. and Elliott, Kimberly Ann (1990) *Economic Sanctions reconsidered: History and Current Policy.* Washington DC: Institute for International Economics

Intergovernmental Conference (1996) "Memorandum by the United Kingdom on the European Court of Justice.", CONF/3883/96, 25 July

Intergovernmental Conference (1996b) "Note de transmission. Objet: Création de la possibilité de transférer aux Tribunal de Première Instance les procédures relatives aux questions préjudicielles. Presenté par la délégation allemande..", CONF/3862/96, 22 October

Intergovernmental Conference (1997) "Proposition d'amendement de la délégation française sur la Cour de Justice.", CONF/3853/97, 25 March

Jacobson, Harold K. and Brown-Weiss, Edith (1995) "Compliance with International Environmental Accords." Global Governance *1*(1), pp. 119-48.

Keohane, Robert and Hoffmann, Stanley (1990) "Conclusions: Community Politics and Institutional Change," W. Wallace, *The Dynamics of European Integration.* London/New York: Pinter Publishers,276-300.

Lampinen, Risto and Petri Uusikylä (1998) 'Implementation Deficit – Why Member States

do not Comply with EU directives?', Scandinavian Political Studies 21(3): 231-251

Landes, William M. and Posner, Richard A. (1975) "The Private Enforcement of Law." Journal of Legal Studies *4*(1), pp. 1-46.

____ (1981) "An Economic Theory of Intentional Torts." International Review of Law and Economics *1*, pp. 127-54.

Lane, Robert (1996) "The Fisherman's Tale: National Liability for Breaches of Community Law." The Edinburgh Law Review *1*, pp. pp. 91-105.

Lee, Ian B. (1999) "In Search of a Theory of State Liability in the European Union." Harvard Jean Monnet Working Paper 9/99.

Lewis, Clive (1996) *Remedies and the Enforcement of European Community Law.* London: Sweet & Maxwell

Magee, Stephen et al. (1989) *Block hole tarrifs and endogenous policy theory: Political economy in general equilibrium.* Cambridge University Press

Mattila, M and Lane, J.E. (2001) "Why Unanimity in the Council? A Roll-Call Analysis of Council Voting." European Union Politics *2*(1).

Mattila, Mikko (2004) "Contested Decisions-Empirical Analysis of Voting in the EU Council of Ministers." European Journal of Political Research *43*(1), pp. 29-50.

Mattli, Walter and Slaughter, Anne-Marie (1996) "Constructing the European Community Legal System from the Ground up: The Role of Individual Litigants and National Courts," *Jean Monnet Working Papers No. 6/96,* New York.

Mbaye, Heather (2001) 'Why National States Comply with Supranational Law. Explaining
Implementation Infringements in the European Union 1972-1993', European Union Politics 2(3):259-281

Mendrinou, M. (1996) "Non-Compliance and the European Commision's Role in Integration." Journal of European Public Policy *3*(1), pp. 1-22.

Miceli, Thomas J. (1997) *Economics of the Law. Torts, Contracts, Property and Litigation.* Oxford: Oxford University Press

Moravcsik, Andrew (1993) "Preferences and power in the Euopean Community: a liberal intergovernmentalist approach." Journal of Common Market Studies *31*(473-524).

Moravscik, Andrew (1995) "Liberal intergovernmentalism and integration: a rejoinder." Journal of Common Market Studies *33*(4), pp. 611-28.

Müller, Dennis G. (2003) *Public Choice III.* Cambridge University Press

Neyer, Jürgen; Wolf, Dieter and Zürn, Michael (1999) "Recht jenseits des Staates," *Zentrum für europäische Rechtspolitik Discussion Paper 1/99,* Bremen.

Niskanen, William (1971) *Bureaucracy and Representative Government.* Chicago: Aldine-Atherton

____ (1975) "Bureaucrats and Politicians." Journal of Law and Economics *18*, pp. 617-43.

Pape, Robert A. (1997) "Why Economic Sanctions Do Not Work." International Security *22*(2), pp. 90-136.

Paraskevopoulos, Christos (1998) "Social Capital, Institutional Learning and European Regional Policy: Evidence from Greece." Regional and Federal Studies *8*(3), pp. 31-64.

Plötner, Jens (1995) "The European Court and National Courts - Doctrine and Jurisprudence: Legal Change in its Social Context (Report on France)," *European University Institute Working Paper RSC 1995/28,* Florence.

Polinsky, A. Mitchell (1980) "Private versus Public Enforcement of Fines." Journal of Legal Studies *9*(1), pp. 105-27.

Polinsky, A. Mitchell and Shavell, Steven (2000) "The Economic Theory of Public Enforcement of Law." Journal of Economic Literature *XXXVIII*(1), pp. 45-76.

Posner, Eric and Sykes, Alan (2004) "Optimal War and jus ad bellum," *Public Law and Legal Theory Working Paper No.63* Law School, University of Chichago.

Puttfarken, Hans-Jürgen and Franke, Nicole (1999) "Die Action Civile der Verbände in Frankreich," H. Basedow, Kötz, Baetge, *Die Bündelung gleichgerichteter Interessen im Prozeß.* Tübingen: Mohr Siebeck

Rawlings, Richard (2000) "Engaged Elites, Citizen Action and Institutional Attitudes in Commission Enforcement." European Law Journal *6*(1), pp. 4-28.

Renwick, Robin (1981) *Economic Sanctions.* Cambridge, MA: Center for International Affairs, Harvard University

Sales and Cole (1984) "Punitive Damages: A Relict That Has Outlived Its Origins." Vanderbilt Law Review *37*(1117), pp. 1124.

Salmon, Pierre (2002) "Accounting for centralisation in the European Union: Niskanen, Monnet or Thatcher?," *LATEC Working Paper 2002/05.*

Schäfer, Hans-Bernd and Ott, Claus (2000) *Lehrbuch der Ökonomischen Analyse des Zivilrechts.* 3rd Edition, Heidelberg and Berlin: Springer Verlag

Schäfer, Hans-Bernd and Van den Bergh, Roger (2001) "Member States Liability for Infringement of the Free Movement of Goods in the EC: An Economic Analysis." German Working Papers in Law and Economics *2000*(Article 2).

Schlueter, Linda L. and Redden, Kenneth R. (2000) *Punitive Damages.* 4rd Edition, Michie

Schwartz, Thomas (1975) "Vote Trading and Pareto Efficiency." Public Choice *24*(Winter), pp. 101-9.

Shapley, L. and Shubik, M. (1954) "A method for evaluating the distribution of power in a committee system." American Political Science Review *48*(787-92).

Shavell, Steven (1984) "The Design of Contracts and Remedies for Breach." Quarterly Journal of Economics *99*, pp. 121-48.

____ (1993) "The Optimal Structure of Law Enforcement." Journal of Law and Economics *36*(1), pp. 255-87.

____ (1997) "The Fundamental Divergence between the Private and the Social Motive to Use the Legal System." Journal of Legal Studies *26*(2), pp. 575-612.

____ (2003) "Economic Analysis of Public Law Enforcement and Criminal Law," *Harvard Law and Economics Discussion Paper No. 405* Boston.

Siaroff, A. (1999) "Corporatism in 24 industrial democracies: Meaning and measurement." European Journal of Political Research *36*, pp. 175-205.

Smith, Adam (1776) *An Inquiry into the Nature and Causes of the Wealth of Nations.*

Snyder, Francis (1993) "The Effectiveness of Euopean Community Law. Institutions, Processes, Tools and Techniques." Modern Law Review *56*, pp. 19-54.

Stefanou, Constantin and Xanthaki, Helen (1995) "Article 224 of the Treaty of Rome and the Repercussions of Case C-120/94." Web Journal of Current Legal Issues *3*.

____ (2000) *A Legal and Political Interpretation of Article 215(2) [new Article 288(2)] of the Treaty of Rome - The individual strikes back.* Ashgate

Steiner, Josephine (1993) "From Direct Effects to Francovich: Shifting Means of Enforcement of Community Law." European Law Review *18*(1).

Steunenberg, Bernhard; Schmidtchen, Dieter and Koboldt, Christian (1999) "Strategic Power in the European Union: Evaluating the Distribution of Power in Policy Games." Journal of Theoretical Politics *11*(3), pp. 339-66.

Stigler, George (1971) "The Theory of Economic Regulation." Bell Journal of Economics *2*(1), pp. 359-65.

Stone Sweet, A. and Caporaso, James (1998) "From free trade to supranational Polity: the European Court and Integration," W. Sandholtz and A. S. Sweet, *European Integration and Supranational Governance.* Oxford: Oxford University Press

Stratmann, Thomas (1992) "The Effects of Logrolling on Congressional Voting." American Economic Review *82*(5), pp. 1162-76.

____ (1997) "Logrolling," D. G. Müller, *Perspectives on Public Choice.* Cambridge: Cambridge University Press,322-41.

Sugarman, Steve (1985) "Doing Away with Tort Law." California Law Review *73*, pp. 558.

Tallberg, Jonas (2000) "Supranational Influence in EU Enforcement: The ECJ and the Principle of State Liability." Journal of European Public Policy *7*(1).

____ (2002) "Paths to Compliance: Enforcement, Management, and the European Union." International Organisation *56*(3).

____ (2003) *European Governance and Supranational Institutions: Making States Comply*. London: Routledge

Tallberg, Jonas and Jönsson, Christer (1989) "Compliance and Post-Agreement Bargaining." European Journal of International Relations *4*, pp. 371-408.

____ (2001) "Compliance Bargaining in the European Union," *Paper presented at the ECSA International Conference* Madison, Wisconsin.

The Internet Center for Corruption Research (1994-2002) "Corruption Perceptions Index.", online at http://icgg.org

The World Bank Institute (2003) "Governance Matters III: Governance Indicators for 1996-2002," Washington D.C.. Online at: http://www.worldbank.org/wbi/governance/govdata2002/.

Tridimas, Takis (2000) "Enforcing Community Rights in National Courts: Some recent developments.," D. O´Keeffe, *Judicial Review in European Union Law, Liber Amicorum Slynn.* The Hague: Kluwer Law International

Tullock, Gordon (1959) "Some Problems of Majority Voting." Journal of Political Economy *67*(December), pp. 571-9.

United Kingdom Parliament-House of Commons (2001) "Committee on European Scrutiny-Tenth Report.", 12/12/2001, available for download online at: http://www.publications.parliament.uk/pa/cm200102/cmselect/cmeuleg/152-x/15205.htm

Van Bergeijk, Peter (1989) "Success and Failure of Economic Sanctions." Kyklos *42*(3), pp. 385-404.

Ward, Angela (1995) "Effective Sanctions in EC Law: A Moving Boundary in the Division of Competence." European Law Journal *1*(2), pp. pp. 205-17.

Weiler, J. (1992) "The White Paper and the Application of Community Law," R. Bieber, R. Dehouse, J. Pinder and J. Weiler, *One European Market?* Baden-Baden: Nomos,337-58.

____ (1993) "Journey to an unknown destination: a retrospective and prospective of the European Court of Justice in the arena of political integration." Journal of Common Market Studies *31*(4), pp. 417-46.

White, Nigel (1994) "UN Peacekeeping - Development or Destruction." International Relations *12*, pp. 129-58.

Wooldridge, Jeffrey W. (2002), *Econometric Analysis of Cross Section and Panel Data,* MIT Press, Cambridge Massachusetts

Yeazell, Stephen (1980) "From Group Litigation to Class Action." UCLA Law Review *27*, pp. 514.1

FSC
www.fsc.org
MIX
Papier | Fördert
gute Waldnutzung
FSC® C083411

Kolibri 360 GmbH
Ferdinand-Jühlke-Straße 7
99095 Erfurt, Deutschland
produktsicherheit@kolibri360.de